The Successful On-Site Manager

Keith F. Levine, Publishing Manager
Mark Ingebretsen, Project Editor

The Successful
On-Site
Manager

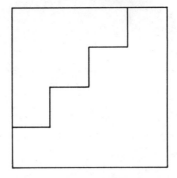

Carol Stone King, CPM®
Gary Langendoen, CPM®
Lyn H. Hummel, CPM®

Institute of Real Estate Management
of the NATIONAL ASSOCIATION OF REALTORS®
430 North Michigan Avenue
Chicago, Illinois 60611-4090

International Standard Book Number: 0-912104-62-7
Library of Congress Catalog Card Number: 83-82536

Printed in the United States of America

Fifth Printing, 1989

Foreword

The Institute of Real Estate Management (IREM) of the NATIONAL ASSOCIATION OF REALTORS® is an organization of professional property managers that certifies property managers who have distinguished themselves in the areas of education, experience, and ethical conduct. IREM offers property managers and the public an expansive program of courses, seminars, books, periodicals, audiovisual kits, and other educational activities and materials. *The Successful On-Site Manager* has been prepared as part of this professional program.

About the Authors

Carol Stone King, CERTIFIED PROPERTY MANAGER® (CPM®) and Graduate, REALTORS® Institute (GRI), is the owner of King Associates, a Denver, Colorado, real estate firm that offers property management consulting and investment property brokerage. Ms. King began her property management career in Indianapolis, Indiana. From 1966 to 1978, she was property manager for Willowbrook Development Corporation, developers and managers of multifamily housing and commercial buildings.

Ms. King is a popular speaker and instructor. Her seminar on "Managing Your Own Real Estate" has been offered by REALTOR® boards and IREM chapters in many parts of the

United States. Past president of IREM's Southern Colorado Chapter, Ms. King received that chapter's Manager of the Year Award in 1982.

Gary Langendoen, CPM®, is president of Conreal Equities, a real estate syndication and property management firm in Encino, California. In the past five years, Mr. Langendoen has been responsible for the management of 12,000 apartment units in five states and for the acquisition of 10,000 rental units with a market value of $400,000,000.

Mr. Langendoen is a governing councillor of IREM and a past president of IREM's Los Angeles Chapter. He has written several articles on property management; in 1978 his article "The Growing Field of Asset Management" earned him the *Journal of Property Management's* "Author of the Year" award. Mr Langendoen is a member of IREM's Academy of Authors, IREM's national faculty, and the editorial review board of IREM's *Journal of Property Management.*

Lyn H. Hummel, CPM®, CCIM, GRI, is director of management services for Western Skies, Inc., real estate developers, managers, and leasing agents. Ms. Hummel is responsible for overseeing Western Skies's management and accounting departments and for developing new business. Previously, she was vice president of Equity Builders, Ltd., a real estate development, management, leasing, and consulting firm.

Ms. Hummel is a member of IREM's national faculty and teaches property management for the NATIONAL ASSOCIATION OF REALTORS® GRI program in Colorado. She is also a member of the REALTORS NATIONAL MARKETING INSTITUTE® and holds their CCIM (Certified Commercial-Investment Member) designation.

Disclaimer

This publication is designed to provide accurate and authoritative information in regard to the subject matter covered. It is provided with the understanding that the publisher is not engaged in rendering legal, accounting or professional service through its distribution. If legal advice or other expert assistance is required, the services of a competent, professional person should be sought.

Contents

2 The On-Site Manager

4 Personnel Policies

5 Resident Policies

6 Rental Rates and Collections

7 Legal Aspects

8 Marketing the Property

9 Opening the New Property

10 Leasing the Apartment

11 Maintenance Management

12 Maintenance Procedures

13 Energy Conservation

Preface

Recently, an ad was run in a major metropolitan newspaper for an on-site manager position. The ad stated that the candidate for the position needed to possess (among other things) the ability to "prepare a yearly budget and control expenditures" and "experience in long-range planning." Many on-site managers have paid little attention to these two areas—budget preparation and long-range planning—and perhaps justifiably so. These are areas which have traditionally been the responsibility of a higher-level manager. But the ad quoted above is evidence that the role of on-site manager in property management is becoming increasingly sophisticated. On-site managers are assuming greater responsibilities than ever before, and the successful on-site manager will be the one who is continually widening his or her own scope of knowledge and experience.

We have written *The Successful On-Site Manager* with this goal in mind. We have attempted to provide the reader with a broad background in property management combined with specific advice on day-to-day on-site management. Many true-to-life problems drawn from our own experience are discussed, along with their resolutions. (Although drawn from real life, the situations have been made hypothetical, and any manager or staff member who is given a name is to be considered fictional.)

Though we have written this book specifically for on-site managers with some experience, almost all property management terms and concepts are defined in the text and in the glossary. The book is filled with sample forms for the on-site manager. The beginning on-site manager as well as the layperson interested in entering the field will find this book a useful introduction to property management.

The *on-site manager* is the person in charge of the daily operations of an apartment building or complex. An on-site manager who also lives on the premises is commonly called a *resident manager*. The on-site or resident manager generally reports to a *property manager*, an employee of the owner or the management firm operating the community. A property manager usually works off-site and is responsible for more than one community. For the purposes of this book, we will refer to the on-site and resident manager simply as the *manager*. The property manager will be referred to as such.

The first step in becoming a truly successful on-site manager is to gain a basic understanding of the property management field and how on-site management relates to it. Chapters 1 through 3 discuss the various forms of ownership and management, the responsibilities of the on-site manager and the skills and abilities needed to perform them, and the three basic aspects of management planning: the management plan, the budget, and the operations manual.

The on-site manager serves as the connecting link between management, personnel, and residents. While a property manager on a higher level may deal primarily with other managers, the on-site manager must deal with all levels, from management to personnel to residents. The on-site manager must make sure that employees perform their duties, must resolve problems that arise between residents, must make sure the rent is collected and a profit is produced for the owner, and all the while keep residents and employees as happy and as comfortable as possible. The key to dealing with personnel, resident, and rent problems is to have effective policies in effect beforehand, and chapters 4 through 6 provide numerous examples. Though on-site managers are usually not responsible for legal action, it is important for them to be aware of the legal implications of their actions. Chapter 7 provides a concise overview of the legal aspects of on-site management, including federal, state, and local regulations regarding employees and residents.

Another large area of the on-site manager's responsibility is the area of marketing. As the management's representative on the premises, the on-site manager often determines the success of the marketing program. Without a successful marketing program, there will be a high vacancy rate and reduced income for the owner. Chapters 8 through 10 take the manager step by step through the marketing process: how to establish a marketing theme, how to create and place a newspaper ad, special problems associated with *renting up* a new property, and how to successfully "close a sale," among many other topics.

Much of the on-site manager's time will be taken up with maintenance of the physical property itself. Our section on maintenance is divided into two chapters. Chapter 11 discusses how to establish, manage, and administrate a maintenance program. Chapter 12 details the actual maintenance that must be performed on the property.

As an addendum to the maintenance section, the last chapter of the book provides an introduction to energy conservation. Although many on-site managers may not yet be involved with energy conservation, it is an important maintenance issue that will only become more important as the decades progress. By keeping on top of such trends, the on-site manager of today will become the truly *successful* on-site manager of the future.

We would like to acknowledge several individuals who have made important contributions to this book. Irma M. Schretter, CPM®, president, S-C Management Corporation, Boston, Massachusetts, and Mildred Jan Brown, ACCREDITED RESIDENT MANAGER™, (ARM®), property manager, Jack and Robert Alfandre, Reston, Virginia, reviewed the manuscript prior to editing. Frederic A. Bovais, CPM®, residential management consultant and trainer, Sherman Oaks, California, is to be especially commended for his diligence, perseverance, and dedication in reviewing the first two drafts of this book. The chapter on "Management Planning" was reviewed separately by Robert H. Murray, ARM®, regional property manager, Mid America Corporation, Fort

Wayne, Indiana; "Energy Conservation," by David Holtzman, CPM®, president, Dabar Management Co., Inc., Bronx, New York; "Legal Aspects," by Jenner & Block, Chicago, IREM's legal counsel. E. Robert Miller, CPM®, senior vice president of property management, the Robert A. McNeil Corporation, San Mateo, California, reviewed the entire manuscript prior to publication. John F. Brandstatter, CPM®, vice president, Mellon Bank, N.A., Pittsburgh, Pennsylvania, and chairman of IREM's Publishing Committee, 1983 and 1984, reviewed selected portions of the manuscript.

Harry Voigt of Oak Park, Illinois, provided the attractive cover design and the internal layout. Keith F. Levine, IREM's publishing manager, effectively coordinated our efforts. Mark Ingebretsen, project editor, took our mountain of manuscripts and expertly fashioned them into a cogent whole.

Carol Stone King, CPM®
Gary Langendoen, CPM®
Lyn H. Hummel, CPM®

1

Ownership
and Management

In the past 40 years, the apartment has become a way of life for many Americans, joining the single-family home as a traditional place of residence. The 1960s and 1970s, particularly, saw a boom in the apartment construction industry. Methods of development, ownership, and management evolved over the years have produced the complex and multifaceted rental market of today.

The on-site manager, although not responsible for acquisition of property or major management decisions, will find it useful to understand how these decisions come to be made. As an introduction to property management, chapter 1 will provide a broad overview of the industry: types of residential properties, the various forms and objectives of ownership, and the development of property management.

Types of Apartment Buildings

Forty years of change and growth in the apartment industry have resulted in several distinctive types of properties which share the rental market today.

1

Low-Rise Buildings

Apartment buildings considered low-rise are usually not more than five stories in height. Those with more than three stories are usually equipped with elevators. The traditional urban walk-up building is a low-rise, as are the newer garden-style apartment and the townhouse.

Garden-style apartments. The proliferation of garden-style buildings came out of an effort to build a greater number of units on a piece of land while avoiding the appearance of overcrowding. Garden-style apartments are usually only two- or three-story walk-up buildings. In some, the first floor is one-half flight lower than ground level; only its windows appear aboveground. Apartments on this level—often called the garden or terrace level—command a higher rent than a basement unit but slightly less than a unit completely above ground. The suburbs have proved an ideal locale for large complexes of two- or three-story garden apartments, which often provide complete amenities and recreational facilities and are usually operated by an on-site manager.

Townhouses. Another type of low-rise rental housing, the townhouse, first appeared in densely populated urban areas and enabled city dwellers to live in close proximity to each other while maintaining a sense of privacy. Usually two stories in height, the standard townhouse shares a common side wall with neighboring units but has its own front and rear entrances. Some units may also have patios, basements, and garages or carports. In the difficult economic times of the 1970s, townhouses rose in popularity as an alternative to owned homes, since townhouses combine the privacy of a single-family home with the relatively low cost of rental housing. Due to this popularity, townhouses are now found throughout the suburbs as well as urban areas.

Mid-Rise Buildings

Mid-rise buildings, found in both urban and suburban areas, are designed to use the space they are constructed on as efficiently as possible. In older buildings, this may mean that adequate parking and aesthetics were not primary considerations in the design. Six to nine stories in height, almost all mid-rises provide elevator service. A central lobby, trash chutes, and laundry and storage rooms are usually standard features. Each floor in a mid-rise is laid out in nearly an identical fashion, creating stacks of kitchens above kitchens, baths above baths, and bedrooms above bedrooms. All units open onto a common central hallway on each floor.

High-Rise Buildings

Apartment buildings with 10 or more stories are usually classified as high-rises, although urban high-rise apartment buildings may be as tall as office buildings. Similar to a mid-rise in construction and layout, the high-rise very often provides extra amenities, such as a security guard, parking garage, health club, shopping, services, and restaurants.

Forms of Ownership

Many different forms of ownership have been developed over the years to keep pace with the growing complexities of the housing market.

Sole Proprietorship

Sole proprietorship is the traditional form of ownership from which other forms have evolved. The sole proprietor may be a part-time investor in real estate, or an individual or family who owns the property. The sole proprietor may also manage the property and/or live on site. This latter arrangement is suited best for smaller properties; it was the development of larger, more complex properties that created the need for other forms of ownership and management.

Limited Partnerships

A partnership or syndicate consists of a number of individuals who band together to invest in the development or purchase of residential property. The most common form of partnership is called a *limited partnership*, which consists of *general* and *limited partners*. Limited partners are primarily investors, and have no voice in the management of the property or the partnership. The limited partner's liability is equal to the amount of money invested. The general partner has the authority to speak for the partnership, selects the management, makes all financial and management decisions, and assumes liability for the general risks of the partnership.

The economic goals of the investment—as well as the regulations of the Securities and Exchange Commission (SEC)—dictate the number of partners in the venture. The financial earnings of apartment ownership are divided among the partners according to the partnership agreement, often in proportion to the share of ownership held. In most partnerships, operational responsibilities are turned over to a professional property manager.

Although partnerships are a very popular form of investment, they do have potential problems. Limited partners may become dissatisfied with their lack of voice in management operations. They may also be asked for additional contributions of capital. Unless the specific goals of the investment are clearly defined, disagreements can and often do occur.

Corporations

Corporations enter the rental housing field for three primary reasons: (1) as a tax shelter, (2) as an investment, and (3) to provide employee housing. Large corporations that enter the business in an attempt to diversify may find that their real estate investments provide some tax shelter, but that as a corporation they lack the agility needed to succeed in a speculative field. Corporations that invest in residential property in order to provide attractive and comfortable housing for their employees are often located in places such as resort areas where decent housing is hard to find. They must provide housing in order to attract employees into the area.

Institutional Lenders

Institutions such as large insurance companies, pension funds, banks, and savings and loan associations enter into a wide range of investments, including multifamily housing. (National banks are not allowed to own real estate except for their own use.) Some properties are purchased or developed as part of an investment program; others come into the institution's ownership through default on a loan. Institutional lenders may protect their loan by retaining a percentage of ownership of the property. If the developer defaults on the loan, the institution can bypass the normal foreclosure process and take over the property.

Real Estate Investment Trusts

The real estate investment trust (REIT) first appeared in the early 1960s and is one of the few forms of ownership to have completely changed by the 1980s. The original purpose of a REIT was to attract small, unrelated investors to property ownership without the use of the partnership structure. REITs planning to acquire a property offer shares of ownership in the REIT to investors. The REITs then take the funds and purchase the property or loan the funds for the construction of a particular property, thereby acquiring an interest in ownership. The Securities and Exchange Commission regulates the sale of shares in the REITs and oversees their operation.

REITs were enormously successful, and it was their success that led to their downfall in the sagging real estate market of the mid-1970s. Lending institutions, which had become deeply involved in the creation and operation of REITs, pursued very speculative investment and lending policies in order to sustain the huge rate of growth. REITs were required to distribute excessive amounts of profits, eliminating the possibility of establishing reserves. These policies eventually backfired, and the growth of REITs collapsed. Many REIT investors, who had little to say in the management of the REIT, suffered heavy losses. Legislation was enacted in many states prohibiting lenders from sponsoring REITs. Since then, REITs have slowly made a comeback, adopting more conservative investment and management policies along the way.

Cooperatives and Condominiums

As forms of ownership, cooperatives (co-ops) and condominium associations operate in a similar fashion. There is, however, an important difference between the two. Cooperatives issue shares of stock that include the right to occupy a particular unit as well as a share of ownership in the corporation which owns the real estate in its entirety. In condominium associations, it is the units themselves that are titled and sold, along with a proportionate share of common areas. These two forms of ownership accomplish the same purpose: a number of real estate investors are given a means of banding together to share in the operation and financial gains of a real estate investment.

Cooperative buildings are found predominantly in the eastern part of the United States. The co-op resembles a corporation: it sells shares of stock and is operated by a board of directors who are elected by the shareholders from among themselves. In some cooperatives, matters such as budgets, procedures, and policies must also be ratified by a majority of the stockholders.

Condominium ownership is a more recent development than cooperative ownership. The owner of a condominium unit owns the title to the unit and a share of the *common area*. Common areas include everything but the units themselves, such as land, lobbies, basements, parking areas, and recreational facilities.

Various names are given to different types of condominium units. A typical unit is found in an apartment-style building and includes all space inside the apartment "from the paint in." The owner of a condominium unit does not own the walls, floors, and ceilings of the unit, but the *air space* (as it is commonly called), the invisible cube of air inside the unit. Low-, mid-, and high-rise buildings, as well as townhouses, can all be condominium properties.

The name of the legal entity that operates a co-op is generally the name of the building followed by *cooperative*. The terminology for condominiums is more varied. *Homeowners' association*, *council of co-owners*, and *condominium association* are some of the terms commonly used. In some states these designations are prescribed by law.

One purpose of forming a cooperative or condominium association may be to minimize housing costs through income generated by the public use of the recreational facilities. For example, an association may also own facilities such as a country club, restaurant, or sports center which are open on an optional or low fee basis to the individual homeowners of the association and on a much higher fee basis or by special membership to nonowners. Even if residents do not make use of these facilities, many will still feel that such facilities are a benefit of membership in the association.

Planned Unit Developments

Planned unit developments (PUDs) are often quite large in scope, containing shopping facilities and office space as well as residential apartments. Developers, market analysts, and zoning boards work together to thoroughly plan the development before construction starts, paying close attention to such considerations as landscaping, population density, and parking. The period of construction and development usually lasts for several years. The residential space available may be a mix of garden-style apartments, low-rises, mid-rises, townhouse units and condominiums. A homeowners' association is often responsible for the maintenance of common areas such as streets, lawns, parks, and in some cases, utilities.

Government

State and local governments as well as the federal government are involved in apartment ownership through foreclosures, direct investments, or subsidy programs. As the private sector began to fall behind in meeting the demand of moderate- and low-income families for inexpensive housing, the Department of Housing and Urban Development (HUD) and the Federal Housing Administration (FHA), a division of HUD, began to take a more active role in the housing field through subsidies and loan guarantee programs. These programs are often referred to by the section number of the particular act authorizing them, such as Section 236, Section 8, or Section 221(d)(4).

Some subsidies were loans at below market interest rate (the BMIR programs); others provided that a minimum-income family would pay only a certain percentage of their income with the balance of the rent subsidized by the government. Significant funding, sometimes with subsidies, became available to developers who wished to construct apartment buildings on an FHA-guaranteed loan through a commercial lender.

The combination of subsidies and loan guarantees has created a large volume of additional housing, but serious problems arise when developers and managers of these projects lack the necessary management expertise. Buildings fall into disrepair and must be taken over by the government to keep them operating. Guaranteed loans are defaulted on and must be foreclosed. The government, an unwilling partner in these ventures, must pay off the commercial lender, rehabilitate the physical facilities, upgrade the management, and operate the properties until new owners and management can be found. As a result, the FHA is now one of the largest owners of apartment properties in the United States.

Objectives of Ownership

High profits are, of course, the primary objective in apartment ownership. Reasons beyond this, however, vary among the different forms of investment. Major reasons are for a return on investment (ROI) and for the creation of tax shelters.

Return on Investment

There are three ways a property owner can receive a return on an investment:

Cash flow. The monthly net income derived after all items of expense have been met and all necessary reserves put away is called *cash flow.* Some on-site managers may find themselves in the position of operating a property under *negative cash flow* conditions, which means that the property is operating with a deficit. The property owner will have to supply the necessary funds to offset this deficit.

Appreciation. Appreciation is the amount the property gains in value between the time it is bought and the time it is resold. Appreciation can take two forms. One form is the increase in the property's value which the marketplace creates through inflation. The second form is forced appreciation, which the ownership creates through management expertise and cosmetic improvements to the property. These management efforts should result in a higher cash flow and a more aesthetically appealing property. Cash flow and appearance represent two bases on which apartment building values are set when the property is put up for sale.

Equity buildup. Equity is the difference between the current market value of the property and the claims of any loans against the property. Equity builds up as the mortgages and debts are paid off. Say that a property is purchased with a $900,000 mortgage, and by the time the property is sold, $150,000 of the mortgage has been paid off. The equity is then $150,000. When the property is sold, the equity that has been built up goes to the benefit of the investor.

Tax Benefits

Interest paid on mortgages is tax deductible, as are many operating expenses. A primary form of tax benefits for the real estate owner is tax deductions for depreciation, called *capital cost recovery deductions* by the Economic Recovery Tax Act (ERTA) of 1981.

Depreciation is the property's gradual loss in value due to physical deterioration and obsolescence. Owners are allowed to deduct a certain percentage of the value of the property from their gross income each year as depreciation. There are different methods by which depreciation may be deducted. When the amount deducted for depreciation is larger than the property's actual depreciation, a tax shelter is created on paper, and the property owner's ordinary income is protected.

By creating a tax shelter through cost recovery deductions, the investor is only deferring income tax until the end of a certain number of years or the time the property is sold. In a sense, the investor is simply borrowing money from the government without paying interest. In complicated cost recovery systems, however, a savings over ordinary income tax exists. The overall tax savings may turn out to be substantial, because the capital gains tax the owner pays on profits from the sale of the building will be less than what would have been paid as regular income tax. The federal government uses cost recovery deductions as a way to promote stability by encouraging owners to hold onto their property for a longer time. It is also used as an incentive for investment by the private sector in low-income housing.

Tax matters are generally the concern of the owner, property manager, and/or accountant, and only rarely the responsibility of the on-site manager. However, it is important for the manager to be aware of the tax benefits available to the apartment building owner, since this will have an effect on cash flow.

Other Reasons for Ownership

The status of owning a real estate property, whether an income-producing property or not, should not be overlooked as a reason for the acquisition and ownership of property. Coupled with the pride of ownership is the pride that comes with increasing the property's value through conscientious management.

Sometimes an apartment building is acquired involuntarily. For example, a property might be placed in receivership by the government, trustee-appointed by a court of law, or inherited. All are examples of involuntary ownership.

Many investors acquire apartment buildings for speculative purposes; their acquisitions are often called *turnaround investments*. A turnaround, also called a "pump and dump" acquisition, occurs when an investor sees potential for quick profit in a substandard and improperly managed property that has the potential for being rehabilitated. This investor believes that with changes in

management and maintenance, it will be possible to
renovate the property rapidly, maximize rental income while
efficiently managing the property and its expenses, and
resell the building in a short time for a realistic profit.

Another type of investor finds no major management or
maintenance problems with a property, but believes an
increase in value will occur. This increase may be caused by
changing trends in the local market or because of favorable
changes in the makeup of the neighborhood. These
investors, therefore, speculate by purchasing the building in
advance of market and neighborhood changes, usually
making only routine management adjustments and cosmetic
improvements, and then reselling the property after it has
increased in market value.

Other investors look to apartments as a means of
diversification. They hope to attain a greater range of
security by spreading investment dollars through real estate
as well as the stock market and other financial investments.

Development of
Residential Property Management

Whatever the form or objective of ownership, the owner of a
residential property usually seeks professional help for the
management of the property. To understand the function of
the property management firm, we must examine the trends
that created professional property management.

Urban areas began to experience enormous growth
around the turn of the century. With this growth came the
construction of large amounts of multifamily housing.
Property management as we know it today, however, did not
begin until the 1920s. Even then, apartments were not
managed by managers as such, but by agents who looked
after buildings belonging to absentee owners. Often, the
agent was simply a real estate broker who performed the
necessary services in order to make a favorable impression
on potential customers. The volume of these management
services grew, and real estate firms soon formed
departments to handle their management business. Because
of the profits involved, these firms began to strengthen their

efforts at management. These management departments eventually evolved into today's management firms.

The Great Depression saw numerous foreclosures on rental properties, and the lending institutions that now owned these properties had a great need for professional property managers. The Institute of Real Estate Management (IREM) was founded in 1933 to address this situation. The founders of IREM were concerned about the ethics and competency of property managers, and so created a Code of Ethics and a certification program for property managers meeting certain requirements of experience and education. The founding of the Institute marked the beginning of high, professional standards in the property management field.

In the 1950s, the urban exodus to the suburbs began, bringing with it vast changes in apartment development and management. Instead of focusing attention on urban buildings of 50 units or less, developers began to eye the expansive land areas in the suburbs where zoning would permit large apartment communities of 100 units or more. New types of apartment buildings were built and new patterns of ownership emerged, creating a greater need for professional on-site management.

These trends continued into the 1960s, as large communities of 300 units or more became financially feasible. Institutional and corporate ownership of property became common. Business people drew upon their expertise in other areas of business and applied their knowledge to the management of apartment buildings.

Some large apartment communities began to provide a complete lifestyle for their residents in the 1960s and 1970s. The on-site manager's responsibilities expanded to include supervision of budgets, large staffs, elaborate clubhouses, and recreational facilities. The largest of these communities hired their own social directors. On-site managers of medium-size communities (100 to 300 units) were also given more responsibilities.

The mid-1970s saw a dramatic increase in the number of rental buildings converted into condominiums. Owners found that rental increases—circumscribed by rent control in some areas—could no longer keep up with skyrocketing operating costs. Many middle-income households could afford neither the inflated price of single-family homes nor the high mortgage interest rates needed to finance their purchase, yet still desired ownership of real estate as a hedge against inflation. The burgeoning market for condominiums and the potential for profit led to the creation of the condominium conversion market.

The early 1980s were a very poor time for apartment construction. The combination of high interest rates, the lack of substantial new construction, and the massive conversion of rental units to ownership reduced vacancy rates in most urban areas. At the time of this writing, the national economy seems to be experiencing a slow recovery from recession, but the outcome of this recovery is far from certain. If the current trend of belt-tightening continues in the economy, several trends in the housing industry are likely to emerge.

It is likely that apartment buildings being constructed will be smaller and less costly. Amenities offered will continue to be fewer. Owners will be less willing to spend the money necessary to provide these amenities, and residents will be less willing to pay for them in higher rents. Smaller, energy-efficient apartments close to public transportation will continue to be in high demand. The singles population will probably continue to share living quarters, exchanging a degree of privacy for the lower rental rate of a shared unit. This, in turn, is likely to create a greater demand for two items per unit—two baths, two parking spaces, two bedrooms.

The Property Management Firm

Property management firms vary in the scope of their operations. Some firms simply provide accounting and maintenance, but take no part in marketing and leasing. Other organizations take care of the day-to-day management of the property, but leave most management decisions to the owner. The most comprehensive form of management is offered by the *asset management firm*. This type of firm is responsible for all aspects of the property's operation and makes recommendations to the owner for major management decisions.

As management firms increased in size, property
managers became individually responsible for more and
more properties. They hired assistants to work on the site.
Often these assistants were only maintenance workers, but
the position slowly gained responsibility. Depending on the
firm and the particular property being managed, today's
on-site manager may be responsible for leasing, purchasing,
hiring and firing, settling resident grievances, and even
budgeting. The position of on-site manager—its
responsibilities and the skills needed to perform them—will
be discussed in the next chapter.

Summary

Forty years of change and growth in the multihousing
industry have resulted in a wide variety of properties which
share the rental market. Methods of development,
ownership, and management have also evolved over the
years.

Common types of residential properties are *low-rise*
buildings (5 stories or less), *garden-style buildings* (2- or
3-story walk-ups with sunken first floor), *townhouses*
(separate entrances), *mid-rise* buildings (6 to 9 stories), and
high-rise buildings (10 or more stories).

Common types of owners and forms of ownership include
sole proprietorship, limited partnerships (consisting of
general and *limited* partners), corporations, institutional
lenders (pension funds, banks), real estate investment trusts
(REITs), cooperatives, condominiums, homeowners'
associations in planned unit developments (PUDs), and
state, local, and federal government.

The major objectives of owning and investing in
residential property are for a return on investment (by *cash
flow*, *appreciation*, or *equity buildup*), tax benefits (especially
capital cost recovery deductions for *depreciation*), pride of
ownership, quick profit on a *turnaround investment*, and
diversification of investments.

The modern-day property management firm developed as
the multifamily housing industry developed. The first
property managers were real estate agents who looked after
buildings belonging to absentee owners. As the volume of
the management business grew, firms organized

management departments; these departments eventually evolved into today's management firms. There are different types of management firms; the *asset management firm* offers the most comprehensive range of services.

2
The On-Site Manager

The on-site manager is vital to the success of any apartment property, from the smallest "mom and pop" operation to the largest multibuilding complex. The manager's performance directly affects the property's reputation in the neighborhood, the property's vacancy and turnover rates, the cooperation of the residents, the performance of the staff, and ultimately the financial achievement of the property. The on-site manager serves as the connecting link between ownership, the property management firm, on-site staff, residents, prospects, suppliers, and the neighborhood. If the interaction between these parties runs smoothly, few problems should arise in the operation of the property. This chapter will examine the on-site manager's duties and responsibilities, as well as the abilities, skills, and management techniques needed to perform the job successfully.

Responsibilities of the On-Site Manager

The responsibilities of the on-site manager lie in four areas: *marketing*, which includes merchandising and renting the apartments; *public relations*, which includes communication and maintaining the property's reputation; *administration*,

which includes rental collections and record keeping; and
operations, which includes maintenance and supervision of
staff. All four areas overlap and interact. All require
balancing the needs of the residents with the goals and
objectives of the owners and upper management.

The typical duties of the on-site manager vary with the
size of the property. The manager of a medium-sized
apartment property would have the following
responsibilities and duties:

Marketing

1. Prepare a marketing plan (or assist the property
   manager in its preparation) and implement it. The
   marketing plan should include the creation of an
   advertising logo and other symbols. The plan
   should also establish rental rates for the property
   after giving consideration to the available
   competition.

2. Set up and operate the model or rental office.

3. Use good salesmanship in leasing the units, and
   train any staff involved in leasing to use the same
   techniques.

4. Qualify the prospects and process the applications,
   including credit checks and verifications.

Public Relations

1. Communicate with the residents, staff, property
   manager or owner, suppliers, and the neighborhood
   in a professional manner to create a good image for
   the property. Participate in a neighborhood
   association if one exists.

2. Resolve any conflicts with or between residents or
   resident organizations as smoothly as possible.
   Strive to communicate as clearly as possible to
   avoid problems before they arise.

3. Stimulate resident pride in the property by
   providing professional services and, where possible
   and appropriate, planning and organizing both
   recreational and social activities.

Administration

1. Work within the guidelines of the formal management plan, reviewing it regularly and modifying it as needed. The manager may also be called upon to assist in the creation of the management plan (to be discussed in chapter 3).

2. Maintain complete records for rental collections, maintenance, staff, and payroll. Maintain orderly files for each unit and resident.

3. Maintain a system of accounts payable and receivable. Make all bank deposits.

4. Prepare a budget and finalize it with the property manager. Monitor the budget, comparing monthly and year-to-date expenses. Meet with the property manager to adjust the budget at quarterly or semiannual intervals.

5. Create (or assist in the creation of) a complete operations manual that provides written guidelines for all policies and procedures. Continually review and update the manual, noting suggestions for modification from the staff.

6. Create a resident handbook or manual, containing all items of information that residents would wish or need to know, such as property rules and regulations. Periodically update the resident handbook.

7. Continually upgrade security and safety procedures. Train staff and residents to take wise precautions.

8. Collect all rents, issue all notices, and complete paperwork for evictions when necessary. Become familiar with all state and local regulations regarding management and residents.

9. Handle all aspects of move-ins and move-outs, consulting with the property manager on lease terminations.

10. Report any accident, injury, or property damage immediately to the property manager. Complete

the necessary insurance and OSHA (Occupational Safety and Health Act) paperwork.

Operations

1. Hire, train and regularly evaluate all employees.
2. Supervise the staff on a daily basis, delegating both authority and responsibility where appropriate.
3. Supervise the operation and use of recreational facilities.
4. Coordinate the ordering of office and maintenance supplies, maintaining an adequate inventory of necessary items. Create a system for signing out supplies, parts, and tools.
5. Obtain preliminary cost estimates for projects large enough to require bids from outside contractors. Coordinate the work of contractors and occasional labor with the work of the staff.
6. Set up a complete control system for both service requests and preventive/routine maintenance. Inform the residents of the expected completion time for their requests. Follow up service requests to ensure that the work was satisfactorily performed.

Responsibilities in the Smaller Property

Smaller properties—of around 50 units or less—are often managed by a couple who reside on site. One may handle management or administrative duties while the other handles maintenance, or they jointly may handle all responsibilities. Office hours tend to be shorter, since the manager's apartment often serves as office and show model. Managers of smaller properties may feel that many of the systems and procedures described in this book and other textbooks are too complicated for their operations. While this may be true to some extent, the principles of good management can be applied in any size of property. Forms and record-keeping procedures, for instance, may be limited in a smaller property, but cannot be ignored if a smooth operation is to be maintained.

Exhibit 2.1 Responsibilities by Size of Property

	Small (50 units or less)	Medium (50–150 units)	Large (150 units or more)
On-site manager?	Yes	Yes	Yes—one on-site manager and one assistant
Leasing	Manager	Manager and assistant	Staff with supervision
Rental collection	Manager	May be on-site or by mail	Usually by mail
Accounting	Manager	Bookkeeper	Main office
Maintenance	Manager and maintenance worker	Staff	Staff
Cleaning	Manager	Staff	Staff
Painting	Can be service contractor	Staff or contractor	Staff or contractor
Landscaping/ yard work	Contractor	Staff or contractor	Staff or contractor
Inspections	Manager	Manager	Manager and staff

Responsibilities in the Larger Property

In larger properties (150 units or more), the on-site manager is often largely involved with public relations, administration, and operations. Although the manager will still be heavily involved in marketing, leasing duties will probably be shared with several people. The larger the property, the more likely it is that all maintenance service will be handled in-house, since the property's size makes an in-house maintenance shop feasible. In the larger property, record keeping is often handled by a central office; marketing becomes the primary on-site responsibility. Exhibit 2.1 compares typical management responsibilities in three sizes of properties.

Responsibilities in a Community Association

In chapter 1 we discussed the manner in which community associations are operated: homeowners elect a board of directors to set management policies for the community. The on-site manager is an employee of the association and cannot dictate policies or establish procedures. Instead of a supervisor, the manager is a mediator and coordinator, charged with the operation of the management plan.

The Management Function

Besides possessing an awareness of the basic responsibilities of the position, the successful on-site manager must also possess an understanding of the way in which management works. Effective management—on any level and in any field—always consists of five basic functions:

Planning

Decision making

Organizing

Directing

Controlling

The five functions of management need to occur in order in every situation; true management does not occur unless all five functions take place in order. Without planning, for instance, decision making can be ineffective guesswork. Without both planning and decision making, organization is necessarily limited, direction becomes mere aim, and control is nonexistent.

Let us examine how the five functions of management relate to the various responsibilities of the on-site manager. (The tasks discussed and the terms used in the following two examples will be explained in greater detail in later chapters.)

A manager whom we will name Tom is setting up the maintenance work schedule. He sees that he has two service requests from yesterday and four from today. His preventive maintenance schedule also indicates that the swimming pool is due to be vacuumed today.

1. **Planning.** Tom gathers all the facts and information—in this case, he determines all the tasks which need to be accomplished.

2. **Decision making.** Tom asks these questions: Which

tasks are the most critical? Can all be accomplished today? Which staff member should handle which assignment?

3. **Organizing.** Tom lays out the schedule, prepares the work orders, and checks inventory for supplies and tools.

4. **Directing.** Tom supervises the staff. He starts them on the maintenance assignments, making sure each employee understands what is to be done.

5. **Controlling.** The employees turn in the work orders, marking each complete or incomplete and indicating which supplies or parts were used. Tom notes that inventory on a certain part is now low and makes a note to order more. Tom checks back with a staff member to discuss one work order which could not be completed. He reschedules it for the next day, notifying the resident of the reason for the delay.

It is important to observe that Tom performed the five functions of management in order.

A manager whom we will name Mary anticipates that rents should be raised.

1. **Planning.** Mary completes a market survey of rents in the area and reviews the current rents in her building. She checks the current budget, income, vacancy and turnover rates, and the proposed budget. The planning function in this instance includes gathering all the data necessary to analyze the current situation within the property and within the surrounding area.

2. **Decision making.** Mary establishes a proposed new rent schedule and assigns a new rent to each unit, balancing the proposed rents until the new income meets the property's needs. After she reviews the proposed schedule, she presents it to the property manager for approval.

3. **Organizing.** Mary puts the new rent schedule into effect by meeting with her staff to explain the

changes and by establishing a schedule whereby the new rents will be implemented as each lease is renewed. She makes sure that all the necessary forms are ready for use.

4. **Directing.** Each month, Mary processes the rent increases for the appropriate units. She gives her assistant manager the responsibility of sending the renewal notices and following up with the residents. Mary checks with her assistant to ensure that the proper procedures are followed.

5. **Controlling.** Mary follows the vacancy and turnover rates carefully to make certain that the rental increases are not affecting the property adversely. She checks the monthly financial statements against the budget as a further control. Mary and her assistant meet with the residents to make sure that the rent increase is properly explained in a fashion acceptable to the residents.

These examples demonstrate that the five functions of management are applied to every responsibility of the on-site manager, whether it is the day-to-day assignment of service calls or the long-range planning and implementation of rental increases.

Profile of the On-Site Manager

Besides being able to incorporate the use of all five functions of management, the successful on-site manager must possess skills and abilities in communication, judgement, delegation, and organization, and must be aware, alert, and goal-oriented.

Communication

The importance of communication—in on-site management as in all of life—hardly needs to be stressed. At some time or another, everyone has found themselves in some unpleasant situation that better communication might have avoided. We mentioned earlier that the on-site manager serves as a connecting link between the owner, the property manager, on-site staff, suppliers, residents, and the surrounding neighborhood. It is the on-site manager's skills in communication—or lack of them—that make this link strong or weak.

Communication primarily affects three areas of on-site management: marketing and public relations, resident relations, and employee relations.

Marketing and public relations. *Marketing* is the entire process of moving goods to the consumer. In marketing apartments, the degree of success is increased by the on-site manager's ability to interpret the reaction of the public and act or react accordingly. As an on-site manager, you are the property's primary marketing tool on the property: you are largely responsible for selling the prospect on the idea of living in the building, whether you talk with the prospect directly or through the staff you have hired and/or trained. To market effectively, communication skills are especially needed. An on-site manager who is a good communicator will be able to put prospects at ease and impart all the information the prospect needs in a positive fashion.

The manager's communication with the public—that is, public relations—makes a great impact on the marketing effort. By communicating effectively with the public, the manager creates a good public image for the property. A positive image will not only make current residents feel better about their building, but will also serve as a marketing tool aimed at prospective residents. These prospects—friends of current or former residents, or referrals from suppliers or merchants—will have already formed an opinion of the property before entering the office. In any dealings with the public, therefore, the manager and staff must always strive to communicate effectively and appear to be involved, concerned, and above all, professional.

(Chapter 8 is entirely devoted to the subject of marketing.)

Resident and employee relations. Enthusiasm and diplomacy are needed to establish and maintain good resident and employee relations. A moody, temperamental person is probably unsuited to be an on-site manager, since the position requires communication with many different types of people at all hours and on any issue. Good communicators can resolve even "impossible" conflicts. They are able to get tenants to cooperate with each other and know how and when to praise or constructively criticize their staff.

When communication breaks down, work is often performed ineffectively. Misunderstandings often result in bad feelings between the manager, the staff, and residents. The rather common example of the misunderstood maintenance request illustrates this.

The manager receives a telephone call from an angry resident complaining that a leaky faucet had not been fixed as promised. The manager apologizes profusely, then checks the maintenance records and discovers that the person assigned to the job has marked it completed. The maintenance worker is called in, sternly reprimanded, and told to complete the job properly. Later, however, the manager realizes that since the first work order did not specify "kitchen faucet" as the resident intended, the maintenance worker simply looked for any leaky faucet in the apartment. A leaky faucet had, in fact, been found in the bathroom and had been repaired.

In this situation, poor communication occured at four levels. First, the manager did not interview the resident properly when the first service request was made. The particular leaking faucet should have been specified by the resident and noted on the work order. Second, the maintenance worker should have been directed to check all faucets if the work order did not specify the faulty one. Third, no notice was left indicating that a repair had been made. Fourth, the manager should have probed deeper into the situation, asking for an explanation before criticizing the worker.

It would not be surprising if this situation, were it actually to occur, resulted in antipathy towards the manager. The maintenance worker might feel unjustly put upon, while the resident might conclude that the management is incompetent or uncaring. Diplomacy is the solution to this situation. The manager should express real concern over the misunderstanding and explain the mistake made, once discovered. The maintenance worker should be criticized in as positive a fashion as possible. Instead of being blamed for the situation, the worker should be trained to make a more thorough check of the apartment the next time.

(Communication with employees and residents will be discussed further in chapters 4 and 5.)

The communication process. In the preceding example, the parties involved in the problem became angry with each other. When people are hesitant to express anger out loud, it is often communicated nonetheless through gestures, posture, or facial expressions. It is important to remember that communication can take several different forms:

Oral—what is said.

Written—what is written down, such as a work order.

Inferred—what is assumed, with or without evidence.

Garbled—information that is poorly presented and difficult to interpret.

Body language—hidden meaning or emphasis conveyed through body movement or facial expression.

Intonation—emphasis given through variations in voice quality.

Effective communicators are aware of each form of communication, and base their responses appropriately.

If a message has not been understood by the person receiving it, effective communication has not taken place, no matter how logically and accurately the information was presented. To make certain that your communication was received and understood, you need to analyze the feedback from the person receiving the message. Feedback takes the form of facial expressions and body language, or acknowledgement comments from the recipient, such as, "Yes," "No," or "I don't understand." After the information has been communicated, ask the recipient to repeat the information back to you, or ask specific questions about the information to determine that it was accurately received.

Judgement

Good judgement in on-site management consists of the
ability to know exactly what action to take in a given
situation, exactly which moment to take it, and the possible
consequences of that action. Good judgement is also the
ability to anticipate and solve potential problems before they
occur.

An overloaded maintenance schedule is an example of a
situation needing good judgement to be satisfactorily
resolved. Say that in the property you manage, the
maintenance list for a certain day is full of routine but
important service calls. Then a water line breaks, disrupting
the entire schedule. The emergency situation needs your
sole maintenance worker's immediate attention, but you
have also promised several residents that their service calls
would be completed that day without fail. Do you ask the
maintenance worker to work overtime to complete both
tasks? Do you stall the residents by waiting until the end of
the day, then telling them that your maintenance worker
simply ran out of time?

To correctly judge which action to take, you need to
examine the consequences of each option you have to make.
The maintenance worker may not be available for or desire
overtime. Your residents may not be too understanding if
you postpone your explanations to them until the end of the
day.

In this type of no-win situation, good judgement may
dictate a change in your management routine. Your policy
has traditionally been to handle all repairs in-house. A
broken pipe is an emergency, and the difference between an
employee's overtime rate and a plumber's straight-time rate
may be minimal. Bringing in a plumber would free your
maintenance worker to finish the service calls with a
minimum of postponement. Your next step would be to
contact the property manager or owner for authorization to
hire the plumber. Good judgement requires review of *all*
options—even the option of handing the decision to your
superior—before making the decision.

Delegation

Successful managers in all fields know how to delegate both
responsibility and authority, thereby using their staffs in the

most effective way possible to achieve their goals. Responsibility is the obligation to carry out the duty; authority is the power to take specific steps. If you delegate responsibility without authority, you are still forcing your staff to rely on you. It is very easy for on-site managers to get in the habit of solving every problem on their own, because, as they explain, they can do the work in less time than it would take to teach the job to their staff. Though the manager may save time in the short run through this method, valuable time will be wasted if the problem is a recurring one and the manager has to solve it again and again.

Some managers refuse to delegate authority to assistants. These managers feel that if they delegate too much authority, they will no longer be needed and their own job security will be threatened. An assistant whose work is hampered by too much supervision, however, is unlikely to contribute to the security of the manager's job.

Other obvious problems also arise when one person tries to take on too many responsibilities. An overworked, harried manager may become rude and short-tempered when dealing with current or prospective residents. Furthermore, such managers cannot properly monitor the work of their staff—they are too busy "doing" to be watching and evaluating.

The test of a good manager is the efficiency of the staff. If your staff cannot accept responsibility or conduct business as usual in your absence, you have probably failed to delegate tasks by training each staff member in appropriate areas. Delegation is the discipline of depending on the skills of others, even when you possess those skills yourself.

Organization

Organization, as we discussed earlier, is the third of the five key functions of management; it is impossible to manage effectively without it. Policies, procedures, and methods of organization need to be developed in advance to ensure smooth operation of the property. Accurate record keeping, for instance, can support effective rental collection, and effective rental collection can help to avoid legal action. The myriad details of operating a property will be forgotten and confused if there is no system for keeping track of them. Many otherwise competent and hard-working managers perform their functions with their hands tied behind their backs, as it were, because their working habits lack organization.

For the sake of example, let us consider a manager whom we will name Alice. Were it not for her problems in keeping organized, Alice would be an ideal on-site manager. She is a very outgoing person, enthusiastic about the property and her job. Her office, however, is extremely cluttered and disorderly. Alice knows in general where things are kept, but would find it difficult to explain her illogical system to her staff. When a resident calls with a service request, Alice jots the request down on a small piece of paper—which she promptly misplaces. Fortunately, Alice has a good memory. Residents like her and are willing, for the most part, to accept her occasional errors.

Alice also has problems organizing her time. When the property manager inquires about a weekend traffic count, Alice can respond quickly—she was in and out of the office the entire weekend, her scheduled days off. She is never able to leave things organized enough to delegate two days of managing the property to the weekend staff. Because she does not take any time to plan her activities, she wastes a great deal of time in turning constantly from one task to the next before the first is finished. Alice's time needs to be reorganized as thoroughly as her office needs to be.

Alice's disorganized management methods could spoil her otherwise bright career. Successful on-site managers will develop a system of organization that is tailored to their personal needs, but which the rest of the staff can easily understand. One manager may find that the best method is keeping a log with daily entries of all transactions between current and prospective residents, staff, and upper management. Another manager may prefer a daily checklist, with general goals listed for each day. Whatever the method, organization is essential to effective management.

Awareness and Alertness

Alert and aware managers reveal themselves through seemingly small actions. As they walk through their grounds, they will step off the walk to pick up litter and jot down notes about potential maintenance problems. They are astutely aware of the condition of their property.

This awareness does not simply come with time as the manager gets to know the property better—the manager must continually make a firm effort to stay in tune with the property. Familiarity can breed neglect; it is surprisingly easy for managers to adjust to slightly worsening conditions while failing to take note of the problems that exist. If broken glass in the parking lot is not swept up the moment it is noticed, the manager may become accustomed to seeing the broken glass and fail to realize that it is still there. A prospective resident, however, will not fail to notice it, and may be influenced by the property's unkempt appearance to look elsewhere. Residents may view poor upkeep and maintenance as a sign of indifference on the part of the management, and may take that same attitude towards the upkeep of their own apartments and the payment of their rent. The manager may not have a second chance to make a good first impression.

Being aware and alert means continually noticing and recording small problems, even while concentrating on bigger problems.

Goal Orientation

Goal-oriented managers attack their problems by dividing them up into a series of goals to be achieved. By focusing attention first on short-term, attainable goals, the manager can eventually turn to the investment's long-range objectives.

The management plan and budget provide the basis from which management goals are set. (The budget is the financial plan for the property; the management plan sets forth operational guidelines; both will be discussed more thoroughly in chapter 3.) To understand this process better, let us consider another manager, whom we will name Ron. The management plan and budget for Ron's property shows that, among other things, the property's turnover rate is higher than the neighborhood average. Ron knows that senior citizens are less transient than younger people. He therefore sets a monthly goal to attract more senior citizens into the building. Ron also sees that he may be able to affect the turnover rate by increasing communication with residents. If the residents come to feel valued and important, they may decide to stay in the building rather than move. Ron puts this idea into the form of a goal by planning to meet with at least ten percent of the current residents each month. He holds the meetings and reviews the feedback he has gained from them.

By setting a goal and following through upon it, Ron has used the five functions of management

1. **Planning.** Identifying the situation and objective.
2. **Decision making.** Setting the goal of lowering the turnover rate.
3. **Organizing.** Establishing the details of the meetings with the residents.
4. **Directing.** Holding the meetings.
5. **Controlling.** Reviewing the feedback from the meetings, following up on ideas and requests, and tracking the changes in the turnover rate during the year.

Management Style

All managers develop their own style of management, a style that often reflects their own personality. Generally speaking, however, a manager is either pro-owner or pro-resident.

Pro-Owner

Pro-owner managers always keep the interests of the owner in mind over the interests of the residents. *Career managers* do so in order to further their own careers. They follow the management plan to the letter. Whenever possible, they select residents who closely match the ideal profile and discourage prospective residents who do not. *Business managers* are the type of managers most property owners prefer. Administration is thoroughly professional. The rental office is well organized and collections are prompt.

Problems arise when the pro-owner manager rules the property with too heavy a hand. Residents are always prompt with rent, never play their stereos too loud, rarely have maintenance problems, and never inadvertently lock themselves out of their apartments—but only because they fear incurring the manager's wrath. The owner may realize profits with a minimum of fuss and bother, but the high turnover rate in this property will eventually erode those profits. The manager runs a "tight ship," but the residents do not like living in the atmosphere.

Pro-Resident

Pro-resident managers operate the property primarily with the resident in mind. *Sociable managers* believe that the best way to manage is to keep the residents happy. These managers know many residents on a first-name basis and plan many all-community social events. They put much effort into services that maintain or increase the desirability of the property. *Parental managers* take a personal interest in everything happening in the building. They seem to be able to solve every problem and are greatly admired by residents and staff alike.

The pro-resident manager's warmth and humanity may result, however, in unprofessional management of the property. The manager who has become a good friend of the resident may have great difficulty in enforcing rules, collecting rent, and especially in announcing rent increases. Parental managers may become so involved that they take on their residents' responsibilities themselves. They may try to find jobs for unemployed residents or finance unpaid rental debts. The result is a poorly managed, disorganized property that turns a decreased profit for the owner.

Ideally, the manager will possess all of these traits to some degree and be able to use them appropriately as the situation demands. Problems with rent collections or security obviously call for a more autocratic or pro-owner approach. In situations involving communication, such as conflicts between residents, social activities, or marketing to prospective residents, a warmer, pro-resident approach will be much more successful. A manager who lacks any of these traits will be a less effective manager.

The On-Site Manager's Office

We have emphasized the necessity for order and organization in managing the property. The arrangement of the manager's office can provide a warm, comfortable, and organized working environment for the manager and staff; enhance the property's image in the neighborhood; and impress prospective residents visiting the office.

The office needs to be convenient to the leasing area. If the property is small the office may simply be a corner of the manager's own apartment. In medium-size properties the office may be one room in the model. In large complexes where furnished models are open, the manager's office should be located in the same building as the models, and should be close to recreational facilities and amenities.

The appearance and layout of the office should be professional—not only businesslike, but orderly, organized, and attractive. Since this is the office where many rental applications will be completed, all supplies should be readily accessible. It should not be necessary to go to another office to find applications, leases, receipts, or other forms. Maintenance operations should be kept separate from the rental office at all times.

Good lighting and comfortable chairs are important. The office does not need to be luxurious, but should reflect positively on the manager and the property. Because the manager will be asking for confidential information from prospective residents, the office should provide privacy. If a separate room is not possible, the desk area should be screened or partitioned from the rest of the room so that the prospect's privacy is ensured. Privacy will also prove useful for the manager when it is necessary to speak to a current resident with a prospective resident also in the office: it would be inappropriate for discussions about violations of rules and regulations with a current resident to be overheard by a prospective resident.

If the manager has a staff doing most of the office work in

a separate area, the supplies in the manager's office should duplicate what is used in the other area. The office should be equipped with the proper record books and receipts. Copies of the property's latest ads from newspapers or apartment guides should be on hand for reference. While it may not be the manager's responsibility to collect rents, receive service requests, or prepare leases, there will be times when the manager will handle all three. The manager is the backup for the staff, and the manager's office should be ready to handle any emergency.

Evaluation of the Manager

The manager is evaluated on an ongoing basis by the residents, management staff, and the general public—but most importantly by the manager's direct superior, the owner or property manager. A formal review of the on-site manager's performance will take place once or twice each year.

The performance review consists of an examination of the on-site manager's reports and records and a private interview. The evaluator will be trying to determine how well the manager has fulfilled the position's responsibilities and duties, the quality of the manager's performance, how well the management plan and budget are being followed, and whether or not the property's investment goals are being reached.

During the interview the evaluator and manager will review the manager's performance. The manager may also be asked to submit a self-evaluation of job performance. Before the interview ends, the manager and evaluator should reach an agreement on how to appraise the manager's performance in the past year. Problems that the manager needs to correct in the coming year should also be noted. It is appropriate at this time to discuss salary and benefits, whether or not increases or changes are appropriate at this time.

Methods of Self-Improvement

It may be that the evaluation of the on-site manager detected the need for improvement in certain areas. It is easy for the on-site manager to become stale in the position, particularly if the property is running smoothly. Managers who wish to progress are always looking for opportunities to improve their skills and increase their knowledge.

The manager can stay abreast of current trends in management by regularly reading books and magazine articles. Methods of improving efficiency and saving money will pass the manager by unless they are noted and implemented as soon as possible.

Exchanging ideas and information with other managers is an excellent method of increasing awareness. The manager's town, city, or area may have a local chapter of a professional association that holds meetings and offers programs on a regular basis. These associations, along with local universities and management companies, often schedule courses in management for on-site managers. Formal classroom courses are helpful to the experienced and novice manager alike.

The Institute of Real Estate Management offers the ACCREDITED RESIDENT MANAGER™ (ARM®) program, specifically designed to enhance the professionalism of on-site managers. Those who complete the ARM® education program, meet an experience requirement, and subscribe to the ARM® Code of Ethics are awarded the ARM® accreditation. Many employers look for such an accreditation in a prospective employee.

The more skills and experience the on-site manager can acquire, the better the manager's chances to advance to the next level of management: the property manager.

Summary

The on-site manager is at the center of the apartment management process, serving as a connecting link between residents, management, ownership, and the surrounding community. The position's responsibilities are in four areas: marketing, public relations, administration, and operations.

Marketing duties include leasing the apartments to prospective residents in accordance with the marketing plan. Public relations involves keeping all lines of communication with residents and suppliers open, as well as maintaining a good public image in the neighborhood. Administrative duties include creating and updating an operations manual and resident handbook, maintaining a complete set of records, and rental collection. Operations includes the areas of maintenance and employee supervision.

Any type of successful management, including on-site management, consists of five functions: planning, decision making, organizing, directing, and controlling. All five actions must take place in proper order for effective management to occur.

On-site managers need skills and abilities in several areas to be successful. They must be able to communicate clearly and concisely, avoiding all unnecessary conflict. They must be able to make quick, correct judgements on which course of action to take in any given situation. They must be able to delegate authority and duties properly and appropriately. They must be highly organized in order to avoid being swamped by a morass of management details. They must be continually aware and alert to immediate and long-range problems on their property. They must take a goal-oriented approach to problem solving, dividing all problems into a series of goals to be achieved.

Each on-site manager has a unique style of management, but most fall into one of two categories: the pro-owner manager or the pro-resident manager. Pro-owner managers try to operate their property in a fashion that pleases ownership and management; pro-resident managers, in a fashion designed to please the residents. Each style has its own set of problems; effective managers use a blend of both viewpoints.

The on-site manager's office must be thoroughly professional and organized, not only to impress prospective residents, but to ensure the smooth operation of the property.

Once or twice a year the on-site manager's performance

in the position will be evaluated by the ownership or management. This evaluation includes an examination of the preceding year's records and a formal interview. If a need for improvement is noted, there are several avenues the on-site manager can take: professional associations, courses in management, and keeping track of current trends in the industry are but a few.

3

Management Planning

The management plan, the budget, and the operations manual are necessary tools for the on-site manager; without them the property cannot be managed effectively. The management plan provides short-range strategies and procedures and a long-range forecast for the property; the budget provides income and expense guidelines for the property; the operations manual provides policies and procedures for the day-to-day operation of the property. These documents are traditionally prepared by the property manager or management firm staff, often with the on-site manager's input and assistance. In order to offer knowledgeable help, it is necessary for the manager to understand the components of a management plan and budget and how they are created. As we pointed out in the preface to this book, these responsibilities are already being included in the position of on-site manager. Whatever the scope of your own responsibilities, it will be important for you to know how the management plan, budget, and operations manual are created.

Management Plan

The management plan outlines the method by which the owner's goals for the property will be achieved. The first step in formulating a management plan (after the owner's goals have been determined) is gathering information on the region, the neighborhood, the competition in the immediate area, and the subject property itself. The information can come from a wide range of sources, from the chamber of commerce to city and county governments, lending institutions, industrial development agencies, zoning commissions, apartment and building associations, and property management firms. Many of these groups will provide results from their own surveys. Once the information is assembled, projections about the property's short- and long-term profitability are possible. The plan is finally presented to the owner with recommendations for the property's future operation.

Regional Analysis

The first information gathered is on the property's surrounding region. For the purpose of analysis, a *region* is defined as a sphere of economic influence or a specific trading area. The size of the region varies greatly in different parts of the country. For example, the region for a property located in a suburb of a major city might encompass the entire metropolitan area. The trading area of a small, rural town, however, might include five other small towns and cover as much as a quarter of the state.

The following information is gathered as part of the regional analysis:

1. **Economic base.** The major type and other types of employment available in the region, the extent to which availability of employment draws people into the region, and the number of major employers in the region. If a large portion of the region's population depends on only one or two major types of employers for employment, the entire region's economic health depends greatly on the strength of these employers. The economic growth of Detroit, for instance, was seriously curtailed in the late 1970s and early 1980s when the city's major employer, the automotive industry, suffered a severe cutback.

2. **Political climate.** The local government's general

attitude towards growth and new business. The region may have a no-growth policy which discourages new housing, employment, and expansion through restrictive zoning and rent controls or heavy local and state income taxes.

3. **Growth patterns.** The direction and speed in which the region has grown in the past, is growing in the present, and is expected to grow in the future.

4. **Population.** The median age, family size, and income of the region. Any trends in family structure: whether there is a growing predominance of families or singles in the region. Ethnic makeup of the region. Whether people are primarily moving into or moving out of the region.

5. **Transportation.** The forms of transportation that are most widely used in the region. If most people in the area own their own cars and drive to work, then ideally the property will be located near a major highway. If the study reveals that public transit is the most desirable mode of transportation, the property located near a public transit stop will be more attractive. Any major problems with transportation should be identified, along with the steps that are being taken (or are not being taken) to solve these problems.

6. **Property taxes.** The current rate of taxes and anticipated changes. Includes both real estate and personal property taxes.

7. **Police and fire protection, municipal services.** Whether or not these services are adequate for the area. Deficiencies in these services that could affect the property adversely in any way.

Neighborhood Analysis

After the regional analysis, attention is turned to the property's immediate neighborhood. A *neighborhood* can be described as an area that has consistent patterns of use and residence. The exact boundaries of a neighborhood are

sometimes difficult to ascertain. Many neighborhood
boundaries can be visually defined by such features as a
lake or major arterial street. Other boundaries are more
abstract in nature, such as a zoning change from residential
to commercial. Zoning boards or planning agencies may be
able to define the precise boundaries of a neighborhood. The
following information should be obtained in the
neighborhood analysis:

1. **Transit accessibility.** The common modes of
   transportation in the neighborhood and their
   accessibility.

2. **Physical appearance.** The condition of the
   neighborhood: whether or not it is stabilized,
   expanding, deteriorating, or in the process of being
   renovated; the amount of vacant land that
   competing properties hold; new construction or
   renovations that can be expected from the
   competition; the similarity of other properties in
   the neighborhood to the subject property. Certain
   prospective residents may not be attracted to the
   property because of what is or is not occurring in
   the surrounding neighborhood.

3. **Population.** The number of family units in the
   neighborhood; their average size; average income
   of the family; primary occupations; primary form of
   marital status. This information will help determine
   the policies, rules, and regulations that will best
   suit the property. In most areas, it can be assumed
   that the types of people currently living in the
   neighborhood will more or less remain the same,
   and that similar types of people will be attracted to
   the property. The population may change, however,
   if a nearby major employer shuts down or similar
   events occur.

4. **Ratio of homeowners to renters.** Generally
   speaking, homeowners do better than renters in
   the careful maintenance of their property. A
   neighborhood composed primarily of homeowners
   will very likely be more aesthetically desirable to
   prospective residents.

5. **Services and amenities.** The quality of the

educational and recreational system may have a large impact on a property's ability to attract families with children. If the property's marketing efforts are geared towards senior citizens, the proximity of medical facilities and shopping will be important. The effectiveness of fire and police protection is also a factor.

Property Analysis

After the region and neighborhood have been studied, focus shifts to the subject property. The property analysis begins with the general physical characteristics of the property and moves to matters concerning the property's management. Information is gathered on the following:

1. **Buildings.** First to be evaluated is the property's *curb appeal*—the impression a prospective resident would form upon seeing the property for the first time. If the property is attractive, well maintained and landscaped, and has an appealing and functional layout and good signage, the property undoubtedly has good curb appeal. After the curb appeal has been ascertained, the buildings (both interior and exterior), grounds, amenities, and equipment are all thoroughly inspected. (Interior and exterior inspections are discussed in greater detail in chapter 11.)

2. **Staff.** The current number of employees on the property, their responsibilities, the services they provide, and whether or not the number of employees is proportionate to the size of the property.

3. **Management policies.** All current management policies, an analysis of the policies, and a summary of the operation's results.

4. **Income/expense analysis.** This analysis determines whether the property's scheduled income and expenses match the property's actual income and expenses. Income is analyzed unit by unit. The

terms of each lease (often summarized on the
resident's ledger card) indicate the income that
should be received from the unit. The ledger card is
compared to the rent roll, which indicates both the
scheduled income and the income actually
collected. Any discrepancies between the ledger
card and rent roll are noted. (Ledger cards and rent
rolls are discussed more fully in chapter 6.) The
expenses for the preceding two years are then
reviewed and compared to the budget. The effect
of major repairs is noted. Anticipated major
expenditures are estimated. Expense categories are
compared to a statistical reference—such as
Income/Expense Analysis: Apartments, published
and annually updated by the Institute of Real
Estate Management—to determine whether
expenses for particular categories are out of
proportion with those of other properties.

Market Survey and Analysis

The last part of the management plan is the market survey
and analysis. The purpose of a market analysis is to
determine how competitive your own property is in
comparison with nearby properties. A market survey is
taken of three to six nearby properties. The survey should
start with the competitive property closest in location to
your own, then move to the next closest competitive
property, and so on. It is important that the properties
included in the market survey are similar to your own. If
your property caters to middle-income residents, it will not
be helpful to compare it to the luxury high rise next door.

Exhibit 3.1 shows the types of information which are
gathered in the market survey: condition of the property,
rental policies, rents, and amenities. The rental figures are
very important. The rental rate for each type of unit is listed
and then divided by the number of square feet in the unit to
get the rental rate per square foot. (Allowances must be
made if what is included in the rent varies from property to
property.) This system provides you with a simple but
significant way to compare your own rents to those of your
competitors.

The market analysis is the set of conclusions drawn from

Exhibit 3.1   Market Survey

	Subject	Area Competitors				
Name of Property						
Location Rating						
Age						
Percentage of Occupancy						
Overall Condition and Appeal						
Amount of Security Deposit						
Minimum Length of Lease						
Children Allowed						
Pets Allowed						

Unit Rents	Rate	Per Sq Ft	Rate	Per Sq Ft	Rate	Per Sq Ft	Rate	Per Sq Ft	Rate	Per Sq Ft	Rate	Per Sq Ft
Efficiency												
One-Bedroom												
Two-Bedroom												

	Subject	Area Competitors				
Appliances						
Furnished						
Unfurnished						
Utilities Included						
Parking						
Recreational Facilities						
Clubhouse						
Pool						
Tennis Courts						
Sauna						
Exercise Facilities						
Other Inclusions						

the market survey. You may conclude, for instance, that your next rental increase should be a small one, in order to bring your rents in line with your competitors. Conversely, you may realize that you are undercharging your residents, and could still remain competitive while making significant rental increases. You may decide that extra amenities might draw prospective residents away from your neighbors, or that capital improvements are needed.

Summarizing the Information

After all the information about the region, the neighborhood, the property, and the competition has been gathered, analyzed, and summarized, the information is assembled into a report with recommendations for changes in the operation of the property. A basic coding system can be used to indicate each recommendation's degree of importance. A change coded with the letter A could indicate a change that is mandatory if the investment is to achieve its stated goals; the letter B could indicate recommended changes that are less critical; and the letter C could indicate changes that should eventually be made for the long-term prosperity of the investment. The latter category of recommended changes should carry an explanation of how their implementation would affect the income and expenses of the property.

The timing of each suggested expenditure should also be noted and explained. For example, roof repairs need to be done before the first snow and exterior painting done during a nonrainy season.

A Management Plan Example

To demonstrate more clearly the solutions to problems which a management plan provides, let us examine a hypothetical management plan created with the assistance of a manager we will call Margaret.

This particular management plan was prepared for a 25-unit apartment property whose income had fallen quite drastically and whose turnover rate was quite high. Although rental rates were significantly lower than others in the market, the property still had a 20 percent vacancy rate in a market where 5 percent was typical. Much of the property was in need of repair or replacement. After completing property and market analyses and reviewing vacancy and turnover rates, Margaret reported her recommendations for upgrading the property. The costs were based on estimates from a local contractor. Her recommendations were as follows:

1. Repaint the interior and exterior $13,000
   of the building.
2. Landscape the main entrance area   3,500
   and improve lawn areas.
3. Repaint entrance signs.   150
4. Add dishwashers to all units.   6,000
5. Update the obsolescent bathrooms by   16,000
   installing new wallpaper, floors, and
   vanities.
6. Have the property thoroughly cleaned;   1,000
   if necessary, by hiring extra temporary
   labor.
                                          _____
                              Total $39,650

Margaret reported that if her recommendations were
followed, the rental rates could be raised $65 per month per
unit and still be slightly below the market rate. Vacancy and
turnover rates would be reduced to normal. The period for
renovations would be two months; the entire cost would be
recouped in less than three years. Margaret indicated that if
the needed improvements were not made, the vacancy rate
could be expected to climb. The following were her specific
recommendations:

Maintenance. Up to this point, no records of necessary
maintenance on the property had been kept. Margaret
recommended that a maintenance recording system be
established, containing a detailed list of all necessary
maintenance tasks, to ensure that preventive routine and
emergency maintenance services are handled in a
professional manner. (Maintenance recording systems will
be discussed more thoroughly in chapter 11.)

Staffing. Margaret suggested that the full-time staff of
three be replaced with a couple that would manage the
property and live on-site. Together they would be
responsible for maintenance, landscaping, rental collection,
and leasing. The off-site property management office would
handle record keeping and marketing as necessary.

Margaret discovered that the contracted landscaping company, being paid $200 per month to care for the lawn, was doing an inadequate job. She recommended discontinuing the service and hiring a part-time student during the summer to assist the managers with lawn care.

Marketing. Margaret recommended that steps be taken to make the property more attractive to prospective residents. She noticed that the property had poor curb appeal: the landscaping was poor and the main entrance sign was missing several letters. She suggested the sign be replaced and the landscaping improved.

Leases. Prior to the analysis, all tenancies in the property were month to month. Margaret learned through the market survey that the main competition used six-month leases, and recommended that a standard six-month lease form be devised and instituted. Margaret proposed a substantial increase in rent, but believed that a third of the residents would be willing to pay the new rate for the renovated units.

Rules and regulations. Previously, the management policy of the property had forbidden children and permitted no more than 2 singles in a unit. (It should be noted, however, that a number of states have either specific or interpretable provisions that prevent the exclusion of children as residents.) Although 6 of the 25 units had 3 bedrooms, there was little demand for these larger units, and 3 remained empty. If the management policy permitted children, Margaret believed that the $285 now being asked for these units could be increased to $425, which would be in line with the competition.

Margaret noted that many singles in nearby properties shared 3-bedroom units. She believed that since the majority of these singles were not car owners, there would be no parking problems created if the property were to accept more singles. Margaret did recommend that in the future no pets be allowed in the complex, which was the general policy in the area.

Security. Up to this point the property had employed a security guard, providing him with a salary and a rent-free apartment. Margaret believed that the position could be eliminated if better lighting were installed in the parking area and lobby and new deadbolt locks were added to each unit. If the property were to remove the security guard, special training in security awareness for residents would have to be offered. Because the security arrangements are stated in the lease, a signed acknowledgement of the change in security arrangements would also have to be obtained from each resident. The lease would be rewritten to reflect the new arrangements.

Furnished vs. unfurnished. At the time of the analysis, all units in the property were offered as furnished apartments complete with lamps, couch, tables, and beds. The furniture, however, was 10 years old, unfashionable, and in poor condition. The competition rented unfurnished units and recommended a local furniture rental company, if needed. Margaret suggested that the old furniture be donated to charity and that the property employ the competition's marketing method. This change would reduce rents by about $45 per month, but the loss would be offset with lower furniture expenses.

Insurance. Margaret reviewed the property's insurance coverage with the insurance carrier and found it satisfactory. She did recommend, however, that a clause in the new lease acknowledge that the property does not provide coverage for the furniture and other personal belongings of the residents. Margaret also found that workers' compensation insurance could be added at a moderate premium and recommended it be done.

Timing of renovation. Margaret's schedule for renovation proposed that the five vacant units be renovated first. When those were completed, residents wishing to remain in the property could transfer to the five units while the rest were being renovated. Rents would be increased as the renovated units were leased. Renovation of occupied units was considered unfeasible. If a resident did not want to move to a renovated unit, he or she would have to vacate.

Income and expense projections. Margaret has prepared two reports for the owner. The first is an "as is" projection for one year and for the next five years—short-term and long-term—to demonstrate how the property would fare without renovation. The second is a projection for one and one-to-five years presuming renovation and upgrading is completed, to indicate the possible effects and the expenses involved.

The Owner's Decision

The final decision on which of Margaret's recommendations to implement would rest with the owner. When the renovation proposal is reviewed, the owner will ask the following questions:

Why should $40,000 be spent to improve the property?

Will the renovation extend the economic life of the property and increase the net operating income?

Is the alternative of maintaining the property's status quo a realistic one?

Is there a combination of the two plans that might work?

After answering these questions, the property owner will determine the best possible plan, based on the investment's current financial position and long-term goals and the data contained in the proposed management plan.

The management plan is a step-by-step, detailed program for the successful operation of a property. The plan involves the collection of a great deal of information concerning the region, the neighborhood, the subject property, and the competition. After the information has been analyzed, a summary report is prepared which indicates the possibilities for both short-term and long-term action.

Budget

The budget is the property's financial foundation; it establishes believable financial goals for the property and provides guidelines for accomplishing them. The financial performance of the property is measured by comparing the monthly financial statement, which reflects income and expenses, to the budget. Both monthly and year-to-date comparisons can be made. A budget serves as both a guide and a safety check: a guide in that it sets realistic financial goals for the property, in light of the owner's requirements and the investment's ability to generate income, and a safety check in that it establishes expense limitations and income requirements.

Types of Budgets

One of the first decisions to be made in the budgeting process will pertain to the type and style of budget that will best suit the property's and the owner's needs. Most budgets fall into one of two general categories: *annual* or *long range*.

An annual budget is a one-year projection that breaks down income and expenses into 12 month-long periods. A long-range or *stabilized* budget covers a longer period— usually from 3 to 5 years. It contains both averaged figures for the entire period and figures for each individual year of the period.

Both annual and long-range budgets provide reserves for capital expenditures—money to be spent on major repairs and upkeep. If the capital reserve in an annual budget is to be spent in later years, it must be carried over to the next annual budget. In a long-range budget, capital expenditures can be averaged out over a longer period of time. The long-range budget also takes into consideration changes in the area's economic conditions that are expected to occur during the budget's duration. A manager will often have both types of budgets on hand for reference.

A variation of the annual budget used frequently in new properties is called a *fill-up* or *rent-up* budget. Fill-up budgets attempt to account for the wide variances in income and expenses that occur in new properties. During the initial period as apartments are being leased, marketing expenses will be higher than normal due to the need for extra advertising, promotional programs, and leasing personnel, while income will be lower than normal due to the high percentage of vacancies. Other expenses may still be minimal at this point: maintenance costs may be lower because new equipment is still protected by warranties. The fill-up budget must be able to accurately estimate the rate at which vacancies will be filled, but must be flexible enough to be easily adjusted.

Styles of Budgeting

Just as there are different styles of management, so are there different styles of budgeting that reflect the investment's objectives.

Traditional budgetary guidelines are drawn with great attention to past operating budgets and to accuracy, with little provision made for additional income or the possibility of increased expenses.

Upward budgeting, preferred by many property managers, refers to the practice of allotting more money in the budget than will probably be needed. The principle behind this practice is to cover most contingencies, thereby ensuring the presence of sufficient funds. Rents are conservative and reserves are generous; substantial funds often remain at year's end as a result. In upward budgeting, caution must be exercised to avoid deliberate padding of the budget that compensates for poor planning and provides for unnecessary frills.

A *conservative* budget approach favors the annual budget. If the money is not in the budget to be spent, the theory goes, the manager will be forced to be prudent and conservative in expenditures. Frills will be avoided—only the basic needs of the property will be met. Conservative budgets tend to provide more for preventive maintenance than for capital expenditures.

Preparing the Budget

After a decision has been reached on the type of budget to be used, much information needs to be assembled before the budgeting process can begin. All aspects of the property's operation must be known, and the figures on the property's current and past operating income and expenses must be easily available. The budget should be prepared far enough in advance of implementation to allow the plan to be reviewed and, if necessary, revised and adjusted. For a fiscal year beginning January 1, it would be best to begin the budget preparation as soon as the income and expense figures for the previous September are known. This will allow the property manager and owner enough time to discuss and evaluate the coming year's goals and put any changes in management strategy into effect before the year begins.

A budget has five basic components: (1) income, (2) operating expenses, (3) finance expenses, (4) capital reserves, and (5) owner's requirements. *Income* includes rent, miscellaneous sources of income, and any other fees collected (minus an allowance for vacancies and bad debts). *Operating expenses* consist of all regular expenditures made for the operation and maintenance of the property, including fixed costs such as property taxes, insurance, and professional services. *Finance expenses* are the cost of financing the property, including all payments on mortgages and loans. *Capital reserves* are funds set aside for the replacement, improvement, and upgrading of the *capital*, which in this sense refers to the physical assets of the property: the building itself and the furniture and equipment within it. *Owner's requirements* are the owner's financial objectives for the property scheduled in the budget—for instance, the owner might have an objective of a 15 percent return on the original investment. The final figure of the budget, after all expenses have been subtracted from all income, is the *cash flow*, which is expected to meet or exceed the owner's requirements.

Exhibit 3.2 is a sample annual budget form. A real budget would be more detailed, containing all subcategories under each major category of expenses. In addition, each item in the budget would have its own account number. These numbers are usually keyed to the particular account. For instance, the account numbers for each category of maintenance expenses might begin with the digit 5: 511.00 for apartment cleaning, 512.00 for carpets, 513.00 for plumbing, etc. The next major category of expenses would begin with the digit 6.

Exhibit 3.2   Annual Budget

Property _____   For Year _____

	Jan.	Feb.	Mar.	Apr.	May	June	July	Aug.	Sept.	Oct.	Nov.	Dec.	Annual
Income													
Gross Scheduled Income													
Less:													
Vacancies													
Bad Debts													
Total Projected Income													
Miscellaneous Income													
Effective Gross Income													
Operating Expenses													
Employee													
Payroll													
Payroll Taxes													
Utilities													
Maintenance													

Income

Various calculations must be made to determine the final income figure—the *effective gross income*. Earlier in the chapter we mentioned the rent roll, which shows the base

Exhibit 3.2 (Continued)

	Jan.	Feb.	Mar.	Apr.	May	June	July	Aug.	Sept.	Oct.	Nov.	Dec.	Annual
Miscellaneous													
Office Supplies													
Insurance													
Taxes and Licenses													
Real Estate Taxes													
Other Taxes, Fees, Etc.													
Property Management Fee													
Total Operating Expenses													
Net Operating Income													
Less:													
Capital Reserves													
Finance Expenses													
Cash Flow													

Prepared by _____ Date _____

Approved by _____ Date _____

rent for each unit, the date of the next rental increase, the amount of the increase, and a monthly cumulative total. This total is the *gross scheduled income*.

Subtracted from the gross scheduled income is an allowance for *vacancies and bad debts*. This allowance is an estimate, often in the form of a percentage of gross income.

Several sources should be consulted to estimate this figure: the previous year's records, the normal range of vacancies and bad debts in the neighborhood, the vacancy and turnover rates anticipated, and the effectiveness of the rental collection procedures to be used in the upcoming year. The figure gained from the subtraction of vacancies and bad debts from the gross scheduled income is the *total projected income*.

Miscellaneous income—income from sources other than unit rent, such as parking, lockers, recreational facilities, late fees, and guest fees—is then added in. Money collected from vending and laundry machines is also included as miscellaneous income. The property's share of the income from these machines can be projected by verifying the arrangements with the vendors.

Another type of income comes in the form of residents' security deposits. In most states, the security, cleaning, pet, and other types of deposits cannot be mixed with general funds. They must be placed in a separate escrow account, which may or may not be permitted to earn interest for the owner, and are not listed as income on the budget. (Chapter 7 will discuss the legal aspects of security deposit escrow accounts.)

The sum of the total projected income and the miscellaneous income is called the *effective gross income*. This formula for determining income can be expressed as follows:

Gross Scheduled Income

−

Allowance for Vacancies/Bad Debts

=

Total Projected Income

+

Miscellaneous Income

=

Effective Gross Income

Operating Expenses

Operating expenses are often difficult to categorize, but must be kept quite distinct from each other for accounting purposes. There are seven major categories: (1) employee; (2) utilities; (3) maintenance; (4) advertising; (5) miscellaneous expenses, which can include office supplies, professional fees, and property insurance; (6) taxes and licenses; and (7) property management fees. All expense categories should reflect any anticipated increases in costs.

Employee expenses. All costs that relate to the hiring, training, and paying of employees are considered employee expenses, including all state and federal payroll taxes and the employer's contributions to social security and workers' compensation insurance. The previous year's figures can be used to project the current year's increases. Hidden employee costs, such as the expense of vehicles assigned to employees for work duties and/or transportation to and from work, must be taken into consideration. A careful assessment of the costs of fringe benefits, vacation pay, salary increases, and bonuses should be made.

Utility expenses. Utilities include electricity, gas, water and sewage, and telephone. In determining utility costs, seasonal variations must be considered. If the area's climate is extreme, utility expenses can rise and fall dramatically with the season. There may not be any watering of the landscaped areas during the winter or rainy season. Air conditioners, furnaces, and swimming pools are only used during certain months. The local utility company can often supply detailed cost projections along with an audit of the property's energy usage. An allowance for increases in utility rates, based on the utility company's projections, should also be built into this category.

Maintenance expenses. A thorough review of the property will provide a starting point for budgeting maintenance expenses. The age of the building, the size of the property, and the amount of renovation or preventive maintenance already performed at the property will all affect budgeting. Turnover rates will also have an effect on the maintenance budget: the higher the turnover rate, the greater the redecorating and cleaning expenses.

Certain maintenance costs are seasonal, such as air conditioning repair, snow removal, and pool maintenance. These costs should be budgeted accordingly, even though the seasons vary from year to year and are impossible to predict with complete accuracy. During an unseasonably hot spring, a compressor which was budgeted for repair in the summer might demand immediate attention. A winter of heavy snowfall could greatly increase expenses for snow removal and roof repair.

Advertising expenses. This category includes all outlays for brochures, ads, signs, posters, and specialty items used to promote the property. Also included are commissions paid to apartment referral services (see chapter 8) and the cost of specialty items used to promote the property. Advertising expenses can increase during the seasons when the greatest number of vacancies could occur.

Miscellaneous expenses. A miscellaneous category provides for expenses that do not readily fit into an individual category or warrant their own categories. (Care should be taken, however, not to use this category for unnecessary frills.) Miscellaneous expenses could include office supplies, professional fees, resident and security services, and insurance. Attorneys and accountants provide estimates of their fees; costs for resident and security services are usually estimated by taking competitive bids. An examination of the insurance portfolio should be made to determine if the property is appropriately covered.

Taxes and licenses. Rates for real estate and personal property taxes are often not available until the end of the year. If this is the case, it is appropriate to use the latest known assessment for budgeting purposes. License fees are not as variable; the various federal, state, and local licensing agencies can provide the necessary information.

Property management fee. The fee charged by the property management firm for its services is usually a percentage of the rent collected. In the budget, it is based on the new projected income. The fee usually only covers management not performed on site.

Other Costs

The combined operating expenses are totaled and subtracted from the effective gross income to obtain the *net operating income*. The following costs are then subtracted:

Finance expenses. Finance expenses include payments on all loans, whether they are property mortgages or furniture and equipment loans. Each loan payment should be split between the amounts paid on the principal and on the interest. The term of each loan should be noted. Ground or land lease payments would also show as finance expenses.

Capital reserves. Capital reserve funds are a means of setting aside cash for anticipated future expenditures on the physical assets of the property, such as the replacement of the roof, mechanical equipment, appliances, carpets, furniture, and draperies. If this fund is not established and money deposited into it regularly, the money will have to be obtained from the owner or borrowed when major repairs and replacements are needed. Money may be available from neither source when the need arises. A structured reserve fund is required when the property is managed as a Department of Housing and Urban Development (HUD) property.

The following steps are taken in setting up a capital reserve fund:

1. Decide the items for which reserve funds are to be set aside.
2. Estimate the remaining useful life of each item.
3. Estimate the cost for the repair or replacement of each item, figuring in the anticipated effect of inflation.
4. Divide the cost for repair or replacement by the number of years left in the remaining useful life of each item.
5. Divide that sum by twelve.

The resulting figure is the amount that should be budgeted monthly into the reserve fund. The worksheet in exhibit 3.3

Exhibit 3.3 Capital Reserve Worksheet

Property _____

Item	Replacement Cost	÷	Years of Remaining Useful Life	=	Annual Reserve Requirement	÷ 12 =	Monthly Reserve Requirement
Building							
Painting, Interior							
Painting, Exterior							
Roof							
Heating/AC System							
Water Heater							
Carpet and/or Flooring							
Appliances							
Refrigerators							
Ranges							
Dishwashers							
Garbage Disposals							
Washers							
Dryers							
Grounds							
Fencing							
Landscaping							
Driveway and/or Parking							
Amenities							
Swimming Pool							
Tennis Court							
Recreation Room							
Furnishings							
Total Reserve Requirement					$		$

Prepared by _____   Approved by _____

Date _____   Date _____

expresses this formula. The following example should also illustrate:

Cost

Driveways: resurface in 3 years	$7,200
Exterior trim: repaint in 2 years	4,800
Disposals: replace in 4 years	1,200
Total	$13,200

Broken down into monthly calculations, the following
amounts result:

Per month reserve

Driveway reserve fund (3 years)	$200
Exterior trim (2 years)	200
Disposals (4 years)	25
Total amount needed per month in reserve fund:	$425

When the list is totalled, the property manager should
review it to determine if it is realistic and manageable. The
list should then be reviewed by the owner to ensure that it
meets the owner's objectives.

Condominium or homeowner's associations use reserve
funds extensively. Here, the calculations are taken one step
further: the total monthly amount needed is divided by the
number of units to indicate how much each homeowner
should contribute monthly to the reserve fund.

Owner's requirements. We discussed the various forms of
ownership and their objectives in chapter 1. Some owners
may require a minimum rate of return or maximum
short-term cash flow, while other owners have investment
goals of improving the value of the property and
maximizing the long-term income from the investment. An
owner who intends to resell the property in three years will
probably not set up a large reserve for repairs or
replacements needed after that time. The owner's
requirements will determine how the property is managed
and will therefore influence every aspect of the budget.
Depending on the nature of the owner's requirements, they
can appear as a category in the budget.

Finalizing the Budget

After the finance expenses and capital reserves are
subtracted from the net operating income, the resulting
figure at the bottom line of the budget is the cash flow, or
profit. In its final form, the budget should be expressed in
percentages of gross scheduled income as well as in dollars.
An example of a budget summary is shown in exhibit 3.4.

After the budget has been put into effect, the financial
results of the property's operation will be charted against
the budget. Each month the budget will be analyzed for

Exhibit 3.4 Budget Summary

	Total		% of GSI
Income			
Gross Scheduled Income	$75,200		100.0
less Vacancies & Bad Debts	3,700		4.9
Total Projected Income	$71,500		95.1
plus Miscellaneous Income	3,100		4.1
Effective Gross Income		$74,600	99.2
Operating Expenses			
Employee	$ 3,200		4.3
Utilities	2,300		3.1
Maintenance	7,700		9.9
Advertising	100		0.1
Miscellaneous	1,400		1.9
Taxes and Licenses	13,200		17.6
Property Management Fee	3,000		4.0
Total Operating Expenses		$30,900	41.1
Net Operating Income	$43,700	$43,700	58.1
Finance Expenses	32,600		43.3
Capital Reserves	4,200		5.6
Cash Flow	$ 6,900		11.3

accuracy and, if necessary, adjusted. The following questions should be answered:

How did actual expenses relate to the budget?

What caused any variances?

What can be done to correct the variances?

How would these changes affect the management plan of the property?

Budgets must present an accurate forecast of income and expenses. If a large budget adjustment is needed at the end of the first or second quarter, it may be an indication that a completely new one-year budget should be prepared. The manager should never use a budget that has become meaningless as a result of errors of omission or calculation.

Operations Manual

The management plan and budget both deal with long-term objectives and strategies. The operations manual is a practical guide for the day-to-day operation of the property.

A good operations manual creates efficiency and continuity, and is an invaluable tool for managing an apartment property.

The size of the operations manual will vary from property to property. An operations manual for a 12-unit building might only consist of a handful of loose-leaf papers in a notebook, while the operations manual for a large suburban apartment complex might consist of several volumes.

Many of the policies and procedures contained in an operations manual will be described throughout the rest of the book. At this point we will simply describe the six main sections of a basic operations manual:

1. **Staff and employment policies.** Details job descriptions, work procedures, responsibilites, and all other employee-related policies. (See chapter 4.)

2. **Resident policies.** Contains both rules and regulations which the resident must follow, such as those contained in the lease, and policies to guide the on-site manager in resolving resident conflicts and settling administrative matters. (See chapter 5.)

3. **Rental collection and record keeping.** Provides the procedures and systems for handling, recording, and reporting rental collections and other financial aspects of the property. (See chapter 6.)

4. **Legal procedures.** Contains procedures for the on-site manager to follow in pursuing delinquent rents and serving eviction notices. States the precise limitations of the on-site manager's position in legal matters. (See chapter 7.)

5. **Marketing and leasing.** Outlines procedures to be followed, responsibilities to be fulfilled, and forms, records, and marketing techniques to be used in the marketing program. (See chapters 8 through 10.)

6. **Maintenance.** Contains both administrative procedures and actual maintenance procedures. This section is further broken down by categories into preventive, corrective, deferred, routine, emergency, and cosmetic maintenance. (See chapters 11 through 13.)

Once the operations manual is prepared, it needs to be revised frequently as policies and procedures are improved. Staff members should be encouraged to write down their specific work procedures, to ensure that the staff members are following the manual and that the manual accurately represents the operation of the property. A copy of the operations manual should be provided to all new employees as part of their training program.

The creation of an operations manual is discussed in greater detail in *How To Write an Operations Manual: A Guide for Apartment Management*, published by the Institute of Real Estate Management.

Summary

The management plan, budget, and operations manual are traditionally prepared by the property manager or management firm staff, often with the on-site manager's input and assistance. They are invaluable management tools; without them, the property cannot be operated effectively.

The management plan provides short-range strategies and procedures and a long-range forecast for the property. In order to make such a forecast, much information must be gathered on the property and its environment.

The *regional analysis* covers the local region's economic base, political climate, growth patterns, population, transportation, property taxes, and municipal services. The *neighborhood analysis* looks into the neighborhood's transit accessibility, physical appearance, population, ratio of homeowners to renters, and services and amenities. The *property analysis* studies the property itself, covering the buildings, staff, management policies, and the patterns of income and expense. Finally, a *market analysis* is undertaken to determine how competitive the property is in comparison to other nearby properties. After this information has been gathered and analyzed, it is assembled into a report with recommendations for changes in the operation of the property.

The budget is a projection of the property's income and a plan for expenses to made during a given year. There are two basic types of budgets: the *annual* budget, covering 12 months, and the *long-range* or *stabilized* budget, usually covering a period of three to five years. A variation is the *fill-up* or *rent-up* budget, often used in new properties. There are also different styles of budgeting: traditional budgeting, which is highly accurate; *upward* budgeting, which allots an amount for expenses above what is expected; and conservative budgeting, which prudently plans only for necessities.

A budget has five basic components: (1) income, (2) operating expenses, (3) finance expenses, (4) capital reserves, and (5) owner's requirements.

Income consists of the basic rent or *gross scheduled income*. An allowance for *vacancies and bad debts* is subtracted to obtain the *total projected income. Miscellaneous income* is added, and the final income figure is the *effective gross income.*

Operating expenses include expenditures for employees (payroll, benefits), utilities, maintenance, advertising, professional fees, insurance, taxes, licenses, and the property management fee. The operating expenses are totaled and subtracted from the effective gross income to obtain the *net operating income.*

Finance expenses include all payments on mortgages. *Capital reserves* are funds set aside for anticipated replacement, improvement, and upgrading of the property's physical assets. (*Owner's requirements* represent the owner's financial objectives for the property, and are not necessarily a category in the budget itself.) Finance expenses and capital reserves are subtracted from the net operating income to obtain the *cash flow*, or profit.

During the year the budget is in effect, the budget will be periodically analyzed for accuracy and adjusted if necessary. These analyses provide the basis for creating the following year's budget.

The operations manual provides detailed policies and procedures for the six basic areas of the property's operation: staff and employment, resident policies, rental collection and record keeping, legal procedures, marketing and leasing, and maintenance.

4

Personnel Policies

Besides providing homes for residents, an apartment property is also a business, and to be successful must be run like a business. The property's staff, large or small, is an essential part of that business. The on-site manager has responsibilities in five areas of personnel relations: (1) selection, (2) training, (3) supervision, (4) evaluation, and (5) termination. Effective procedures and policies must be drawn up and implemented for each area.

Selection

Unless the manager assumes responsibility for an established property, an entire staff must be recruited and trained. It is usually the on-site manager's responsibility, under the supervision of the property manager or owner, to determine staff needs and recruit and select employees.

Staffing Needs

The property's size and condition will determine how many staff members are employed, and whether they are full- or part-time. Small properties of up to 50 units may be managed by a couple residing on site; leasing and

maintenance employees may be hired part-time. In a
medium-sized property of 50 to 150 units, these positions
might be expanded to full-time.

Job Description

Before the recruitment process begins, the manager should
first review the management plan and the individual job
descriptions contained in it. There may be current job
descriptions that need revision, or there may be no written
job descriptions at all for some positions. In any case, a
complete job description should exist for each position on
the staff. The job description must be ready before the
interview of a potential employee. Applicants should already
be qualified for the job for which they are applying; in most
cases, the job description should not be molded to suit the
qualifications of the applicant.

If it is necessary to rewrite one job description, the
manager may find that other positions also need to be
redesigned. For example, say that the property had a
full-time leasing agent during the initial rent-up period.
Now that the property is rented up, a full-time leasing agent
is no longer needed. The agent might now be promoted to
the position of assistant manager, with leasing
responsibilities included in the new job description. The
position of leasing agent might then be redesigned as a
part-time position.

Recruitment

The manager must attract a sufficient number of qualified
applicants for the positions available. There are several
avenues which the manager can explore in the recruitment
process.

On-staff promotions. There may be an employee currently
on staff who could be promoted into a new or vacated
position. Such promotions offer numerous advantages. The
manager has already observed the employee in training and
in work, and is well aware of the employee's on-the-job
skills, strengths, and weaknesses. The need to rely upon the
impression made during the interview is eliminated.

Further advantages are the current employee's familiarity with the property, the work situation, and the manager's supervisory style. Promoting a current employee also provides an incentive for other employees to work towards advancement.

There are two methods of promotion from within the company structure. The first method is to advertise the position openly to all employees and interview all respondents. Problems could develop, however, if a employee who lacks the qualifications applies for the position and, when not promoted or transferred into the position, decides to leave the company.

The second method avoids this complication. The manager reviews the qualifications of potentially promotable employees and ranks them in order of ability. They are then offered the position separately. If the manager's first choice does not accept, the second choice can be approached.

Personal contacts. Present employees, residents, and friends can be excellent sources of qualified applicants. For example, a resident might know a well-qualified, diligent maintenance worker who is out of work, and recommend that the worker call the manager to find out more about the job opening. Referrals of applicants to the property are often preferred to other sources: the manager has some assurance that the referral is coming from a trusted source. Employees, residents, and friends generally have a keen interest in the success of the property, and it is unlikely that they would recommend unqualified applicants for the job. Whenever the property has a job opening, you should spread the news among all your contacts.

Employment agencies. There are certain advantages to using an employment agency. An agency does the initial screening, saving the manager the time it takes to answer the many informational telephone calls an ad would generate. An agency has numerous sources for obtaining available, qualified, and skilled applicants. When specialized skills are needed, an agency might contact prospective applicants who are employed elsewhere.

Nevertheless, employment agencies also have their drawbacks. Agencies usually charge a significant fee for their services to the employer, employee, or both. If the agency is unfamiliar with the field in which an employee is sought, it may send overqualified or underqualified applicants. This problem can be avoided, however, by using an agency recommended by another manager or a management company. In any event, the manager should provide the agency with specific written instructions and qualifications guidelines.

Overzealous agency employees may be very aggressive in their attempt to "sell" a particular applicant to the manager, which may result in the agency's misrepresentation of applicants. There may also be a delay in filling the position. The agency may need to advertise, arrange appointments during its regular office hours, screen prospects, and check references before even sending an applicant to the property for a first interview. An on-site manager usually has the flexibility to arrange evening and weekend appointments, which might be impossible for the agency to arrange.

Schools. Many high schools, community colleges, vocational schools, and universities now provide excellent job referral programs. Many schools offer courses in property management in their business curriculum. Other schools have apprenticeship or work-study programs. In these programs students work part-time for local companies, and the employer provides the school with an evaluation of the student's performance.

Placement offices at these schools attempt to find positions for their graduating students. Job counselors screen members of the graduating class and will send appropriate applicants to the property for an interview. Students from these institutions, though lacking experience, are likely to be well trained and aware of the newest, most sophisticated techniques in areas such as energy conservation. Students coming directly from a learning environment are generally very anxious to gain practical experience and have probably not yet had a chance to acquire poor work habits.

Experienced, long-term employees, however, are an extremely valuable commodity; skills held by a new graduate from a trade school or college cannot replace years of on-the-job training. The manager may wish to develop current employees for promotion, as well as boost their morale, by sending them to a nearby college or trade school for courses.

Advertising. Advertising will reach a wide area and attract many qualified applicants. Advertising does have its disadvantages: the manager may be inundated with responses; as a result, the routine of the property may be disrupted. Applicants may also exaggerate or misrepresent their skills and qualifications on resumes. Nevertheless, advertising can be a very effective means of recruitment.

Advertising can be placed in several different media: newspapers, bulletin boards in local stores, union hall notice boards, trade journals, and city and state employment offices.

The wording of the ad, and just how much information about the position should be revealed, is often difficult to determine. Exhibit 4.1 displays two ads for a maintenance employee. The first ad, if placed in a newspaper, will be short and therefore inexpensive. Its brevity, however, will attract numerous callers, many of whom will be unsuitable for or ultimately uninterested in the position. The second ad, although more expensive to run, will allow prospective applicants to eliminate themselves from consideration. Many job-seekers, for instance, might not want a live-in position or be interested in working on the southeast side of the city.

Even more information can be included in ads placed at a union hall, state and city job service offices, or on the bulletin board of a local store. The ad can include the address of the property and greater detail on the required skills, the type of housing available, the salary range, and any benefits offered. Prospective applicants might also be asked to look at the exterior of the property before calling for an interview.

Many local radio stations broadcast public service announcements of job openings in the area. If the local radio station does offer such a service, the manager might send a brief announcement to the station. If an apartment industry trade show is being held, the manager might arrange for a help-wanted bulletin to be posted at the show. A

Exhibit 4.1   Want Ads for Maintenance Worker

MAINTENANCE worker for apartment complex. Must provide own tools. Good hours, good pay. Call 338-7282 for interview.	**MAINTENANCE**—Experienced maintenance employee for 150-unit apartment community located southeast part of city. Mechanical and carpentry skills required. Must provide own tools. Live-in position with rotating hours. Start immediately. Good salary plus benefits. Call 338-7282 between 4 and 8 p.m., weekdays.

---

help-wanted ad could be read at a meeting of community employees. Many areas sponsor job fairs to bring employers and prospective employees together. In sum, the manager should be alert to all advertising possibilities.

The manager must be prepared for the telephone calls the ad will generate. By specifying in the ad the hours during which applicants should call, the manager can arrange to be free to take the calls personally.

The telephone contact is not an interview, and should not be handled as one. During the telephone conversation, you should reiterate the basic qualifications for the position, and then ask just enough questions about the background and skills of each caller to determine whether the caller should be invited to apply for the position. A short list of qualifying questions on hand will be helpful. Any other discussion about the position should be saved for the interview.

Application

Having selected viable prospects, the manager invites applications. A common method of handling the application process is to receive applications for a specific number of days, review the applications, and then choose the applicants to be interviewed. The disadvantage to this method is that a delay of more than a week between application and interview could result in the loss of desirable applicants.

Another method is to interview each seemingly qualified applicant at the time the application is received. A final decision on whom to hire should be delayed, however, until you have had an opportunity to interview a sufficient number of applicants.

The employment application (see exhibit 4.2 for a sample application) should be designed to obtain only the needed information about the applicant's personal qualifications. Care should be taken in the design of the application to ensure that it seeks only the information relevant to the position being filled. Federal and state regulations single out inquiries about age, sex, race, color, religion, national origin, ancestry, handicap, and military status as discriminatory in most cases.

Key questions in the application are the salary anticipated by the applicant and his or her availability to begin work. If the job will require certain physical abilities, inquiry should be made on the application.

The application should be reviewed for the following:

The information supplied.

Any information not supplied, and the reason it is not supplied.

How well the applicant follows directions.

What the application says about the applicant's spelling, grammar, and general style of presentation.

The candidate's professional strengths and weaknesses.

If upon review of a particular application it becomes apparent that the applicant is not qualified, decline the interview. To proceed with an interview when there is no possibility that the applicant will be hired is a waste of both the manager's and the applicant's time. Interviews should only be arranged for applicants who seem promising.

Interview

All interviews should be conducted in private. Plan for a minimum of interruptions during the interview. Review any notes you have made about the application before the interview begins.

Many interviewers are more interested in selling the applicant on the job than they are in listening to what the applicant has to say. Avoid asking the applicant questions that can be answered with a simple "yes" or "no." Although

Exhibit 4.2   Employment Application

We are an equal opportunity employer, dedicated to a policy of nondiscrimination in employment. Various federal and state laws prohibit discrimination because of age, sex, race, color, religion, national origin, ancestry, handicap, or military status. Inquiries as to handicap are made in good faith for nondiscriminatory purposes. In completing this application, PLEASE EXCLUDE any information which may indicate the race, color, religion, national origin, or ancestry of the applicant.

Please print all information.

Date _____

Personal Information

Name _____

Address _____

City _____ State _____ Zip ____ . _____

Phone _____ Social Security Number _____

Referred by _____

Employment Desired

Position _____ Date you can start _____ Salary desired $ _____

Are you currently employed? _____ If so, may we contact your employer? _____

Have you ever applied to this company before? _____ Where _____ When _____

Education

	Name and Location of School	Years Attended	Date Graduated	Subjects Studied
Grammar School				
High School				
College				
Other (Specify)				

Subjects of special study or research work _____

_____

_____

Activities _____

_____

_____

_____

verbal skills will not be a primary requirement for many positions, the interview should be structured so that the applicant does most of the talking. (It is, of course, important to allow the applicant ample opportunity to ask questions during the interview.) The application only contains the basic facts about the applicant's background and experience. Only by listening to the applicant can the manager discover such information as the reasons the applicant left past jobs, the applicant's long-term career plans, and the financial package that would satisfy the

Exhibit 4.2   (Continued)

Former Employers (List former employers, starting with the most recent)

Month and Year	Employer: Name, Address, Phone, and Supervisor	Salary	Position	Reason for Leaving
From				
To				
From				
To				
From				
To				
From				
To				

References (Give names of two persons not related to you whom you have known at least one year)

1. Name _____ Years Acquainted _____

Address _____

Business _____ Phone _____

2. Name _____ Years Acquainted _____

Address _____

Business _____ Phone _____

Physical Record

List any physical handicaps which may hinder you from performing the job applied for

_____

_____

Nearest relative _____

Relative's address _____ Phone _____

Person to contact in the event of an emergency:

Name _____

Address _____ Phone _____

I authorize investigation of all statements contained in this application. I understand that misrepresentation or omission of facts called for is cause for denial of employment.

Signature _____ Date _____

Do Not Write Below This Line

Interviewed by _____ Date _____

Remarks _____

_____

_____

Neatness _____ Character _____

Personality _____ Ability _____

Hired _____ Department _____ Position _____ To Report _____ Salary $ _____

applicant. This information can be quite important. It is costly to lose an employee shortly after the training period, particularly for reasons which should have surfaced in the initial application and interview.

Appearance in the property management profession is critical. The on-site employees reflect the image the management projects. An applicant who comes to an interview sloppily dressed will not, in all likelihood, look professional after he or she is hired. A prospective leasing agent who chews gum loudly and smokes during the interview will bring those unattractive habits into the leasing office.

In the interview, the manager must determine the applicant's skills in three different areas: human, technical, and conceptual. Though each position on the staff varies, the employee will need at least some skills in all three areas.

Human skills are primarily skills in communication. The applicant might be presented with a hypothetical situation regarding a dispute between residents and asked how the situation should be handled. Technical skills can be determined by giving the applicant a diagnostic skills test or asking the applicant to outline the procedures for a common maintenance task. The test must be related to the position for which the applicant has applied; any other tests may be found discriminatory.

Conceptual skills are more difficult to assess. Skills in this area involve the ability to see small duties as they relate to the overall management plan. For instance, the rental agent who ignores the responsibility of crossing off a leased unit at the time an application is taken may be shocked at the end of a busy day to discover that another agent has leased the same unit. A person with conceptual skills can determine which duties are important, no matter how small or insignificant they appear to be.

Prospective applicants have been eliminated throughout the selection process: some by the wording of the ad, some by telephone contact, and some by review of the application. The list continues to narrow during the interview stage. If you have already determined that the applicant is unqualified or unsuited for the position, it is appropriate to inform him or her of your decision. If you are certain that the applicant will be considered for the position, you should end the interview by asking about the applicant's interest in the position—some applicants may have eliminated the position from their own consideration on the basis of the interview.

Final Decision

After the interview, the business and personal references of each applicant are checked. Care should be taken in checking the references to ensure that accurate information is obtained. Keep in mind that a bad reference is rarely given. If the applicant has given you permission to call his or her current employer, make sure that the person listed as a reference holds the position listed on the application.

After references are checked, the list is narrowed down to three or four applicants. These applicants can be ranked in order of the manager's preference. A second interview with the top three or four applicants is advisable.

During the second interview, it is appropriate to take the applicant on a tour of the property, allowing the discussion to take place in a more informal setting. In this interview, your questions can be directed to measure the applicant's general enthusiasm. Many managers have a second person, often the property manager, perform the second interview; both evaluations can then be compared. Your final decision will take into consideration the information gained from both interviews, and should be in line both with the property's short- and long-range goals.

Occasionally, a desired candidate may not meet all of the specific requirements listed in the job description. Before offering the applicant the job, the manager must decide on what adjustments should be made to the job description.

The following example should illustrate. A manager, whom we will name Phil, was faced with the choice between Ann and Bob for the position of assistant manager. Ann was Phil's first choice—she was outgoing, she seemed to be very conscientious, and her references were excellent. But there was a problem. The job description specified that housing for the assistant manager was to be a one-bedroom unit. Ann had a husband and two school-age children, and they owned a home nearby.

In reviewing the job description, Phil and the property manager determined that it was not critical for the assistant manager to live on site, as long as the assistant manager could reach the property quickly. Phil decided that the one-bedroom unit could be rented out rather than given to Ann. With the additional cash flow from the rental of this unit, the property could provide Ann with a pager. The budget could be adjusted to provide for Ann's on-call overtime.

Training

The training of new employees should include an orientation, a review of each trainee's job description and the property's policies and procedures, and actual hands-on training. During the orientation, the new employee should be given any necessary keys, sign income tax forms, and complete fidelity bond applications. A checklist, such as the one in exhibit 4.3, can be used in the orientation process.

In training new employees, the manager should go through the following steps:

1. Establish a reasonable amount of time for each task to be completed. Provide a list of equipment needed to perform each task.

2. Explain each task in detail.

3. Use written directions along with demonstrations, and supplement the instructions with the operations manual.

4. Demonstrate the procedure for the employee in as typical a situation as possible.

5. Have the employee perform the assignment while you observe. Ask the employee to repeat the directions back to you while performing the assignment.

6. Review your evaluation of the employee's performance with the employee, and give any feedback or further instruction needed.

Little opportunity for miscommunication will occur if this systematic approach to training is followed.

Many of the tasks a new employee needs to learn are specialized, especially such seasonal tasks as cleaning air conditioner coils or activating sprinkler systems. In these cases it is helpful for the new employee to work alongside a more experienced employee. Occasionally, a new employee may pick up poor or unsafe work habits from an experienced employee. Monitoring the training with observation and review should alleviate this problem.

While most of the new employee's training comes from the manager, many other sources of information can also be utilized. If there are complete shop books about the equipment on hand, provide employees with duplicate

---

Exhibit 4.3   New Employee Checklist

Name _____ Date Employed _____

Address _____ Phone _____

Salary $ _____ Social Security Number _____

Position _____ Job Location _____

Unit Included? _____ If yes, amount of rent $ _____ Unit Number _____

Permanent _____ Temporary _____ If temporary, expected date of termination _____

Full-time _____ Part-time _____ If part-time, maximum number of hours to be worked per week _____

In case of emergency notify _____

Address _____ Phone _____

Action Required	Date Completed	Action Required	Date Completed
IRS Form W-4 to bookkeeper		Employee form completed	
Employee agreement signed			
Fidelity bond application completed			
Business cards ordered			
Keys issued			
Pertinent information to personnel			
General orientation			

Miscellaneous comments _____

---

copies to take home for study. Reference files should be established, containing operating instructions, service manuals, texts on aspects of maintenance and property management, and reprints of trade journal articles.

Other professionals can also be used as resources. The company attorney can provide training in legal matters; the local fire department, in fire safety; and suppliers, in maintenance. Many of these sources will provide free training guides and publicity material for the property and the staff.

Training should not end after the first month of employment. Employees should continually be learning new techniques and methods of performing their jobs. Training must be an ongoing concern.

Supervision

Supervision is a difficult task in any field. To supervise employees effectively, the manager must communicate clearly, present a professional attitude, and establish a system of controls.

Communication

The need for clear, concise communication has been mentioned several times already, and need only be touched upon here. In communicating with employees, the manager must review the work procedures and standards with each employee, provide frequent evaluations, assist the employee when necessary, and communicate with each employee often.

All employees must thoroughly understand the duties and responsibilities of their positions. A written guideline generally serves this purpose. The guideline should include a description of (1) daily work procedures and responsibilities, (2) required standards of performance, (3) quality of work anticipated, and (4) other policies regarding such matters as attendance, vacation, and benefits.

In order to increase your employees' efficiency, you must communicate your evaluations of their work to them regularly. For example, say that it has always taken the maintenance worker a full day each week to complete the lawn-care duties. If the amount of time taken is never discussed, the maintenance worker can only assume that you approve. The time taken, however, may be excessive. It is better to discuss the matter with the worker when the assignment is given and to agree upon a realistic goal for completion.

Attitude

The manager acts as a role model for employees and should be conscientious about his or her performance of duties and general attitude. For example, the rental assistant who sees the manager arriving to work late or leaving early each day may develop a similarly lax attitude about office hours. Likewise, maintenance employees who see that the manager has little interest in the needs of the residents will probably have a similar lack of interest—and lack of respect for the manager.

Controls

A *control* is a method of regulating the amount or quality of work produced by an employee. Quotas, deadlines, and quantity goals are examples of controls. Controls are an important part of effective supervision, but must be handled with tact and care. Some employees may resent the thought of being "controlled" by their supervisor. Any system of controls used must be justified.

The following is a list of documents which are used as controls:

Time clock, time card, and time sheets.

Purchase orders.

Maintenance logs for deliveries, orders, and repairs.

Inventory records.

Bookkeeping forms (including rent rolls, ledger, payroll, and journals).

Unit and resident files.

Operations manual.

Questionnaires.

By establishing a system of controls, employees' work hours can be watched, expenditures can be carefully monitored, procedures for routine tasks can be made consistent, and daily tasks can be performed thoroughly. The amount of work performed will always vary from employee to employee. With a system of control for each job assignment, the manager can minimize the variations.

A system for purchasing, for example, should include built-in controls in the record keeping system to promote honesty in contracting and diminish the opportunity for kickbacks to be solicited or offered. Time sheets should control employees from working overtime hours without permission. A manager's credibility with the property manager and owner can be adversely affected by one employee's inadequate performance.

Employee incentives or bonus programs are a means of control that attempt to boost employee productivity. There are many disadvantages, however, to this system of control. The following plans are often used to create a sense of partnership on the property:

1. Employees receive a share of the gross income. *Possible result*: Employees fight a rental increase because of a fear that residents will vacate.

2. Employees receive a bonus for each unit leased. *Possible result*: Employees seek quantity rather than quality in resident selection.

3. Employees receive a bonus for a lower vacancy rate. *Possible result*: Market conditions are usually out of the employee's control. Even the most efficient employees may be left without just compensation.

This type of control is counterproductive. In a normal rental market, sales quotas are not likely to produce better results by any appreciable amount. Superior work might be better rewarded with a one-time bonus rather than several incentive bonuses.

Salary adjustments are another means of control, and will be discussed later in the chapter.

Evaluation

Just as the manager is formally evaluated once or twice each year, so must the other employees on the management staff be evaluated on a regular basis. Before the meeting, the manager fills out an evaluation form on the employee (see exhibit 4.4). This form, signed by the employee after it is reviewed and any comments from the employee noted, goes into the employee's permanent file. A copy is given to the employee.

In the meeting, the manager and employee discuss the employee's performance in light of the management plan objectives and the employee's own personal goals. If the employee has been given a notice of unsatisfactory performance during the previous year, achievements in those particular areas must be reviewed.

The employee's job satisfaction is an important concern. Many managers find it uncomfortable to discuss job satisfaction with employees. They often ask if the employee is happy and quickly move on to another subject. The following questions, however, might be asked in determining the employee's job satisfaction:

How would you rate your performance?

If you could change some aspect of your job, what would you change?

What changes do you think could be made that would improve your contribution to the success of the property?

If you had more training in a specialized area, how do you think it would affect the property?

Do you believe there is sufficient opportunity for you to advance in this property? What changes might be made that would provide you with means for additional growth?

Are there any aspects of your job that you consider too difficult? Do you think there are certain responsibilities that are a waste of your talents?

Are there any major changes you feel should be made in your job description?

Since these questions require thought, it is appropriate to provide a copy of the questions in advance of the interview. By asking such questions, you are drawing the employee into the decision-making process. Employees need to be made aware of how important their contributions are to the property's success.

Salary

A discussion of compensation is appropriate during the evaluation meeting, whether or not a raise is scheduled for that time. It may be helpful to review the entire compensation package, not only the salary. Many employees will be unaware of the full range of benefits to which they are entitled, and to which the employer contributes. If profit sharing or a retirement fund is available, the details of each program should be reviewed.

Adjustments in salaries and benefits should keep pace, as much as possible, with market trends. Occasionally, however, managers are faced with the dilemma of being unable to offer a raise to valuable employees because the property's profits during the year have not been sufficient.

Exhibit 4.4   Employee Evaluation

Name _____ Review Date _____

Property _____ Salary $ _____

Factors for Review	Unsatisfactory	Satisfactory	Excellent	Comments
Personal Appearance				
Attitude				
Towards work goals				
Toward coworkers				
Other				
Cooperation				
Works effectively with others				
Willingness to accept assignments				
Ability to be flexible in various jobs				
Knowledge				
Of company procedures				
In area of responsibility				
Productivity				
Amount of acceptable work produced				
Ability to self-direct				
Ability to meet time schedule				
Quality				
Accuracy and efficiency of work produced				
Dependability				
Attendance				
Punctuality				
Responsibility				
Responsible performance of duties				
Responsible care of equipment used				
Utilization of time				

The manager should be prepared to explain to the employee the reasons why no raise (or why only a very small raise) can be given at this time. Additional vacation time and the opportunity for overtime work may compensate for a small or nonexistent raise. Another solution could be a generous one-time bonus, given at the time of the evaluation rather than at the traditional end of the year. This should assure the employee that your failure to offer a raise at this time does not reflect on the employee's job performance.

Exhibit 4.4 (Continued)

Factors for Review	Unsatisfactory	Satisfactory	Excellent	Comments
Communications				
Ability to communicate verbally with others				
Ability to communicate in written form				
Supervisory Ability				
Planning				
Decision making				
Organizing				
Directing				
Controlling				

Definitions of Rating Terms:

Unsatisfactory - - Performance indicates corrective action is necessary.

Satisfactory - - Performance is adequate and meets the requirements of the job.

Excellent - - Performance is extremely good, consistently exceeding what is expected of the job.

Overall Review _____

_____

_____

Recommended Action _____

_____

_____

Date Reviewed with Employee _____

Signature of Evaluator _____   Signature of Employee _____

Employee Benefits

At one time, elaborate benefit packages were offered only to upper level management executives. Within the last decade or so, however, regular employees have come to expect benefit packages as a normal part of their compensation. These packages might include any or all of the following benefits:

1. Insurance, including hospitalization, major medical, income insurance, and life insurance. These benefits might cover the employee and the employee's family.
2. Overtime compensation.
3. Vacation time, paid holidays, bonus days.
4. Sick leave, including good health bonus time.
5. Bonus plans that reward work achievement.
6. Company housing.
7. Transportation to and from work.
8. Uniforms and uniform care.
9. Meals.
10. Tools (or tool allowance).
11. Expense allowance.
12. Retirement funds or pension funds.
13. Stock options.
14. Training and continued education.
15. Reimbursement for higher education costs.
16. Compensatory time off for education.

The benefits provided can vary from one employee to another, depending on the position and salary level. For example, a point value may be set for each benefit, with each employee given a set number of points, depending on the position, numbers of years of service, and current salary.

The employee benefit program should be reviewed annually and updated as needed. The hidden costs of employee benefit packages can be quite substantial. The manager should prepare a chart that indicates (1) the actual cost in dollars of benefits, (2) the value in dollars of the time the employee spends away from work, and (3) expected increases in the costs of benefits.

Benefits should not be offered simply as a way to avoid paying employees a fair market wage. Whenever possible, the employee should be given the opportunity to waive certain benefits in return for a wage increase.

Termination

Although the manager has used the best possible judgment in hiring and supervising a particular employee, it may turn out that the employee is unsuited for the job. Documentation of the employee's problem must be thorough. Proper notification that the employee's performance is unsatisfactory must be made. The employee should have the opportunity to correct the problem. If a joint effort between manager and employee fails to remedy the situation, the employee should be fired decisively and professionally. To allow an incompetent employee to remain in a position will only damage the operation of the property and weaken the morale of other staff members.

Defining the Problem

The need to fire an employee usually becomes apparent when a problem or series of problems with the employee's performance develops. In defining the problem, the following questions should be answered:

1. What is the problem?
2. How serious is the problem?
3. What is the specific cause of the problem?
4. Is the employee definitely responsible for the problem?
5. Can the employee resolve the problem?
6. Would the problem be solved if the employee were simply made aware that it exists?
7. If the problem involves a certain assignment, can the assignment be charged to another employee?
8. How much time should be allowed for solving the problem?
9. If the employee was warned earlier about the problem, but the problem has not been solved, should the employee be fired?
10. If the employee is fired, will the next employee have the same problem; that is, is the problem inherent in the position? Are the requirements and expectations for the job unrealistic?

Disciplinary Action

If it is determined that the problem stems from the employee's inefficiency, some disciplinary action must be taken. If it appears that the employee can readily solve the problem, no disciplinary action need be taken if the employee agrees to resolve the problem immediately. If the employee's ability to deal with the problem is questionable, however, the employee should be placed on probationary status. At the end of the probationary period, another meeting is held and the employee's performance reviewed. If the problem has not been solved, termination can proceed.

Garnishment of wages can be an effective disciplinary action in cases of absenteeism and tardiness. Employees who are habitually late or absent can be told that their paycheck will be docked. The amount of money withheld must correspond exactly to the time missed.

Proceeding with Termination

If after disciplinary action the problems are not resolved, it will become necessary to fire the employee. The termination will probably be quite upsetting to the employee, although in many instances, the employee is actually not surprised.

A reasonable period of time should elapse between the last disciplinary meeting and the termination. The entire termination process must be thoroughly documented in order to counter any lawsuits or false unemployment benefit claims. The employee should be given a brief statement of exactly why the termination action has become necessary. In many states, a form for validating termination is supplied by the unemployment bureau. Copies of the completed form are sent at the time of the termination to the bureau and to the employee.

Decisiveness is necessary in firing employees. If the employee is guilty of an act of misconduct—arriving to work drunk, for example—and is aware that the act automatically results in termination, you must fire the employee on that day. Any delay may create liability to unemployment benefit claims and possibly lead to lawsuits.

It is usually impractical to begin the search for a new employee before the unsatisfactory employee has been fired. If it appears that the employee cannot be quickly replaced, overtime may be given to willing employees, or an

---

Exhibit 4.5 Employee Termination Checklist

Date _____ Job Location _____

Reason for Termination _____

_____

Employment Dates	From _____ To _____	
Vacation Pay Due	S_____	
Sick Pay Due	_____	
Other Compensation Due	_____	Explain_____
Less Amount Owed to Company	_____	Explain_____
Net	S_____	

Forwarding Address _____ Phone _____

Action Required	Date Completed	Action Required	Date Completed
Keys returned			
Necessary personnel notified			

---

arrangement might be made to use an employee from another property operated by the management firm.

An employee termination checklist (see exhibit 4.5) can be used to keep track of the termination. The employee should be required to return all keys, uniforms, and tools. If the employee lives on-site and receives housing as partial compensation for services, the employment agreement will govern when the employee is to vacate or begin paying rent.

Laws regulating the payment of salary at termination vary from state to state. Some states require the payment of the entire salary through the date of firing, plus overtime, vacation time, or accumulated bonuses. Other states allow up to one month for the final paycheck to reach the employee. The manager should be familiar with the state's specific regulations. It is not appropriate to grant severance pay to an employee who is discharged for cause.

At the time of the termination, the performance of other employees may improve. This may be an appropriate time to hold a general staff meeting to review goals and responsibilities.

Unemployment Compensation

Laws regarding unemployment compensation are quite complex and vary from state to state. As an employer, you contribute payroll taxes into a state unemployment insurance fund. You also pay a federal unemployment tax (FUTA). State taxes vary with how many unemployment claims are made against the employer—if your employee turnover rate is low, your unemployment taxes should also be lower.

To receive unemployment compensation, the fired employee must file a claim. The eligibility requirements for unemployment compensation vary from state to state, and the employer against whom the claim is filed has the right to dispute the claimant's eligibility by supplying documentation about the termination. Generally speaking, if the employee has been laid off or is fired for undocumented reasons, the employee may be eligible for benefits.

In order to properly question a claim, the termination must be completely documented and have proceeded in the manner specified by state law. The state department of labor will provide you with information on unemployment compensation law in your state.

Notification of Termination

While the reasons for termination should be kept confidential, it is proper to notify both the staff, the property manager, and owner that the employee has been fired. (The property manager and owner, of course, should be given the reasons for termination.) Judgment should be used in notifying the residents and suppliers of the employee's termination.

For example, if the employee will remain in the property until the end of the month without performing after-hours service, the residents should be sent a notice similar to the following:

> Sam Jones is no longer a member of the staff. He will continue to reside at Park Manor. All service calls taken by Sam will be taken by Allan Brown at 123-4567. Our answering service will take your after-hours calls.

The following notice should be sent to suppliers:

> We have a house charge account with you which authorizes Sam Jones to sign for materials picked up at your store. Please be advised that effective February 1,

1988, Mr. Jones is no longer an employee of Park Manor.
Allan Brown, Mr. Jones's replacement, is hereby authorized
to sign for purchases.

Resignations

When an employee resigns, the employee's final workday
should be agreed upon. Employees are traditionally required
to give two week's notice that they are leaving. Any special
responsibilities and duties the employee may have during
that time—training another employee to take over, for
example—should be clearly understood.

It is desirable that a good employee leave with a feeling of
goodwill. When an employee resigns to take a higher paying
position, it is a reflection on your own professional skills in
providing appropriate training and experience. If, on the
other hand, an employee is leaving because of some
dissatisfaction with the job, an effort should be made to
understand the reasons for dissatisfaction. It may be too late
to keep this employee, but rectifying the situation that
caused the employee's dissatisfaction could prevent the
departure of other employees.

Summary

On-site employees are essential to the successful operation
of the property. Policies and procedures must be drawn up
for five areas of personnel relations: (1) selection, (2)
training, (3) supervision, (4) evaluation, and (5) termination.

The property's size and condition will determine how
many staff members are needed. A complete review and
updating of job descriptions should take place before the
recruitment process begins. The manager can use several
different methods and sources for recruitment: on-staff
promotions, personal contacts, employment agencies,
schools, and advertising. Each has its advantages and
disadvantages.

The employment application should be designed to obtain
all the information needed to qualify the applicant while

meeting federal, state, and local guidelines for fair employment practices. Interviews should be arranged for promising applicants.

The interview should take place in private. The manager should encourage the applicant to speak as much as possible, and should avoid "selling" the applicant on the job. The manager should form an evaluation of the applicant's appearance, qualifications, and ability to handle the position's responsibilities. Applicants who are unqualified for the position should be told at the end of the interview that they will not be considered. The list should be narrowed down to three or four applicants, who should be given a second interview. The person chosen for the position should receive an orientation to the property, a review of the job description and the property's policies and procedures, and actual hands-on training.

To supervise employees effectively, the manager must communicate clearly and concisely, present a professional attitude, and establish a system of controls, such as quotas, deadlines, time clocks, and purchase orders. Employee incentives and bonus programs are sometimes used as a means of control, but are usually counterproductive.

Employees should receive a formal evaluation of their performance once or twice each year. The employee's personal goals and any areas of unsatisfactory performance are discussed. The entire compensation package, including benefits, is also reviewed.

When an employee's performance is unsatisfactory, the problem should be defined and a plan of action to solve the problem agreed upon. In certain circumstances, the employee should be placed on probationary status. If disciplinary action fails to rectify the situation, the employee must be discharged decisively and professionally. If the employee is guilty of an act of misconduct, such as arriving to work drunk, he or she must be fired on that day. The termination must be thoroughly documented and proceed according to state law in order to counter any lawsuits or false unemployment benefit claims. The staff, property manager, owner, and suppliers should be notified that the employee has been dismissed.

Employees who resign are usually required to give two week's notice. Any special responsibilities or duties they have during that time should be clearly understood.

5
Resident Policies

Much of our discussion of on-site management has focused on setting up the business aspects of operating the property. The residents living on the property are the "customers" of this business; their money is the primary source of the business's income. They must be served well by the management, but must also abide by the contract. The residents are also part of a community of people, and must live together and cooperate with each other.

In order to accomplish this, a complete set of resident policies must be implemented. These policies will consist of guidelines for the manager to use in dealing with residents and guidelines for the residents regarding the use of the property. Leases, rules, and regulations are the primary forms of resident policies. Areas covered by these policies include communication, administration, and safety and security.

Leases

The *lease* is the agreement to rent between the property and the resident. The name for this agreement can be as specific as *lease* or as general as *rental agreement* or *contract*. Though leases in the past have tended to be simply a means of protecting the owner from loss, leases are now looked upon as an agreement between equals, each of whom has responsibilities towards the other. A lease which waives the resident's rights in many situations may be both impractical and legally unenforceable. Common sense should be exercised in drawing up the lease terms so that the end result is a useful document.

The on-site manager must follow three rules in preparing a lease: (1) the lease must comply with local, state, and federal law, (2) the lease should be in writing, and (3) the lease should be specific and enforceable. The manager must also consider the form of lease traditional in the marketing area. In some states, the majority of tenancies are month-to-month; in others, a one-year lease is standard. Some states provide a state-approved lease form, others provide guidelines for leases.

Clauses in a Standard Lease

Each lease must contain certain items of information and certain agreements. Clauses in a standard lease would include:

Names of the parties. There are two parties to the lease: the *lessor*, who is the owner or the property management company; and the *lessee* who leases the apartment from the lessor. All occupants of legal age should sign the lease and be *jointly and severally* (as a group and individually) responsible for the lease. If one party to the lease later decides to live elsewhere, the lease should be either rewritten or modified to reflect the change.

Address. It is not enough to state, "building 8, unit 3, parking space 25," as a means of identification. The complete address, zip code, parking space, and storage space number should be included in the lease.

Term of lease. The lease should state the beginning and ending date of the rental period, as well as state what will happen at the end of the lease term. At one time many leases were automatically renewed for a similar period of

time unless notice to the contrary was given. A current
trend is for the lease to convert to a month-to-month
tenancy at the same or a higher rental rate. In any event,
the lease should state the amount of notice the resident
needs to give in order to renew, terminate, or convert the
lease at expiration.

Rental amount, escalation clause, conditions of payment.
The rental amount may be stated as a monthly amount or as
a term-of-lease sum with payment instructions (for example:
$3,600 annually, payable at $300 per month on the first day
of each month in advance). In some states it is difficult to
collect more than one month's rent in a lawsuit when the
lease is broken by the resident unless the rental amount is
expressed both as a monthly amount and as a full-term sum.

Escalator clauses, which became popular in the mid-70s,
permit the rental rate to increase automatically either by
increments in comparison to a standard index or as certain
costs (such as utilities costs) increase. The manager who
incorporates any escalation clause in a lease should call
attention to the clause and not assume the resident has read
and understands the clause. It may prove helpful to stamp a
notice on the face of each lease saying, "escalator clause
included," and to have the resident initial the notice.

Security deposit. The lease must state the amount of the
security deposit, what it secures, and how it will be held
and refunded. Some security deposits are partially for lease
performance and partially for cleaning when the unit is
vacated. Other deposits include a nonrefundable credit
report fee. Laws vary from state to state regarding payment
of interest on security deposits, the amount which can be
charged, and the time limit for returning the deposit.

Occupancy restrictions. The lease must state the names of
anyone allowed to reside in the apartment besides those
who sign the lease. The names and ages of minor children
are taken from the rental application.

Pet restrictions. If no pets are permitted, the lease should
include this restriction. If pets are permitted, the lease

should refer to an attached pet agreement. The pet agreement should be specific and detailed. It should include not only the rules regarding the pet but a description of the pet as well: name, age, breed, size, and weight.

Use restrictions. The lease must state that the premises will only be used for private residential use. Any other uses must be identified and in compliance with zoning restrictions.

Utilities. The utilities clause states which utilities are provided and which party—the lessor or the lessee—is to pay for each.

Services, maintenance, and repairs. This clause of the lease states what services are to be provided, what maintenance standards will be maintained, and who is responsible for each. Traditionally, the resident's responsibility is limited to "maintaining the premises in good repair, normal wear and tear excepted."

Inspections, access, keys. The lease should state what access the manager has to the unit in routine and emergency situations, as well as the manager's privileges in showing the premises for leasing after the resident has given notice of vacating. A prohibition against installing additional locks or changing locks should be included in this clause.

Liability and insurance. This clause, sometimes referred to as a *hold harmless* clause, states who is liable (and who is *not* liable) in the event of loss or damage to the premises or the resident's property. It often requires the resident to carry apartment insurance protecting the property owner as well as the resident in the event of personal injury or loss.

Assignment, subletting, transfer. The lease must state what privileges the resident has to either assign or sublet the apartment. If there is an allowance for lease termination due to employment transfer, the guidelines should be specific and require complete documentation as well as sufficient notice.

Casualty loss. This clause spells out the resident's and owner's rights in the event of a fire, flood, or other disaster. It provides for continuation or cancellation of the lease, abatement of rent, or similar action when the premises are rendered either partially or totally uninhabitable.

Default, eviction, abandonment, bankruptcy. The lease must provide for appropriate legal action to be taken in the event the resident fails to pay rent, abandons the property, or files for bankruptcy.

Condemnation. The lease must make provisions in the event that a local, state, or federal governing agency takes over the property by condemnation—more formally, by right of *eminent domain*. The resident needs protection in the form of a realistic amount of time to vacate upon notification of condemnation. The owner needs protection against being unable to honor the lease term because of the condemnation. The owner should also be protected from any obligation to share with the resident any award made by the government in settlement of the condemnation action.

Quiet enjoyment. This clause, dating back to 18th-century English law, promises that the resident is entitled to exclusive possession of the premises without interruption or interference from the owner.

Rules and regulations. Current rules and regulations should be included in the lease, either as part of the lease itself or as an attachment. The clause should provide that revisions and additions to the rules automatically become part of the current lease once proper notice is given.

Notices. This clause covers two areas. First, it generally contains a waiver of notice for rent due. Without this waiver it would be the owner's responsibility to send a statement for rent each month. Second, the clause specifies the legal address for both the lessor and lessee to which notices must be delivered.

Independence of clauses. This clause states that if any one clause of the lease is in violation of law, the clause becomes void but the balance of the lease remains in full force and effect. This protection is usually provided because of changes in local, state, or federal law that might render a particular clause illegal.

Signature block. This section of the lease usually contains a statement that all parties have read and understand the lease and that the rental application automatically becomes part of the lease.

Specialized Clauses

Additional clauses may be needed for specialized situations. For example, an older resident may request a "death clause" allowing the lease to be terminated by notice from the executor of the resident's estate. A young couple may want a clause allowing termination if a home is purchased. A single resident may want to be covered for "any one roommate" while retaining complete liability and responsibility for the lease. The manager must consider whether the requested clauses will compliment the lease or whether they will serve as a one-sided termination agreement. Leases are difficult to enforce if a maze of clauses exist. A straightforward, commonsense lease will do much to promote long residencies in your property.

Reviewing the Lease

The lease terms and rental policies should be reviewed at regular intervals to keep them timely. Careful records should be maintained throughout the year on lease problems. If problems appear to be related to a particular clause, the difficulty within the clause should be identified and the clause revised or removed.

Creating Rules and Regulations

While the lease exists to outline the responsibilities and preserve the rights of the resident, the property's rules and regulations exist primarily to preserve harmony. Rules and regulations also promote safety and encourage responsibility.

For rules to be successfully enforced, they must be kept simple and sensible. Too many rules can be distracting. An endless list of rules which governs everything from the pool to the parking lot can create frustration.

Let us examine the case of a manager we will name Martha. Martha started her position as on-site manager with a basic lease and some simple rules. Every time something went wrong, she added a clause to her standard lease to cover that particular situation. Soon her lease was four pages long, and she decided to stop adding to the lease—she began adding new rules, instead. Soon her list of rules became as long as her lease. There were rules for what time to wash cars, the volume at which the bass on a stereo could be set, and when to turn out patio lights at night. The inevitable happened: her residents stopped honoring *any* rules. When the residents threatened to form a tenant union, Martha finally made her lease and rules sensible and general in nature. Once a standard lease and no-nonsense rules were implemented, resident cooperation improved.

Rules and regulations for the property will cover four areas:

1. **Safety and security.** Building security, use and replacement of keys, fire safety procedures, storage locker use, speed limits.

2. **Resident comfort.** Noise, parties, number of occupants, and guests.

3. **Property use.** Use of fixtures and equipment, recreational facilities, parking facilities, and common areas; pets and children; resident decoration or improvements; legality of use.

4. **Communication.** Notices, notifications, service requests.

Exhibit 5.1 contains examples of typical property rules and regulations.

Exhibit 5.1   Sample Rules and Regulations

Safety and Security

1. For your protection we suggest you lock your car at all times and register it with our office. Do not let anyone unknown into the building or your apartment. Please be sure the building door locks behind you when you enter or leave. Lock your deadbolt at all times.

2. Locks may not be added or changed without the written authorization of management.

3. If you are locked out, contact the office or night number for assistance. There is a $5 fee for lockouts after office hours. Extra keys may be obtained from the office for both your apartment and mailbox.

4. The storage room is in the basement with an individual locker available for each unit. Do not leave or store anything in the hallway of the storage room. Place your lock on the door and your name and apartment number in the slot provided. The management is not responsible for loss or damage to items in the storage room.

Resident Comfort

5. Occupancy is limited to those named in the lease agreement. If a change becomes necessary, please contact the manager promptly.

6. As outlined in your lease, excessive noise which disturbs your neighbors is prohibited. Please be considerate of your neighbors' privacy by keeping your stereo and other audio equipment at a level which will not disturb them.

7. Overnight guests are welcome for periods not to exceed two weeks. If special circumstances require an extended visit, please contact the manager to make arrangements.

Community Use

8. Parking places are assigned. If you find another car in your space, please call the number posted in the parking lot to have it removed. Guests must park in spaces at the ends of the building marked *Guests*. Extra cars belonging to residents should be parked in the extra lot—not in our guest spaces.

9. Reservations are accepted and rules are available for use of the party rooms at the management office.

10. Pet guidelines are covered under the separate pet agreement attached to your lease. Permission and guidelines for visiting pets should be obtained from the office.

11. Any decorating or changes made to your apartment must have the advance written consent of the management. Please contact the office.

12. Visiting children should be under the supervision of an adult at all times while in the common or public areas.

13. All window coverings shall show white to the exterior.

14. Awnings, blinds, or other patio/balcony enclosures or screens are not permitted.

Exhibit 5.1   (Continued)

15. Residents shall not interfere with any portion of the heating, cooling, or lighting apparatus.

16. Personal property of residents shall not be placed or left in lobbies, hallways, or common areas. Bicycles shall be kept locked in the bicycle racks provided or in the resident's apartment or storage locker. Motorcycles, trailers, boats, and other nonautomobile vehicles shall be parked in the areas designated for this purpose.

17. Any damage caused to the common areas of the building by residents moving in or out shall be paid for by the resident.

Communication

18. In the event damage occurs to your apartment, please notify the management immediately so that insurance coverage can be arranged without delay.

19. Plumbing stoppages can affect other apartments. For this reason, please notify the management immediately of any plumbing breakage or stoppage. If the cause of the stoppage is found to be the resident's fault, the resident will be billed for the service call.

20. Names shall be displayed on doors or mailboxes only in the uniform manner prescribed by management.

Communication Policies

As in every area of on-site management, the manager must adopt effective methods and policies of communication with residents. The objectives of the manager's communication policies should be to ensure that (1) residents are comfortable and safe, (2) residents are treated equally and professionally, and (3) residents are made to feel that the property is their home. Through effective communication policies, the manager strives to meet the residents' needs, preferences, and desires while maintaining the standards necessary to successfully operate the property.

Resident Handbook

The resident handbook is a primary form of communication between manager and resident. It serves as a public relations tool and a method of education. It contains information on every policy affecting the resident.

The handbook should be carefully prepared; if possible, with the aid of an experienced writer or editor. It may be a spiral-bound notebook or an assemblage of neatly duplicated pages in a simple binder, but should present a professional appearance. The handbook includes information on the following subjects:

The neighborhood. Information on shopping, transportation, recreational facilities, churches, library, post office, etc.

The property. A map of the property locating the manager's office, recreational facilities, laundries, mailboxes and storage areas.

Rental policies. Leases, renewals, occupancy limits.

Maintenance procedures. Arranging for repairs, emergency service, operation of appliances, etc.

Safety and security. Information on contacting the fire or police departments, emergency medical assistance, keys, lockouts, insurance protection, etc.

Resident comfort. Noise or disturbances, courtesy to neighbors, how to report complaints, etc.

Recreational facilities. Procedures for use, guest policies, etc.

Parking. Assignments, vehicles permitted, guidelines for repair/washing, motorcycles, recreational vehicles, etc.

Miscellaneous information. Staff names, deliveries, waterbeds, social programs, voting, etc.

Telephone numbers. Maintenance, manager, emergencies.

The handbook cannot be a substitute for good communication as the resident moves in; it is designed rather to reinforce your policies and procedures. For this purpose, it should be kept completely up-to-date. When time permits, it is helpful to offer the handbook to the incoming resident in advance of occupancy.

Newsletters

A monthly or bimonthly newsletter can be a major means of communication for the manager. The newsletter can help

---

Exhibit 5.2   Acceptable and Poorly Stated Rules

Acceptable	Poorly Stated
Laundry room open from 8 A.M until 10:00 P.M.	Keep out after 10:00 P.M.
Please run dishwashers prior to 11:00 P.M.	No noise after 11:00 P.M.
Clubhouse may be reserved for private parties—contact office for rules.	Clubhouse only available for parties with $100 deposit.
Tennis courts open to residents and accompanied guests.	Non-residents: keep off courts.

---

create good public relations by fostering a good image for the property. Items that could be included in the newsletter are: (1) mentions of maintenance rules that are being abused, including clarifications of the reasoning behind the rule; (2) explanations of new security procedures; (3) announcements of social or recreational activities and events; (4) announcements of activities that occur on a regular basis, such as window cleaning; (5) small feature stories about residents or staff who have received awards or who are involved in interesting projects; and (6) requests for resident input.

A newsletter should *not* be used to issue major new rules and regulations. In these cases, residents should receive an individual letter.

Signs and Notices

While the resident handbook contains all the rules and regulations, it will be necessary to post many rules, especially those regarding the use of facilities. In order to preserve good public relations and to encourage compliance, these rules must be stated diplomatically. Exhibit 5.2 shows acceptable and unacceptable forms of stating rules.

Routine communication can take place through the property newsletter. In some situations, however, immediate notification to all residents is necessary. A standard location for emergency notices should be established *before* the need arises. The most typical location is over the mailbox or near the entrance door of each building.

For nonemergency notices, a flyer may be used as well as a notice. A typical notice of this kind might inform residents that water will be turned off at a certain time for water-line maintenance, or it might inform residents that the maintenance worker is going on vacation. In any event, the notice must state (1) what is to take place, (2) when it is to take place, (3) why it is taking place, and (4) where to go for further information.

Government regulations require that certain licenses and notices be posted, such as those for swimming pools or elevators. To prevent tampering with the license, a standard notice may be posted instead stating that the inspection certificate is on file in the management office.

Resolving Resident Conflicts

A sense of privacy is sometimes difficult for apartment residents to maintain, which makes privacy all the more important to them. The manager's policies regarding resident comfort must be designed to create harmony between residents. But because resident comfort depends largely on the behavior of other residents, it is very difficult to come up with cut-and-dried rules and regulations. Most resident conflicts will have to be resolved by the manager as they occur. Complaints about other residents' behavior must be handled diplomatically and confidentially.

The majority of the conflicts that arise will have to do with noise. Most instances of excessive noise occur within the first few weeks of occupancy. The incoming resident needs to know the volume level of music that will not disturb others and what noises will or will not carry through the walls, floors, and ceilings. Many guidelines can be set forth in the resident handbook, others can be discussed in the preoccupancy conference.

When residents do come to you with problems about noise, they are very likely to be quite angry. Say that a resident comes to your office and yells, "I can't put up with those noisy people upstairs any longer!" Your first step must be to define the problem. Calmly ask the resident about the specifics of the problem: What exactly are they doing that causes the noise? Is it happening at any particular time of day? What would the resident consider to be a realistic solution? By showing concern and interest, you will likely lessen the resident's anger as well as discover the exact nature of the problem.

Sometimes residents try to resolve their problems with other residents themselves. This often only magnifies the problem. Instead, offer the resident the opportunity to remain anonymous, assuring him or her that you will take care of the problem. If you can create trust by professionally handling one complaint, the resident will probably trust you to take care of other problems as well. And other problems *will* occur.

Tenant Organizations

A particularly delicate area of manager-resident communication is tenant organizations. Management practices do not necessarily have to be outrageous for a tenant union to form. Tenant unions developed out of consumerism, with its emphasis on consumer rights, and political activism, with its emphasis on action. Dissatisfied residents decided that if what they felt were their rights—such as fewer rent increases or more habitable units—were not granted promptly, they would organize their neighbors and stage demonstrations. When courts rendered judgments on unfit properties and buildings, activist resident groups attempted to apply those judgments to all properties and buildings. Legislators became involved, passing regulations that accorded tenant rights. Many residents want the right to live on the properties on terms and conditions agreeable to them. If this right is not granted, or if the property is in poor condition or poorly managed, the residents will organize. Their action can result in court decisions that severely penalize the property and handicap sensible management.

Preparation for dealing with a tenant union or similar organization begins with the establishment of the management plan and operations manual. State and local requirements on housing should be consulted. By beginning with realistic rules, policies, leases, and rental rates, the chances that your property will be judged unreasonable are diminished. While many properties may have activist groups, the majority of your residents can and will live peacefully and quietly if you are providing good communication, conditions, and services at a fair rental rate.

If you are confronted by a group of your residents who may or may not be formally organized into a coalition or union when they approach you, the following actions will be appropriate:

1. Determine who the group represents. Is it a small minority claiming to represent the entire building?

2. Ask them each to submit individual reports itemizing their complaints and grievances. If they are unwilling to submit individual reports, remind them that each person is entitled to individual consideration since each has an individual lease. Review each complaint carefully and decide whether each complaint is genuine and specific.

3. Offer to meet with each complainant individually. Work with each on resolving problems individually.

4. Act promptly—within days—on each legitimate complaint to defuse the situation.

By taking a businesslike approach and indicating that you are willing to work out difficulties, but only on an individual basis, you are splitting the group's one large grievance into smaller, more manageable problems. By treating each member of the group as an individual, you are lessening the strength they have together as a group.

If the complaints by your residents alert you that an immediate change in policy is needed, or if the residents are already formally organized, treat the situation seriously and enlist aid immediately. Sources for good counsel on handling a tenant union would be your property manager, owner, company lawyer, the local property management or apartment association, and any landlord-tenant mediation commission in your area. The union may create a great deal of media publicity. How professionally you handle and resolve their grievances and complaints will have an impact on your marketing effort as well as on the property itself.

It is important not to make assumptions about the motivation of the tenant union members. Some may be honestly looking for rectification of what they consider to be an unfair condition. Others may be politically motivated, seeking publicity and attention. Still others may simply be confused about a particular policy or requirement. It is up to the manager to sort out the situation and reach a solution which is fair to all parties—but which also meet the owner's goals and requirements. Regardless of who may be right or wrong in the matter, it is your professional responsibility to reach a satisfactory conclusion.

Administration

Requests for Rule or Policy Waivers

In some cases a rule or policy waiver becomes necessary, even though the rule or policy is realistic. The manager should review the request carefully before deciding whether to agree or not agree to the waiver. If the waiver is given, consideration should be given to changing the rule for everyone. If the waiver is not given, the manager's reason must make sense. All waivers should be confirmed in writing as an addendum to the lease.

Apartment Transfers

Residents often like to change apartments when a more desirable unit becomes available. If the resident is an asset to the property, it is generally a good idea to permit a change. Conditions for approving such a transfer might include:

1. Good rental payment record.
2. No history of unnecessary complaints.
3. New lease at current market rate to be executed.
4. Vacated unit to be left in good and clean condition.
5. Resident's willingness to cooperate in timing the transfer to avoid lengthy *downtime* (time the unit is unoccupied).

Resident Improvements

Your residents may wish to wallpaper, change the paint color, add wall mirrors, or even recarpet their unit. Often they are seeking your permission, not your funding, especially if they anticipate staying for many years.

The simplest improvement for residents to make is painting their apartment a different color. A common policy is to allow residents to change paint colors freely, provided that when they vacate the expense of any extra coat or coats of paint to restore the original decor will be at the residents' expense. The resident wishing to repaint should be made aware that some colors are easier to cover over than others. A shade of blue will probably need only one extra coat to be covered; brown enamel may take two or three extra coats.

Wallpapering is more permanent than paint and is very difficult to remove. Your policy might be to allow residents to wallpaper their units provided that when they vacate, the wallpaper is to be removed at their expense, including the cost of labor and surface restoration. If the next resident approves of the vacating resident's choice of wallpaper, no removal need be made. These policies place the burden of responsibility on the outgoing resident.

It is rarely advisable to permit structural changes or dramatic changes in carpeting. If a resident wishes to use his or her own light fixture or refrigerator, permission can be given provided the resident is held responsible for the storage of the unit's original fixtures.

When in doubt as to whether or not a modification or decoration should be permitted, an estimate to restore the unit may be determined and an extra deposit equal to that amount required of the resident.

Parking Assignments

In order to more easily identify unauthorized cars parked in the parking lot, all vehicles owned by residents should be registered with the manager's office. A form similar to exhibit 5.3 may be used.

Once the registration forms have been gathered, there are several useful ways to list registered vehicles. One list might be by vehicle license number; another might list the parking places by space and by resident assignment. Another useful list might be in the form of a map showing the location of each space, its number, and the resident to whom it is assigned. At a glance the manager can identify the problem

Exhibit 5.3   Vehicle Registration Form

Vehicle License Number _____

Property _____

Occupant _____

Unit _____   Phone _____

Make of Vehicle _____

Year _____   Color _____

Operator's License Number _____

State of Vehicle Registry _____

A separate registration form must be filled out for each vehicle.

Occupant's Signature _____

Date _____

space and take action to remove the illegally parked vehicle. The blank map, showing only space location and number, can be given to residents as an aid in reporting parking problems.

Storage Space

Accurate records of storage space assignments can help you identify which lockers should be empty and which are assigned. When residents are about to vacate, they may forget about the storage area; they should be sent a reminder before vacating. Most states have laws which will prevent you from disposing of unclaimed storage area items without notification to the former resident. If you have failed to remind residents about their storage area, it may be difficult to reach them after they have moved, and you may be required to store the items for many years.

Move-In Procedures

Several procedures can be utilized to ensure that the move-in process for new residents goes smoothly.

The unit should be inspected to make certain that it is in

perfect condition. The locks to the unit should have been changed after the previous resident vacated.

The manager should meet with all new residents to orient them to the property. A copy of the lease should be given to the resident if one has not already been sent. Make sure that the security deposit and first month's rent (or prorated amount due) has been received before releasing the keys.

The manager and incoming resident should walk through the unit, noting the condition of the unit and any problems that exist. Use of the HVAC (heating, ventilation, and air conditioning) system, the appliances, and any safety features should be demonstrated. If it is the manager's responsibility to change the utility billing to the new resident, be sure that an authorization form is signed. If the resident is to change the billing, check to see that this has been done. It is important to point out the smoke detector and fire extinguisher and explain their use. Fire exits should also be shown.

The resident handbook should be briefly reviewed. Laundry, trash disposal locations, and recreational facilities should all be shown and guidelines for their use explained. Moving procedures should be reviewed: where moving vans or trucks may be parked, which elevator may be used, where to dispose of moving cartons, etc. Many new residents will have new furnishings delivered during the first month of occupancy; make certain the new resident understands which entrances may be used for deliveries. Emergency and service request procedures should be reviewed at this time.

A typical move-in meeting may take anywhere from 30 to 60 minutes. At its end, new residents should be thoroughly acquainted with their new community.

Move-Out Procedures

Certain steps must be taken when a move-out is anticipated. The manager must confirm the move-out date, provide move-out guidelines, collect the rent, inspect the unit, and return the deposit.

All moving notices should be specific and in writing. If a resident gives notice by telephone, or if the notice is vague about the exact date, the manager should obtain written confirmation of the resident's intention to move. The manager then provides the resident with a written notice explaining the resident's lease liability or nonliability, the procedures for showing the unit, the cleaning requirements, and the procedures for inspection and deposit refund.

In coming to an agreement regarding the vacating date, consideration should be given to prorating the rent to accommodate both the resident's schedule and the property's needs. If residents are allowed to vacate slightly before or after the first day of the month, it will be easier to schedule staff to prepare the unit for the next incoming resident. If the manager is rigid and insists that each vacating resident pay a full month's rent, the residents may stay through the last day of the month. This can create an overload for the maintenance crew if several residents vacate in the same month.

When the resident has vacated the unit and is ready to turn in the keys, the manager and resident together should duplicate the walk-through inspection made at occupancy and agree on the condition of the unit. The inspection form should note any repairs or cleaning necessary and who will be responsible for the cost. It should be dated and signed; a copy should be given to the outgoing resident. If exact charges cannot be determined during the walk-through, they should be calculated as quickly as possible.

It is considered good public relations to return security deposits promptly. Most state and local governments have regulations governing the return of security deposits and the charges that are permissable against them.

Safety and Security

Resident safety and security is becoming an increasingly important issue. Not only must the building be safe and secure, but the residents must be educated in safety and security measures as well. Security and safety policies should be reinforced each month in the property newsletter. Your maintenance staff should be trained to note and report potential problems.

Emergency Procedures

It is not sufficient to simply train the residents in emergency procedures. The manager must have a written plan in the event of a disaster. It can be helpful to enlist the aid of the local fire and police departments in preparing such a plan. Reciprocal arrangements can be made with other nearby apartment properties. In case of fire, they can provide an emergency base of operations and extra temporary staff.

Fire Safety

Many states now have laws requiring smoke detectors and fire extinguishers in apartment buildings. The manager should consult with the local fire department regarding this requirement.

The resident handbook should contain all fire safety information, but individual instruction is also needed. During the move-in orientation meeting with the incoming resident, time should be set aside to thoroughly explain safety measures. The location and importance of smoke detectors, fire extinguishers, emergency exits, and fire alarms should be emphasized. Information on what to do in the event of a fire emergency should be reviewed. The resident should be shown how to test the smoke detector, how to operate the fire extinguisher, and how to check for a fire before opening the unit door. The telephone numbers of the local fire department should be made available. The fire department can also be an excellent source of training for residents. Annually, a local fireman can be invited to come to the property to demonstrate the use of fire extinguishers and stress the importance of smoke detectors.

Building Security

Great care should be taken when promising or guaranteeing security. Legal decisions have shown a trend towards holding owners liable for their residents' safety, especially when security is offered or when the building is in a high-crime area. One such example took place in Miami in the case of *Ten Associates* v. *Mildred McCutchen*, 39 S.2d 860 [1981]. The court in this case awarded $76,000 to a resident who had been attacked in her apartment, which was in a high-crime area of Miami. Because the owners did have

Exhibit 5.4   Key Receipt

Property _____

Occupant _____

Unit _____ Phone _____

The undersigned hereby acknowledges receipt of the following keys:

Number of Keys

Serial Numbers
(If applicable)

_____ Apartment   _____

_____ Mailbox   _____

_____ _____ _____

_____ _____ _____

Occupant's Signature _____

Date _____

knowledge of previous crimes committed in the area, the
court stated that the owners were responsible for providing
adequate security. The likelihood of continuing criminal
conduct was, according to the court, "reasonably
foreseeable."

Residents should be encouraged to lock their cars, use the
deadbolt locks, use a timer light when away, pick up mail
promptly, and be alert to strange cars or visitors on the
premises. Residents should be encouraged to notify the
manager any time an unusual situation occurs. Security is
one area of management where it is better to have ten false
calls than miss one genuine emergency.

Key control. Effective key control policies will be a major
means of providing security. Records should be kept of all
serial numbers and all keys issued to residents. When
issuing keys to new residents, it will be helpful to have the
residents sign a key receipt form (see exhibit 5.4). The
receipt should be kept on file until the resident moves. Any
fines for lost keys should be mentioned on the receipt form.

Any extra sets of keys for the individual units should be
locked away at all times. To provide further security, encode
each key with a reference number rather than the unit

address. The number can be cross-referenced in a log kept
separate from the keys.

If master keys and submaster keys are used, they must be
protected at all costs. Every person in possession of a
master key has access to every unit in the property as well
as all recreational areas, thereby jeopardizing the security of
the property.

It is poor policy to permit a resident who is locked out to
"borrow" the master key for access. The resident may forget
to return the key. The resident may also tell other residents
it is "easy" to borrow the master key. An extra key for each
unit may be kept on a key board for use by residents or
delivery personnel needing access. If no key is available, a
staff member should go to the unit and unlock the door. If a
master key is lost, the expense of rekeying every lock can
cost thousands of dollars, at $10 to $20 per lock, while the
opportunity for theft exists until the changeover is made.

Rather than spending time in deciding whether or not a
resident has returned all the keys upon vacating, a policy
should be instituted of changing the locks at each turnover.
One way to change locks without incurring substantial
expense is to purchase several extra locks which have their
own separate keys but are keyed to the master. When a unit
is vacated, a lock from the stock is installed in the unit. The
old lock with at least two keys is returned to stock. The
locks are thus rotated through the units without the
expense of rekeying each time. A supply of six will provide
enough backup for most properties. When no keys are
available for a unit, the locks can be held until several are
ready for rekeying, thereby reducing cost.

Insurance

We have discussed the steps both manager and residents
must take to ensure the safety and security of the property.
When these steps fail, or when catastrophe strikes in spite
of them, it is extremely important that the property's
insurance coverage is adequate to protect the owner from
loss. The insurance needs of the property will change from
year to year and must be periodically examined and
reviewed. The manager must understand the types of

insurance coverage available to be able to assist in planning coverage.

Coinsurance

At one time, many apartment property owners were not carrying sufficient coverage to insure a major disaster. Since most fires or disasters affected only a partial area of a building, the owners carried only partial coverage. To encourage owners to carry full coverage, insurance companies developed *coinsurance* or *shared insurance*. Coinsurance requires you to carry a policy valued at a certain percentage of the property's value. Eighty percent is the common percentage required. For instance, if your building is worth $500,000 in cash value and your coinsurance requirement is 80 percent, then you are required to carry $400,000 in insurance. If you carry the $400,000, the policy will pay the claim up to the policy's limit. If you carry less than $400,000, however, the amount paid for a loss will only be equal to the percentage carried of the required amount of insurance.

Say that the value of your building increases from $400,000 to $600,000. The coinsurance requirement is still 80 percent, so the new required amount of coverage is $480,000. You however, still carry only $400,000, or 83.2 percent of the amount you are required to carry. A loss of $60,000 occurs. You will be paid only 83.2 percent of the $60,000 loss, or $49,920. One can see that it is extremely important to keep coinsurance up-to-date.

Types of Coverage

The primary types of coverage and the losses they cover are as follows:

1. **Fire and extended coverage.** Traditional losses, such as fire, and non-traditional losses, such as wind damage, flooding, explosions, and other disasters.
2. **Theft.** Losses from burglary, robbery, or mysterious disappearance.

3. **Liability.** Losses resulting from the negligence of the property, its staff, or its actions. A liability loss might occur if someone slips on an icy sidewalk that has not been cleared promptly after a snowfall.

4. **Accident.** Losses or injuries that are accidental or unavoidable. For example, the wind loosens shingles which fall on a parked car, damaging the paint. This type of coverage overlaps at times with liability coverage.

5. **Employee bonding.** Owner's loss from employee dishonesty, theft, or misrepresentation.

6. **Workers' compensation.** Medical coverage (and often loss-of-income coverage) in the event an employee is injured either on the job or on the way to or from work.

7. **Income.** Loss of rental income after the premises become uninhabitable due to a fire or disaster.

8. **Errors and omissions.** Provides for the unknowing or inadvertent acts of the ownership or employees where the injured party claims the property is liable.

Each type of coverage is important. Many will be combined into one general coverage (often called an *umbrella* or *multiperil* coverage). Some policies will contain an escalator clause that provides for the value of the coverage to increase over time.

Other categories of insurance have been designed according to specialized needs. Some of the more specialized coverage available might include plate glass insurance, HVAC insurance, major equipment insurance, contents insurance (for items owned by the property), and fleet automobile insurance.

Deductibles

With any type of insurance, you may also carry a *deductible*. The insurance company deducts a certain percentage of the loss from its payment. It is not uncommon for the deductible in an apartment property to be $500, $1,000 or more per claim or loss. It can be applied to some coverages and eliminated on others. The purpose of using a deductible is

to reduce the cost of insurance coverage by sharing the
initial, or smallest, risks.

Records and Claims

Insurance records must be carefully maintained. A special
file should show the amounts of coverage, the carrier, the
renewal or expiration date of the policies, and the agent to
contact for renewal or claims. Guidelines are provided by
the insurance company for what to do in the event of a
claim. In incidents involving an injury or death, time is of
the essence. Your report must be given to the OSHA
(Occupational Safety and Health Act) Commission in your
state. A prompt call to the insurance broker or agent will
obtain the proper forms and guidance for this report.

Guidelines are also available for reporting to the local
police and fire departments. These reports should also be
made with the counsel of your insurance agent.

Review of Coverage

It is advisable to review the property's coverage annually. In
order to facilitate this review, your insurance coverage may
be summarized on a form similar to exhibit 5.5.
Consideration should be given to installing any additional
safety precautions, such as individual unit smoke alarms,
that would obtain a discount. The insurance savings may
pay for the additional installation costs of the alarms within
a year or two, and your residents will be provided with a
safer environment.

Summary

Resident policies will consist of guidelines for the manager
to use in dealing with residents and guidelines for the
residents regarding the use of the property. Leases, rules,
and regulations are the primary forms of resident policies.
Areas covered by these policies include communication,
administration, and safety and security.

The *lease* is the agreement to rent between the property

Exhibit 5.5   Insurance Coverage Summary

Property _____   Address _____   Date _____   Owner _____

Kind of Coverage	Insured by (Company)	Agent: Name and Phone	Amount of Coverage	Period From	Period To	Annual Premium
Fire and Extended Coverage						
Liability						
Boiler						
Workmen's Compensation						
Rent Income						
Employee Fidelity Bond						
Moneys and Securities						
Plate Glass						
Burglary and Theft						
Vandalism						
Automobile: Collision, Bodily Injury, Property Damage						

and the resident. All leases (1) must comply with local, state, and federal law, (2) should be in writing, and (3) should be specific and enforceable. Clauses in a standard lease—besides listing the parties, term of lease, and rental amount—attempt to cover every contingency that could affect the agreement. The lease terms and rental policies should be reviewed at regular intervals.

Rules and regulations exist to preserve harmony, promote safety, and encourage responsibility. For rules to be successfully enforced, they must be kept simple and sensible. Rules and regulations will cover four areas: (1) safety and security, (2) resident comfort, (3) property use, and (4) communication.

The major means of communication between manager and resident are the resident handbook, newsletters, and signs and notices. The resident handbook should contain information on every policy affecting the resident, including all safety and maintenance request procedures. Newsletters should *not* be used to issue major new rules and regulations. Emergency notices should be placed in a standard location, such as over the mailbox.

Conflicts between residents must be handled professionally and confidentially. The manager should try to act as mediator between residents. Conflicts between groups of residents and management should be treated seriously. If a tenant union has already been formed, legal advice should be sought immediately.

Many resident policies are administrative, covering such areas as rule or policy waivers, apartment transfers, resident improvements, parking assignments, and storage space. Move-in procedures should include an orientation meeting with the incoming resident and a walk-through inspection of the unit. When a move-out is anticipated, the manager must confirm the move-out date, provide move-out guidelines, collect the rent, inspect the unit, and return the deposit.

Residents must be educated in safety and security measures. Procedures and polices must be established to cover emergencies, fire safety, building security, and key control. In order to protect the owner from loss, the property must carry appropriate insurance coverage. Most properties are covered by *coinsurance*. The primary types of insurance coverage include fire and extended coverage, theft, liability, accident, employee bonding, workers' compensation, income, and errors and omissions. Insurance records must be carefully maintained.

6

Rental Rates
and Collections

Rent provides the income needed to operate the property. The rental rates established must meet the income requirements of the property while taking market conditions into consideration. Collection policies and procedures must ensure the security of the rent and provide for every contingency. Delinquencies must be pursued vigorously. Rental records must be complete and accurate; record keeping is perhaps more important for this area of on-site management than for any other.

Forms of Rent

Traditional

Several different forms of rent exist. The most familiar and the most traditional form of rent is an amount levied on an apartment unit (including or not including utilities) in equal monthly amounts.

Seasonal and Term

Seasonal rent, often used in resort areas, is adjusted by season. A higher rate is charged during peak occupancy periods of the year. Seasonal rents can be divided into three levels: *low season*, *high season*, and *off season*. Off season is the time of year most uncharacteristic of the area, such as the summer months in ski areas. Low season is the period just before and after the peak time, and high season is the busiest time of year for the area.

There are two ways to establish seasonal rental rates. The first is to determine the total amount of income needed. The amount that can be obtained during high season is calculated and subtracted from the total income figure. The remainder is divided among the low- and off-season months. The resulting figure is the minimum amount of income that must be obtained during low and off season.

The second method is to establish an annual base rate. Whatever the manager feels can be obtained for the particular season is then added to the base rate. The beginning manager is encouraged to calculate season rates using both methods and comparing the different rates obtained before setting the final rates.

Term rent, similar to seasonal rent, is also often collected in resort areas. Units are leased for one season—in Florida, for instance, from November through April—with the lease terms stating that the rent is payable in full in advance.

Head Rent

A third type of rent is called *head* rent. It can be applied to either traditional or seasonal rent schedules. The lease establishes how many persons may occupy a particular unit; there is an additional charge for each person exceeding that number. The reasoning behind head rent is that the greater the number of people living in the apartment, the greater the use of utilities, the greater the wear and tear, and the greater the number of service calls there will be. Head rent is often used in college towns and resort areas. Because of the high rate of transience in these areas, head rent can be difficult to enforce.

Apportioned

The fourth type of rent is called *apportioned* rent: apartment units are graded according to extra features and a different rent is apportioned to each. A base rental rate is established, to which extra charges are added on a per-unit basis. Here are examples of categories for which extra charges may be assessed:

1. View.
2. Floor level.
3. Exposure.
4. Proximity to amenities and recreational facilities.
5. New(er) carpeting.
6. New(er) or additional appliances.
7. Availability of cable television.
8. Proximity to parking or extra parking.

Miscellaneous Rent Charges

To the rental rates are added miscellaneous rent charges, which are accounted for separately. They might include parking fees, laundry service, use of amenities, pet fees and/or deposits, extra services prorated over the lease term (repainting a unit prior to the scheduled repainting date, etc.), installation of new features (dishwasher, etc.).

Security Deposits

The basic deposit required from the incoming resident is the security deposit, paid to ensure resident performance in accordance with the lease terms. The amount required for a security deposit is often one month's rent, but this is an unwise practice. Residents may not pay their last month's rent in the belief that the security deposit is another form of rent. It should be made clear that the security deposit is for performance of the lease terms, not for rent. In order to avoid confusion, the security deposit should be a different amount than the monthly rent.

The manager should not view the security deposit as a means of generating extra revenue. Excessive or unrealistic deductions from security deposits will only persuade vacating residents to withhold the last month's rent.

Laws regarding security deposits vary from state to state and often from city to city within a state. In most states, either the security deposit or an itemization of expenses must be delivered to the former resident within 30 or 60 days after vacating. Unless the lease or rental agreement specifies certified mail, regular mail or personal delivery should be used.

Security deposits should be placed in a separate escrow account. Security deposits illegally mixed with rental payments are called *commingled funds*.

Other deposits. Additional deposits may also be required, such as a pet deposit or cleaning deposit. These deposits should not be required if they are simply to be used as a means of getting more rent.

The last month's rent is also sometimes required as a deposit. If several deposits are required, the initial payment made by the incoming resident can be quite substantial. For example, say that to lease your $400-per-month apartments you require the first and last month's rent when the lease is signed, plus a $300 security deposit. In addition there is a $150 pet deposit. The incoming resident with a pet would then pay:

First and last month's rent	$800
Security deposit	300
Pet deposit	150
Total due	$1,250

The number of deposits required and their amounts varies with the condition of the rental market and the resident's ability to pay. In a poor rental market, for example, you might only require the current month's rent in advance plus a security deposit.

Establishing Rental Rates

Whether the manager is involved with a new property or a long-established one, it is necessary to review rental rates frequently. In order to keep up with rising costs, especially the cost of utilities, rental rates are often revised quarterly or semiannually.

At one time this was not the case. In the 1960s and 1970s, most states still used the traditional one- or two-year lease (Texas being the exception, where monthly tenancies were the rule). These leases, of course, only provided for a rental increase at the time of lease renewal. During the 1970s the costs of utilities skyrocketed. These increasing costs, along with the institution of rent controls in some areas, caused managers to write shorter leases to allow for more frequent rental increases.

Toward the end of the decade, utility rates had begun to escalate sharply at a rate where rental increases could no longer keep up. One solution has been to install individual meters and submeters. Another solution has been the *Resident Utility Billing System*, or RUBS (see chapter 13), which uses established formulas to pass utility costs on to residents in addition to the rental rate. The policy of passing the utility costs on to the resident has now become critical in establishing rental rates.

Gathering Information

The first step in establishing rental rates is gathering information, much in the way the management plan and budget are established. Four sources are used: (1) a market survey, (2) statistical surveys and trend reports, (3) a budget summary, and (4) occupancy and turnover statistics.

The market survey, which is prepared as part of the management plan (see chapter 3 and exhibit 3.1), should be reviewed and updated. Successful combinations of rental rates, rental policies, and amenities offered by the competition in the neighborhood should be identified and compared to your own property's rates, policies, and amenities.

Statistical surveys and trend reports are issued regularly by a variety of organizations and agencies, including the Institute of Real Estate Management (IREM), the National Apartment Association (NAA), and the Department of Housing and Urban Development (HUD). In many cities, apartment locator services, the chamber of commerce, and major property management firms also keep statistical data on hand. The market survey, statistical surveys, and trend reports should be examined to determine the market trends in your area. You may discover, for instance, that there is now a greater demand for two-bedroom units in your neighborhood.

The budget for your property, including month-to-date and year-to-date statistics, should be reviewed, with a focus on the owner's income objectives and how well past rental rates have met those objectives. Finally, your property's occupancy and turnover statistics (or, in the case of a new property, those of similar properties) must be reviewed. If your one-bedroom units are showing a 33 percent vacancy and 15 percent turnover, while your two-bedroom units are indicating a 2 percent vacancy and 10 percent turnover, you know that the two-bedroom units at the current rental rate are more desirable.

After analyzing the market survey, statistical surveys, trend reports, and budget requirements, the manager will arrive at important conclusions to be used in setting the rental rates.

Grading the Units

The next step in establishing rental rates is grading the units. To *grade* a unit means to assign a value to it in comparison with all the other units in the property. The most typical variables considered in valuing rental units are the floor level, view, square footage (i.e., a "small one-bedroom" as compared to a "large one-bedroom"), and the age of such features as carpeting and appliances.

Units are graded by placing them in a systematic fashion on a rental grid (see exhibit 6.1). Each different type of unit in the building is listed down the left side of the grid and assigned a number. Note that types are divided by floor level as well as by number of bedrooms and square footage. Across the top of the grid are several adjustment columns. The first establishes a base rent for each type of unit. The other columns express the added value of each variable. Each column is assigned a letter. These letters, along with the number assigned to each type of unit, can be used as a code for classifying the units.

Rent Schedule and Summary Report

After the grid has been laid out, a rent schedule (see exhibit 6.2) is drawn up, listing each individual unit, its type, and its value according to the grid. The grid and rent schedule are then reviewed in light of the following questions:

Exhibit 6.1 Rental Grid

Size, Location	Quantity	A Base	B Park View	C Lake View	D Add for New Carpet
1. 1 br, 1st floor	10	$300	$310	$320	$10
2. 1 br, 2d floor	10	310	320	330	10
3. 2 br, 1st floor, 800 sq ft	8	380	390	400	10
4. 2 br, 1st floor, 850 sq ft	8	390	400	410	10
5. 2 br, 2d floor, 800 sq ft	8	390	400	410	10
6. 2 br, 2d floor, 850 sq ft	8	400	410	420	10
7. 3 br, 1st floor	8	440	460	480	20
8. 3 br, 2d floor	8	460	480	500	20

Exhibit 6.2 Rent Schedule

Unit No.	Type	Code	New Amount
101	1 br	1-B	$310
102	2 br, 800	3-A	380
103	2 br, 800	3-A-D	390
104	1 br	1-B	310
201	1 br	2-B	320
202	2 br	5-A-D	400
203	2 br	5-A	390
204	1 br	2-B-D	330

Have the income requirements of the management plan been met?

Has the extra value of the features of each unit been incorporated into the rent schedule?

Are the rental rates balanced, realistic and achievable?

Should any concessions be made in the rental schedule on any particular units?

If the schedule is not balanced and does not achieve the basic objectives, the grid is redrawn and the individual units again tallied. The process is repeated until a satisfactory rent schedule is developed.

In drawing up the rental grid, we assigned values beginning with the least expensive unit and worked our way up to the most expensive. It is helpful to validate your work by reversing the process. Assign values beginning with the most desirable unit and work downwards to the *least*. You may find that you obtain a greater overall rental income when you begin with the most desirable unit rather than the least desirable.

Values can be expressed in two different ways: in dollars/month and in dollars/square-foot/month. The latter figure is arrived at by dividing the monthly rental rate by the number of square feet. Dollars/square-foot figures are usually carried out to two decimal places and rounded to the nearest cent.

Compare the dollars/square-foot figure to those current in the market (use the market survey) to determine whether your rates are realistic. With this system of checks and balances—using a grid, using two approaches to scale the rents, and comparing the proposed rate to the market rates—you should be able to avoid unrealistic rates while maximizing potential income.

The proposed grid and rent schedule is then presented to the property manager or owner along with a summary report. This report should contain (1) the projected monthly income for the next 12 months; (2) the amount of time it will take to achieve this rate, based on expected renewals and estimated vacancy and turnover figures; (3) the percentage of increase each type of unit is being given; (4) anticipated changes in the vacancy and turnover rates; and (5) a contingency plan.

Rental Increases

Once the new rental rate is put into effect, there are three different rates for each unit: (1) the *prevailing* rate, which the current resident pays for the unit; (2) the *renewal* rate, which the current resident will pay when and if the lease is renewed; and (3) the *street* rate, which the new resident would pay if the unit were vacated and subsequently leased. Increases in the renewal rate must keep pace with increases in the street rate. The opposite often happens: Rental rates of long-time residents often lag substantially behind the street rate. In such cases, it is better to implement two small increases rather than one large increase to keep the renewal rate closer to the street rate.

Many managers resist rental increases, hoping to hold turnover to a minimum. It is necessary to estimate the effect on turnover that a rental increase will actually have.

Methods of Increase

Once you have established rental rates using a grid system, it becomes very simple to raise rents at a later time. You have already prepared a grid and categorized the units, and your previous rates will give you a pattern to follow in determining new rates.

After a grid rate is put into effect, it may become apparent that a particular style or location of unit, for unforeseen reasons, is extremely desirable. You may become aware, for instance, that you are able to lease your 2d-floor 1-bedroom units much more quickly than your 1st-floor 1-bedroom units. At the next rental increase, you might make your increase of the 2d-floor units larger than usual, while your rate increase of the 1st-floor units might be smaller than usual. This will increase the desirability of the 1st-floor units but should do little damage to the desirability of the 2d-floor units.

Another method of increasing rent is to build the rental increase into the lease. These escalation clauses or lease escalators are commonly used in commercial leases. They provide that the rental rate will increase by a certain amount (either by a fixed dollar rate, by a percentage, or by a formula tied to a national index) on a certain date. The clause may provide that the increase be automatic or that increases will made due to increases in the cost of services and utilities. The purpose of an escalation clause is to provide extra income for the owner while protecting the resident from sudden, large increases.

Resistance to Increase

No matter how reasonable your planned increase is, there will be at least some resistance from residents. The success of your rental increase depends upon how much notice is given (it should be more than the minimum legal requirement), how specific and logical the explanation is that accompanies the increase, how the new rental rate compares to the street rate in both your neighborhood and region, how long it has been since the resident has had an increase, and how well you answer questions.

Collection Policies

Many managers tend to avoid strict collection policies. They may fear that strict policies will create vacancies and the expense of evictions. They may also feel that they are there to serve the residents and provide them with a place to live, rather than to fight with them over rent.

It should be pointed out that an apartment is a piece of property, just like a house or a car. If residents were to neglect paying their mortgage or car loan payments, their houses or cars could be repossessed. The resident who fails to pay rent on time is borrowing property from the owner without the owner's consent.

Rental collection policies should be designed to encourage and promote the prompt payment of rent. They should be clearly communicated to the residents, both at the time of application and at the time of occupancy. The policies should be reviewed from time to time in the monthly newsletter.

Due Dates and Late Fees

It is recommended that all rents be due and payable on the same day each month, preferably the first. The manager should make sure to inquire if the resident will have any problem paying the rent on the first day of the month when due. Some residents may be on a fixed income, awaiting a social security check which does not arrive until the third or fourth day of the month. The resident in this situation should be encouraged to provide for the current month's rent out of the previous month's check—the March 1st rent, for example, should be taken out of the February 4th check.

For convenience in accounting, it is also traditional to prorate the rent to the first of the next month when occupancy begins on any day other than the first day of the month.

It is common to charge a late fee, commonly $5 or $10, if the rent is not received by the 5th day of the month. It is a good practice to refuse and return any late rental checks which do not include the late fee. In lawsuits against a resident for nonpayment of rent, the court may rule that it is necessary to refuse the check in order to claim the late fee.

Form of Payment

Policies should be established regarding the acceptable forms of rental payment, whether cash, check, or money order. In a 1980 small claims court case in Colorado, a resident claimed to have placed cash for rent through the night deposit slot at the manager's office, even though the rent was not found in the undisturbed collection box the next morning. Because there had been no policy prohibiting cash payments at night, the court found that the resident had paid the rent. In a similar ruling in Indiana where a resident who offered to pay cash was refused, the court ruled that the resident had paid the rent because there had been no prior notice prohibiting cash payments.

It is advisable to encourage payment of rent by check or money order for control and security reasons. Although cash is "legal tender," cash payments may be prohibited if so stated in the lease. Because not everyone has a checking account, money orders should be accepted as well as checks. If you do decide to accept cash, you may stipulate the location at which or the hours during which cash will be accepted. All payment policies should be clearly stated in the lease and posted at the rental office.

Advance Rent

The manager should be prepared to accept rent in advance. Many residents may winter in another area, take extended vacations, or simply prefer to pay rent quarterly or annually. Before setting a policy (which may or may not include a discount for advance payment), each manager should become familiar with the state laws regarding advance rental payments. Some states require rents paid more than 31 days in advance to be in an interest-bearing escrow account. Other states may prohibit the acceptance of

post-dated checks. Advance rent should not be confused
with term rent.

Returned Checks

A check may be returned to the manager by the bank for a
variety of reasons: insufficient or uncollected funds, missing
signature, wrong payee, invalid or missing date, or
disagreement between written and numerical amounts.

If the check was returned for uncollected funds, do not
presume that redepositing the check will correct the
problem. It is not unusual for the uncollected check to take
four working days or more to clear locally; ten or more if it is
written on an out-of-state bank, credit union, or money fund
account.

After receiving a returned check, contact the resident and
advise him or her that the check has been returned, giving
the specific reason. If the check was returned for insufficient
or uncollected funds, the resident should bring in a cashier's
check, cash, or money order to replace the check. If the
resident assures you that the check is now good, telephone
the bank to verify that it will clear. If the check will clear,
the returned check may be taken to the resident's bank for
certification, if it is convenient for you to do so. If it is
inconvenient, insist that the resident replace the check with
cash or certified funds. It is customary to charge the
resident a penalty fee for a returned rent check.

When a check is returned by the bank for insufficient
funds, the manager must decide whether or not to accept
any more checks from the resident. A long-time resident
who has always paid promptly and has not had any
difficulty in the past may have simply made an honest error
and should be afforded another opportunity. The resident
should also be given the opportunity to establish that the
bad check was not his or her fault by producing a notice of
bank error. If there are any doubts about the resident's
ability to pay, however, your policy should be to give the
resident a written notice stating that payments must be
made by certified check, cashier's check, or money order.

Delinquencies

Rental record-keeping procedures, discussed later in this
chapter, are designed to tell the manager immediately who

has and who has not paid rent. It is important to develop a set of delinquency collection procedures that are in accordance with the laws of your state, and then begin those procedures immediately after the rent becomes delinquent. Good delinquency collection procedures either recover the rent efficiently or place the manager in good legal position should eviction become necessary.

There are two types of notices the manager will give the resident delinquent with rent. One is an informal late notice, often an invoice stating the rent and any late fees due. The other notice, required by law, is a legal notice that must be given for some period of time before eviction procedures begin. In some states, a 3-day, 5-day, or 10-day notice is required; in others, it is sufficient to produce a copy of the informal late notice before proceeding with legal action.

One method that may help decrease the number of delinquencies in your property calls for combining the informal and legal notice into one notice. Say that your state requires you to give 3-day notices before eviction procedures begin. On the 2d day of the month, make a telephone call to each resident, informing them that the rent has not been received (this serves as an informal notice). On the evening of the 3d day, deliver the 3-day notices to residents whose rent is still unpaid. By allowing the 4th, 5th, and 6th days as the 3-day wait (and the 7th, if it falls on Sunday), you will be in a position to file for collection and/or eviction on the 7th or 8th of the month. If the rent arrives before the 7th, you need not file the 3-day notice with the court. If the rent does not arrive, legal action can commence (discussed in chapter 7). This procedure is a rigid one, but it may produce the desired results.

In collecting delinquent rents, managers should not play favorites nor become personally involved in the financial problems of the resident. A rigid collection system without variation will often avoid ill will and embarrassment, since it will often be the natural reaction of the resident to pay the creditor who creates the most pressure. The rental payment is often the largest debt the resident has, and if the resident is permitted to delay paying the largest debt, the resident's financial situation may never improve.

Skips

When a resident lags behind in paying rent, the question arises as to whether it will be more appealing to that resident to pay up the delinquency or to *skip* (illegally vacate) and start fresh in another property. The exact point the resident will elect to skip is often difficult to determine. A good rule of thumb is that when the amount of the delinquency is greater than the cost to move, the resident will skip.

When it is reported that a resident who has not paid rent has also abandoned the unit, you should immediately visit the unit to determine whether or not the report is correct and to determine if all of the resident's personal belongings have been removed. If they have not been removed, you should review the laws of the state to determine the right to retake possession. In properties where it is common for residents to obtain furniture from local furniture leasing companies, the vacating resident will probably have left the rental furniture in the unit. If you have a good working relationship with the leasing companies, they will routinely notify you when rental furniture is delivered to a unit. When you do not know the agency from which the furniture was rented, examine the furniture for any identification. If the furniture rental agency's identity is known, a call should be made to them immediately. Agency contracts provide for prompt recovery of rental property when abandoned.

A complete inspection of the unit should be made. If damage exists, it will prove useful to obtain two signatures on the inspection report and accompanying photographs for documentation. You then follow the procedures dictated by municipal or state laws to take possession of the premises legally and relet the unit. It should be standard procedure to change locks immediately in cases of abandonment as well as eviction.

Collection and Banking Procedures

The manager is responsible for accurately handling and accounting for large sums of money in the form of checks, cash, or money orders. To receive, record, and promptly deposit the funds is critical. To ensure the money's safety,

thought must be given to the collection and banking
procedures used.

Collection Locations

On site. The convenience of on-site collection encourages
the residents to pay promptly. On-site collections also
provide an opportunity for informal contact between
residents and manager. The negative aspect of on-site
collection is the risk of theft. The need to make frequent
deposits makes it necessary to build banking operations
into the manager's routine. Extra security and often extra
record keeping are necessary. If a slot for night deposits is
used, there should be a sign stating "no cash payments."
The manager's unit could also have a drop slot. A record
must be kept of all payment collected on-site. The record
could be a simple rent roll on a single sheet (as displayed in
exhibit 6.3) listing the form of payment, date paid, and
amount received. A copy of this summary would go to the
accounting office on a daily basis.

Main office. Rental payments may be mailed to the main
accounting office instead of (or in addition to) being
collected on site. The main office is often better staffed to
handle collections during peak periods, relieving the burden
at the on-site office. Disadvantages to main office collections
is that the resident loses contact with the on-site office,
payments may be delayed in the mail, and the final rent roll
must be transferred back to the on-site office for collection
efforts.

Direct banking. In many areas of the country, banks have
established procedures where the rental payments (cash is
not permitted) may be mailed directly to the bank and
deposited into the property's account. Residents are
provided with encoded or identifiable envelopes; only these
envelopes can be used. Funds are deposited the day they
are received and a daily statement of collection is issued
without a trip to the bank by the manager. These services,
however, can be more expensive than handling the

Exhibit 6.3　Summary of On-Site Collections

Property _____　Date _____

Occupant	Unit Number	Rent	Security Deposit	Other Collections	Method of Payment		Comments
					Check	Cash	
	Subtotals				Total		

Received by _____

collection at the property. It may take a long time to trace errors through the bank computer.

Receipts

Some managers use receipts only for cash payments; others use receipts for all forms of payment. Whatever your policy, any resident who requests a receipt should be issued one. Only one official numbered receipt book should be used for recording all noncheck payments.

Receipts should be in triplicate or quadruplicate,
depending on how many people are to receive copies. One
copy is given to the resident, one is kept by the manager,
and one is given to the accounting office. Receipts should
show the following information:

Date of the transaction.

Amount received and balance due.

Form of payment (cash, check, or money order).

Period of time the payment covers.

Name of resident and name of person paying rent (the
two may be different).

Unit number.

Full signature of the staff member receiving the
payment.

Receipts are numbered to enable the manager to account for
each and every receipt. At the end of the month, the copies
of the receipts are arranged numerically and totalled. The
amount of money receipted should equal the amount of
money that has been deposited at the bank for the same
period of time. In order for this double check to work, every
receipt number must be accounted for. Therefore, never
destroy voided receipts.

Receipts should not be presigned. Prior to the first of the
month, receipts *without* a signature may be prepared but
should never be signed until the resident has paid the rent.

Bank Deposits

It is advisable to make as many trips to the bank daily as is
necessary to avoid having a large volume of checks or cash
on hand. Payments should be immediately placed in a
locked location in the rental office. Rental checks should be
stamped or marked, "For Deposit Only." If a volume of cash
is received, it should be secured in several different locations
in the rental office and deposited as soon as is feasible. It is
unwise to hold checks or cash in the office overnight, even if
a safe is available.

The bank deposit should be prepared in triplicate. One copy is held in the office, and the other two are taken to the bank with the deposit. Of these two copies, one will be kept by the bank and the other receipted and given back to the manager. Each deposit slip should show each resident's name and unit number along with the amount deposited. Cash received should be identified as cash.

The receipted copy of the deposit slip should be used to post the rent received to the rent roll, and then forwarded to the accounting, property management, or owner's office immediately.

Rental Records

Complete and accurate rental records are essential. Perhaps in no other area of on-site management are records so important. Rental records must be simply and logically organized; they will be useless if they cannot be read by anyone but the manager. A section in the operations manual should describe the records kept, how they are cross-referenced, and their location.

Problems arise with the most organized of systems because files are not replaced correctly or promptly. An inventory of the records at regular intervals will decrease the possibility of misfiled or missing records.

The primary method of recording rental information is the resident ledger and/or unit ledger card (see exhibits 6.4 and 6.5). The unit ledger card is an ongoing record for each unit; a resident ledger card is begun with each move-in. The unit ledger card is maintained as a record of rents and other monies collected from all occupants of a specific unit and becomes the statement of all monies earned by that unit, while the resident ledger card serves as a complete financial record of all money transactions between a specific resident and the property. Depending on the property management company and the owner, one or both of these forms may be used.

Many managers use a pegboard accounting system to receipt and summarize rent collections. This system combines receipts and record keeping into one process. Master sheets are held on to a board by pegs down one side of the board. On top of the master sheet is a sheet of carbon

Exhibit 6.4   Resident Ledger Card

Property _____

Name _____ Unit Number _____ Phone _____

Employed by _____ Phone _____

In case of emergency contact _____ Phone _____

Lease Term   From _____ To _____

Monthly Rent   Unit   S _____

_____   _____

_____   _____

                    Total   **S** _____

Date	Rent Period Mo./Yr.		Payment Credited To				Total Amount Received	Remarks
	From	To	Rent	Security Deposit	Miscellaneous			
					Amount	Description		

paper. On top of the carbon are individual receipts overlapping each other, each with a self-carbon writing line. The receipts are overlapped so that each writing line corresponds to a line on the master sheet. The resident's ledger card is slipped under the receipt and above the carbon, lined up with the next receipt and the next line on the master sheet. When the line on the receipt is filled in,

Exhibit 6.5   Unit Ledger Card

Unit Number _____ Property _____

Monthly Rent   Unit $ _____

                                 _____

                                 _____

                   Total $ _____

Date	Occupant	Rent Period Mo./Yr.		Payment Credited To				Total Amount Received	Remarks
		From	To	Rent	Security Deposit	Miscellaneous Amount	Description		

the information is duplicated on the resident's ledger card and the master sheet. If two daily logs are needed, another layer of carbon and a second master sheet would provide the second log.

Many different micro- and mini-computer software systems have been designed for keeping rental records (as well as other records the on-site manager keeps). It is outside the scope of this book to discuss this continually changing field. It will suffice to say that computer systems can fill all of your record-keeping needs, from recording all payments to printing out receipts, to posting each payment to the resident's file, to printing out a daily summary of collections. If the primary accounting is done at a property management office, the manager may transfer the data from the rental office computer to the main office computer by telephone or by delivering a duplicate disk. Direct computer communication with the bank is now available in some parts of the country.

Real Estate Software Guidelines: Property Management, published by IREM and the NATIONAL ASSOCIATION OF REALTORS®, is a comprehensive look at the range of potential software systems applications for property management and how to select the software that will most effectively meet the unique requirements of each property management operation.

Reporting

Through efficient record keeping, the manager will be able to prepare reports for the property manager and/or owner. These reports summarize all activity in the reporting period.

Reports may be issued daily, weekly, monthly, bimonthly, quarterly, or even annually, depending on the owner's instructions. In a new property where records are essential, a simple summary may be reported at the end of each day by telephone, with a written report issued weekly. In established properties, a report may be issued only monthly. The main reports include:

1. **Occupancy.** A daily, weekly, and monthly rent roll showing a summary of move-ins, move-outs, transfers, leases executed and deposits collected.

2. **Delinquency.** Reflects any rents which are delinquent and reports what collection action is being taken and the anticipated resolution of the problem—whether the manager expects to collect the rent or expects to proceed with legal action.

3. **Rent roll and collections.** The rent roll lists every unit in numerical order, the scheduled rent,

miscellaneous fees (parking, pets, etc.) the collected rent for the current month, the balance due (if any), the name of the resident, and the amount of deposit on hand.

4. **Summary.** A summary report is the same as the income portion of a financial statement. It shows how much rent was scheduled, how much was collected, how much is in accounts receivable, how much is for vacancy and turnover, and how much is bad debt. This report may bear footnotes to explain any unusual variations. It will end with a brief analysis of achievement expressed in a percentage.

Summary

Several different forms of rent exist: the traditional form (equal monthly amounts); *seasonal* rent (for the *low season*, *off season*, and *high season* in resort areas); *term rent*; *head rent*, a per-person charge, often used in college towns and resort areas; and *apportioned* rent, which varies with the amount of extra features and amenities of each unit. To the rental rates are added any miscellaneous charges, such as parking fees. Several deposits may be required of incoming residents. The primary deposit is the *security deposit*.

Rental rates are based on information gathered from the market survey, statistical surveys and trend reports, budget summary, and occupancy and turnover statistics. This information is analyzed, and any conclusions that would affect the rental rates are noted. The units are then graded on a rental grid and assigned values in comparison with the other units in the property.

Three different rates exist for each unit: the *prevailing* rate, the *renewal* rate, and the *street* rate. Increases in the renewal rate must keep pace with increases in the street rate. One method of increasing rent is to build the rental increase into the lease through the use of an escalation clause.

The success of any rental increase depends on how much notice is given to residents and how the manager handles resident concerns. Increases should be announced in personal letters to each resident.

Collection policies should be designed to encourage the prompt payment of rent. They must be clearly communicated to the residents and strictly enforced. All rents should be due and payable on the same day of the month, preferably the first. A $5 or $10 fee is usually charged for late rent. Cash payments should be discouraged for reasons of security. Advance payments should be accepted. If a rent check is returned from the bank for insufficient or uncollected funds, the resident should be required to bring a cashier's check, cash, or money order to replace the check.

Delinquency collection procedures should begin immediately after the rent becomes delinquent. There are two types of notices that must be given to the delinquent resident: an informal late notice, and a legal notice that must be given for some period of time before eviction procedures begin. If a resident *skips* or vacates without paying rent, the unit should be examined carefully to determine if all of the resident's personal belongings have been removed. Any rental furniture should be returned to the furniture rental agency.

Rent can be collected at different locations: on the site, at the main office, or by mail directly to the bank. One official numbered receipt book should be used for recording all noncheck payments. Deposits should be made at the bank frequently. Checks or cash should not be held in the office overnight. The receipted copy of the deposit slip should be used to post the rent received to the rent roll.

Rental records should be complete, accurate, and simply and logically organized. The primary method of recording rental information is the resident ledger card and/or unit ledger card. Pegboard accounting systems combine receipts and record keeping into one process.

Four reports summarizing rental collections are prepared for the property manager and/or owner: occupancy, delinquency, rent roll and collections, and a summary.

7

Legal Aspects

When the manager leases an apartment to a resident, a legal and binding agreement exists. Whether the agreement is oral or written, it is a legal agreement and can be enforced by law. Most residents will understand their own legal responsibilities as residents and fulfill them. But for the small number of instances where the agreement between management and resident breaks down, the manager will need the support and protection of legal procedures.

The on-site manager must also comply with a maze of municipal, state, and federal laws and regulations. To successfully pursue eviction, the requirements for proper legal forms and notices must be strictly adhered to. It is outside the scope of this book to fully delineate those requirements. Because the laws in this area vary from state to state and are constantly changing, competent legal advice should be sought when any legal question arises. This chapter merely provides an overview of the information the successful on-site manager needs to obtain regarding the legal aspects of apartment management.

Federal, State, and Local Regulations

The responsibility to comply with federal, state, and local regulations may be delegated to the on-site manager. These complex regulations often seem to extend far beyond their primary purpose of ensuring safe and fair housing. To comply with these regulations, the manager must have a working knowledge of each level—federal, state, local.

Federal

The United States government has two basic modes of involvement with multifamily housing. The first mode is through laws and regulations focused on the health, safety, and well-being of the employees and residents of the property. This involvement extends to equal opportunity and the impact of the property on the environment.

The second mode of federal involvement has been through a number of housing acts, beginning with the National Housing Act approved in 1934. The primary goal of these acts has been to ensure an adequate supply of housing for the nation. Methods of achieving this goal have included subsidies for the construction of low-income housing, mortgage insurance, BMIR (Below-Market Interest Rate) loans, and the rehabilitation of inner city neighborhoods.

The Department of Housing and Urban Development (HUD) was created in 1965 as a consolidation of a number of government agencies. Today, HUD provides financing, regulation, and supervision of subsidized, low-income, and moderate-income rental housing.

Some federal acts require management to display certain notices in open view. They also require management to make available information or resources for additional assistance. The Department of Labor can supply the necessary display posters for the on-site office, which include notices of the Fair Housing Act, the Equal Opportunity Employment Act, and the Occupational Safety and Health Act (OSHA).

State

Prior to 1948, few states had regulations concerning rental housing. In the early 1950s, however, housing and

habitability codes on the state level began to emerge. Each
state attempted to supplement federal guidelines in an
individualized way to benefit the residents of that particular
state. In the 1960s, many states emphasized fair housing
practices through the establishment of state civil rights
commissions.

No federal laws exist governing the licensing or
registration of apartment properties. Registration laws do
exist, however, in many states. California, for example,
requires that all buildings with 16 or more units be
registered. As a condition of registration, each property must
have a resident manager if the owner does not live on site.

In a majority of states, an indirect form of licensing of
managers is required. In some states, the manager must
hold a real estate sales or brokerage license unless the
manager lives on site or is in the direct employment of the
property owner.

No federal law exists regulating security deposits. Most
states, however, have established laws and guidelines for
security deposits. Many states do not regulate what use is
made of the security deposit while it is on deposit; however,
a fiduciary responsibility (for accountability) is often
established. Some states require the payment of interest to
residents on their deposits. Many states forbid commingling
funds; that is, mixing the deposits in with the owner's other
income.

States which require notification of deductions from
deposits also impose strong penalties for the failure to
itemize deductions. Many states have legislation that
restrains management from charging residents for "normal
wear and tear." Deposits should be refunded within the
time specified by state law.

Local

City and county governments affect the multifamily housing
industry in several areas. Zoning ordinances restrict the
number of apartments, their location, and the availability of
land for construction. The particular use for which the land
is zoned influences the value of property. When extreme

zoning restrictions exist, they may be in response to neighborhood pressure for a decreased population density, rather than in response to supply and demand for housing.

One example of a municipal regulation is Ridgefield, New Jersey's Landlord Security Deposit Act, passed in 1972. Under the rules of the LSDA, the owner or manager must place a security deposit of a set sum with the city. When emergency repairs are not made, the city makes emergency repairs using the funds on hand.

As we have mentioned in earlier chapters, local governments have regulations regarding fire safety. An inspection by the fire department can reveal whether or not your property is in compliance. The fire department can provide training in fire safety for your residents and staff.

The manager should meet personally with local police officials. The police can often provide better service in cases of emergency if they have already become familiar with the property. Many law enforcement agencies are eager to send officers or deputies to explain the latest techniques in crime prevention and reporting to your residents.

Wage-Hour and Unemployment Compensation Laws

Several laws and acts make up the body of wage-hour laws in the United States, among them the Fair Labor Standards Act (FLSA) and the Equal Pay Act. Wage-hour laws are a particularly sensitive area of property management. Prior to 1970, it was popular to offer a "free" apartment to an employee in exchange for handling after-hours service calls. Legislation passed in the 1970s and updated more recently still allows for this exchange of labor, but provides for a more equitable arrangement with the employee. There are formulas available to help the manager in determining when rent can be exchanged for labor and when overtime pay or compensatory time-off is mandatory.

The manager should also have an understanding of the laws regarding unemployment compensation, discussed in chapter 4. The guidelines for eligibility vary from state to state and can be obtained from the state unemployment office.

Equal Employment Opportunity

Equal employment opportunity for all people, regardless of race, color, religion, sex, or national origin, is provided by the Civil Rights Act of 1964. Grievances against employers are investigated by the Equal Employment Opportunity Commission (EEOC).

Equal employment opportunity is a complex subject, and interpretations of laws change rapidly. On-site managers may discover that they have unintentionally discriminated illegally against their employees. *Wage-Hour and Employment Practices Manual for the Multihousing Industry*, by Harry Weisbrod (Institute of Real Estate Management, 1979), is a helpful and complete guide to both wage-hour laws and equal employment opportunity.

Occupational Safety and Health

The Occupational Safety and Health Act (OSHA) was passed in 1970 and is enforced by local OSHA agencies through U.S. Department of Labor offices. OSHA's guidelines provide a safe work environment for the employee through the establishment of minimum safety standards and procedures. OSHA regulations are divided into a variety of categories; they define acceptable work environments, minimum age guidelines, and safety procedures. The act requires complete record keeping of all preventive measures taken and all accidents. Immediate reporting of any accident involving injury is required.

OSHA agencies serve to coordinate the efforts of other federal, state, and municipal agencies. For example, the requirements to license and operate the property's swimming pool would usually fall under the local department of health. The requirements for employees operating and performing maintenance on the pool would be detailed by OSHA and enforced by the health department. In the event an accident or injury occurred, OSHA would receive the report and handle the investigation, taking whatever disciplinary action is warranted. By working in tandem with the health department, OSHA can ensure that codes meet a minimum federal standard while providing flexibility for the state or municipal government in tailoring additional regulations.

Many individual states have established their own OSHA codes to supplement the federal OSHA requirements and assist in enforcing them. The two sources for detailed information regarding your state's requirements are the state or federal OSHA office and your property's insurance company. Both can provide guidelines for record keeping and reporting.

Habitability

Property owners are required to provide habitable apartments to residents, whether or not this requirement is spelled out in a lease. This was not always true; at one time, the common law rule of *caveat emptor*—"let the buyer beware"—applied. More recently, courts have recognized an implied "warranty of habitability," based on state and local building codes. Because these codes set minimum standards of habitability, they imply that a "warranty of habitability" exists when an apartment is leased. Included in the general definition of "habitability" would be: (1) adequate protection from the weather; (2) plumbing, electrical, and heating equipment, all in safe operating condition; and (3) clean and sanitary buildings and grounds.

Discrimination

There are several federal laws prohibiting discrimination in housing, dating back to 1866. The most comprehensive is the Fair Housing Act, passed in 1968, which prohibits discrimination in housing because of race, color, religion, national origin, or sex. It is quite specific in describing unaccepted discriminatory practices, such as denying that housing is available for inspection or rent when it is available.

The on-site manager of today often faces a situation which was rarely seen prior to about 1970: unrelated residents of the opposite sex sharing an apartment. Some areas have laws or statutes still on their books prohibiting cohabitation, but these laws are often not enforced. A more important

issue for the on-site manager is whether or not the other
residents will take offense at a cohabitating couple.

Rent Control

Rent control was instituted on the federal level in 1942 in
order to ensure an adequate supply of affordable housing for
war workers and was not completely phased out until 1953.
Rent control was reinstated nationally from 1971 to 1974,
and many cities across the nation—New York being the
most notable—still have some form of rent control. Rent
controls can be based on four factors: (1) the resident's
ability to pay (now used in subsidized housing), (2) a
maximum percentage of the resident's income per year, (3)
formulas which limit the rate of the owner's return or profit,
or (4) a maximum percentage by which the owner may
increase the existing rent.

Rent controls have rarely worked as they have been meant
to work. Rental increases allowed under rent control are
usually not adequate to meet rising costs; the result is often
a decrease in the quality of maintenance and repair and
sometimes the eventual abandonment and destruction of
unprofitable buildings. Since those residents with adequate
incomes try to hold on to their rent-controlled apartments
for as long as they possibly can, low-income families—whom
rent control is meant to help—are often forced into the open
market.

Compliance

To prove your compliance with federal, state, and local
regulations, you must keep accurate and complete records.
Some groups of regulations, such as OSHA, specify the
records which must be kept and the notices which must be
given.

Accurate records are especially important when dealing
with employees. An employee who is discharged for
unsatisfactory work or unreliability can often collect benefits
over the manager's objections simply because good records
were not kept. A recommended practice is to keep accurate
records of all warnings given employees, oral or written,

along with a log of incidents. When an employee is discharged, the manager can immediately file a report with the state unemployment office. If a claim is then filed by the employee, the manager's case will be stronger.

Legal Services

In the past, managers often postponed obtaining legal counsel until their problem proved too difficult to handle themselves. Today, the majority of state laws regarding landlord/tenant cases are so complex that owners or property management firms choose to be represented in court by an attorney rather than a manager. The manager's responsibility is often limited to providing facts, even in small claims court. (In some states, however, attorneys cannot appear in small claims court.)

There are three traditional ways the property management firm or manager hires an attorney: (1) on retainer, (2) by fixed fee, and (3) by metered fee. A combination of all three may be used. When legal questions arise, the on-site manager usually consults first with the property manager, who then decides whether or not to pass the question on to the attorney.

When an attorney's services are secured on a *retainer* basis, a monthly, quarterly, or annual fee is paid in anticipation of the need for services. The attorney is available for consultation during the period of time agreed upon. The fee applies whether or not any legal counsel is requested. Under a retainer fee arrangement, many attorneys will provide training and telephone consultation without additional charges.

When a lawyer's services are obtained on a *fixed fee* basis, a fixed set of charges is established for handling specific legal work. The fee remains the same regardless of the amount of time taken to perform the work. In a *metered fee* arrangement, charges are based on the lawyer's time, experience, and expertise.

The attorney may provide the forms to be used for legal notices and provide guidelines for proper record keeping in order to fully document legal actions. The manager may also be trained to complete the appropriate paperwork which the attorney will use to commence legal action.

Finally, the attorney retained by the property may provide guidelines regarding legal limitations—what may and may not be done in the capacity of manager, and what must be brought to the lawyer for action. In some states, for example, the manager may prepare and serve the eviction notice. In other states, the eviction notice must originate in the attorney's office.

The manager should avoid practicing law. When a legal issue is raised, managers should refer to the guidelines provided by the attorney. If no clear-cut response exists in those guidelines, managers should postpone dealing with the question until they have had a chance to check with their superiors. By avoiding legal decisions and recommendations, the manager does not overstep his or her authority under law.

A guide or plan for managing the property legally should be included in the operations manual for reference. The guide should cover equal employment and fair housing compliance and the use of legal procedures in establishing, raising, and collecting rents, making credit checks, maintaining security deposit accounts, and enforcing the lease terms.

Legal Action by Residents

When a current or former resident brings a lawsuit against the management or the owner, it is usually for *breach of contract* or *constructive eviction*. Breach of contract refers to nonperformance of lease terms; the resident believes that the manager did not live up to the lease agreement. In a constructive eviction, the manager has forced the resident to leave by making the premises uninhabitable, whether intentionally or unintentionally. Constructive eviction might occur when the heating system breaks down and the manager fails to have it repaired promptly. Consumer groups and tenant unions may also instigate lawsuits against management or the owner regarding a number of matters, including rental price fixing and illegal discrimination.

Each type of litigation may be for actual damages or actual damages plus punitive damages. Actual damages are the cost of real damages incurred; punitive damages are fines or penalties imposed by the court. Tenant unions or consumer groups may also be seeking an injunction prohibiting a specific practice or action. Legal action by residents is often accompanied by a great deal of unfavorable publicity both within the community and the area. If the manager is aware that a resident or group of residents is contemplating legal action, regardless of motive or justification, advice should be sought from the property manager. Every effort should be made to resolve the problem immediately. If litigation is commenced, the manager should contact the property manager and/or company attorney immediately, follow the attorney's advice, and not discuss the case publicly or privately until it has been settled.

Evictions

Most legal action the manager takes against a resident involves eviction. There are two common reasons for evicting a resident: nonpayment of rent or violation of lease terms.

It is important to distinguish between the two types of evictions. When a resident is evicted for a violation of lease terms, the burden of proof is on the manager. The court often grants several continuances. A resident may appeal the decision to a higher court. When a resident is evicted for nonpayment of rent, it is the resident's responsibility to prove at the court hearing that the rent was paid or that no rent was due under the lease agreement.

The form of eviction used varies with the particular case. Generally, it is easier to evict a resident for nonpayment of rent than it is to evict for violation of lease terms. Unless the resident's actions are creating a major problem, it may be wise to simply wait until the lease expires and try to find a legal reason for refusing to renew the lease.

Before the manager commences the eviction process, the following questions should be answered:

Is my demand reasonable, legal, and nondiscriminatory?

Have I made every effort to resolve the problem?

Do I have complete records and documents to substantiate the claim being made?

Is there any alternative to commencing legal action?

For either type of eviction, the manager follows six steps: (1) documentation, (2) notification, (3) hearings, (4) judgements, (5) obtaining possession, and (6) collection.

Documentation

Documentation to substantiate the manager's claim must be assembled and made a part of the case to be presented to the judge. The documentation should include copies of the lease or rental agreement, the resident's ledger card, any receipts, late notices and proof of delivery, correspondence between the manager and the resident, and notes on any conversations, which should list the date of the conversation, who participated, what communication took place, and what agreement (if any) was reached.

Notification

For eviction due to nonpayment of rent, the legal requirements for notification to the resident vary from state to state. The notice is sometimes called a *demand to pay or quit*. Most states require a written 3-, 5-, or 10-day notice on a specific form. State laws prescribe how notice should be given if the resident is not home. When the time provided for in the notice expires without payment of rent, the demand is filed with the court, the resident is notified to appear, and a court date is set. Eviction notices are complex. The manager should ascertain the exact requirements for eviction notices in the area and follow them precisely.

Hearings

The manager and the resident have the opportunity to reach agreement to satisfy the lawsuit at any time prior to the case being heard. If agreement is reached by the time of the hearing, information regarding the agreement will be entered into the court record. The original complaint may need to be modified. If a money award is part of the out-of-court agreement, the judge will specify a date by which the reward is to be paid. If the money is paid, the case is closed. If the money is not paid, the manager does not have to refile the case, but simply notifies the court that the agreement was not fulfilled. The physical eviction process can then begin.

It is extremely important that the manager maintain a professional appearance during the hearing. No emotion should be displayed, no facts should be distorted. The presentation of the case should be businesslike and complete. The manager should be prepared to answer questions, not to give opinions. The case will be presented by the attorney for the manager; the resident will be given an opportunity to respond. Examination of witnesses for each side is permitted; the judge may also ask questions.

Judgements

Unless a continuance is granted, a judgement or decision will be rendered by the judge or referee at the close of the presentation of the case. There are two types of judgements. One type occurs when all parties appear in court, the case is heard by the judge, and a decision based on the facts is rendered. Another type occurs when one party fails to appear, and a judgement is issued in favor of the appearing party. If the other party later appeals to the court giving an acceptable reason for his or her failure to appear, the judgement will be set aside or rescinded and the case tried at the earliest possible date.

If the judgement is in favor of the manager, it will state what money has been awarded (rent, damages, court costs, attorney's fees) and when possession must be delivered by the defendant. The judgement merely awards delivery of possession or payment of money to the plaintiff; it does not guarantee either.

Possession

In obtaining possession of the unit, there are more regulations regarding what the manager may *not* do than there are regarding what the manager *may* do. The manager may not change locks, remove doors, interfere with the resident's use of the premises, or reduce services in an effort to secure possession. The manager's only recourse in this situation is further legal action, which requires notifying the court of the resident's failure to deliver possession and, in most states, obtaining a *writ of execution* for possession. The writ is filed with the court, and the local sheriff or other court-appointed officer serves the resident with the writ. If possession is still not delivered after 48 to 72 hours, the sheriff or officer of the court may take possession of the premises forcibly, moving the resident and the resident's possessions off the premises. After a forcible eviction, the resident manager should change the lock on the resident's door. The resident's possessions may have to be boxed up and stored.

Collection

After the manager is in possession of the premises, collection of the money awarded may be pursued. Procedures and options vary from state to state. Methods of recovery include garnishment of wages, seizure of money assets such as bank accounts, or seizure and/or sale of personal assets, such as furniture or furnishings. The manager may contact the former resident and establish a repayment plan. Sometimes a collection agency is hired to collect the payments.

If immediate collection is not possible, the judgement may be recorded with the county. A lien can then be filed against any real estate the former resident comes to own.

Summary

The federal government has two basic modes of involvement with multifamily housing. The first mode is through laws and regulations focused on the health, safety, and well-being of the employees and residents of the property. This area covers the following:

1. Wage-hour laws, including the Fair Labor Standards Act and the Equal Pay Act.

2. Unemployment compensation.

3. Equal employment opportunity, provided by the Civil Rights Act of 1964. Grievances are investigated by the Equal Employment Opportunity Commission (EEOC).

4. Employee safety and health, provided by the Occupational Safety and Health Act (OSHA) and enforced by U.S. Department of Labor offices.

The second mode of federal involvement has been through a number of housing acts, many of which are overseen by the Department of Housing and Urban Development (HUD). This area includes:

1. Discrimination in housing, prohibited by civil rights law, especially the Fair Housing Act of 1968.

2. Rent control.

Housing regulations on the state level vary considerably from state to state. Many states require some form of licensing for apartment properties and apartment managers. State laws also regulate security deposits. Local housing regulations often take the form of zoning ordinances, building codes, and fire codes. The existence of state and local building codes, requiring minimum standards of habitability, have led courts to recognize an implied "warranty of habitability" when apartments are leased.

An attorney may be hired three ways: (1) on a *retainer* basis, (2) on a *fixed fee* basis, and (3) on a *metered fee* basis. The attorney should provide guidelines for dealing with legal questions. If no clear-cut response to a legal question exists in those guidelines, the on-site manager should always consult with the property manager and/or attorney.

Lawsuits brought by residents against the management or the owner are usually for *breach of contract* or *constructive eviction*. Each type of litigation may be for actual damages or actual damages plus punitive damages.

Lawsuits brought by management against residents usually involve eviction and are usually for one of two reasons: nonpayment of rent or violation of lease terms. The eviction process consists of six steps: (1) documentation needed to substantiate the manager's claim; (2) notification, which must follow the forms required by law; (3) hearings; (4) judgements, which may award rent, damages, court costs, or attorney's fees; (5) obtaining possession, which may include forcible eviction; and (6) collection of the money awarded.

8

Marketing the Property

Marketing, as we have defined it earlier in the book, is the process of moving products to the consumer—in this case, leasing available apartments to renters. Effective apartment marketing is almost as important as effective apartment management: poor marketing can result in high vacancy and turnover rates. Close professional attention must be paid to all aspects of marketing. Signage, advertising, brochures, and other marketing devices must all be attractive and in some way unique—they must convey the message in a more effective way than the competition. Marketing, however, is more than just the advertising and "selling" of apartments. It also involves the creation of a public image that affects relationships not only with prospective residents, but with current residents and the entire neighborhood as well. As the person who will actually deal with the public, the on-site manager and the property's rental assistants are a key link in the marketing process. Though much of the marketing plan may be the responsibility of upper management, it must be remembered that in marketing, as in nearly any endeavor, the potential for success can be undermined by one weak link.

Public Relations

Public relations is the art of creating goodwill among the
public towards the property, and is therefore an important
part of marketing. In chapter 2 we stressed that the public
relations aspect of marketing is an area where good
communication skills are needed. A prospective resident is a
customer of the business, as anyone might be the customer
of a department or grocery store. As customers, we demand
and receive courteous and prompt service. If we do not
receive satisfactory service at a particular store, we take our
business elsewhere. We often base our judgement of a store
on the salesperson. As on-site manager, you or your rental
assistants are the salespersons for the property. It may well
be the attitude about the property you convey that is the
deciding factor for a prospective resident.

Manager, Staff, and Residents

The staff must have the same positive, professional attitude
the manager has towards the operation of the property. The
manager can ensure the staff's loyalty by pursuing good
employee relations (discussed in chapter 4). Staff members
will have a positive, loyal attitude to the property if they
understand the owner's goals and if they are getting the
respect and recognition they deserve. The manager may,
however, also need to train the staff in public relations
techniques. Prospective renters may not remember a floor
plan, but they will definitely remember a sullen,
uninterested, or insincere rental agent. In most situations,
current residents should be treated with the same respect
and courtesy as prospective residents. Current residents'
satisfaction or dissatisfaction can spread very easily through
the property and neighborhood by word of mouth.

Suppliers

Suppliers of equipment and services can be the best—or the
worst—reference for the property. The needs of the supplier
are very similar to the needs of the property. Both need from
the other fairness, respect, and above all, loyalty.
Maintaining a good working relationship with a supplier
can result in extra assistance when problems with
equipment arise. A decision to switch suppliers should not

be made lightly. If poor service is adversely affecting the property's image, the property should probably switch suppliers. If, however, the cost difference between competitive bids is small, the advantage of having a loyal supplier may outweigh the risk of using a new and unknown supplier.

Neighborhood

Two apartment properties of similar size and construction are adjacent on the block. One maintains a long waiting list for vacancies, while the other averages a 10 percent vacancy rate and has the reputation of being a trouble spot. The efficient management of the first property has given it excellent rapport with the neighborhood. The second property has allowed its problems to spread throughout the entire area. Even if the second property makes an attempt to solve its problems, the bad public image that has been created will likely linger.

Open channels of communication need to be set up between neighborhood and property. The manager might attempt to meet with the neighbors, or possibly attend meetings of a neighborhood association, in order to better understand the effect the property has on the neighborhood. The similarities and differences between the needs of the neighborhood and the needs of the property must be accurately defined. If an apartment building has a high population of young children in a neighborhood of small single-family homes, friction may easily result if the manager does not establish a play area and rules regarding the privacy of the building's neighbors. When standards and policies for the property are set which meet with the approval of the neighborhood, good public relations are established.

Advertising and Promotion

In the marketing of any product, certain conditions must be met for a sale to be accomplished. The customer must be able to pay for the product, must be aware that the product is for sale, and must want the product or one similar to it. The latter two conditions are fulfilled through the careful use of advertising and promotional materials.

Establishing a Theme

The first step in preparing an advertising and promotional campaign is the selection of a theme for the apartment property. The process begins with an examination of the market survey and analysis prepared in chapter 3 as part of the management plan. After a decision has been made as to the type of resident the management wishes to attract, a theme can be created to appeal to that segment of the market. For example, single people might be attracted by an energetic, socially oriented theme, while retired couples might be attracted by a quiet, peaceful theme. The key to selecting a successful theme is to appeal to the interests of a particular market segment without totally ruling out other types of residents. Once the theme has been decided upon, a name, logo, and graphics scheme are created and carefully coordinated to express the theme. A *logo* is a graphic device by which the property is easily identified; it may consist of a symbol, the property's name in a certain typeface, or a combination of both.

Say that an apartment complex is being established on a large lake, and that the management wishes to attract a combination of active singles and empty nesters. An appropriate theme for this complex would be centered on the lake itself. The word *Lakes* would form part of the name; the lake would be mentioned in all advertising. The logo could be a flock of seagulls, a stylized boat, or perhaps a combination of both. Empty nesters would be attracted by the peaceful appeal of a lake, affluent singles by the idea of boating. Each segment of the market the management wishes to attract should see the property as being designed for its needs.

Choosing the Media

Advertising must be chosen carefully. The objective should be to reach the largest number of qualified prospects with the least amount of money. Marketing statistics on the cost-effectiveness of each type of advertising should be

Exhibit 8.1 General and Specific Signs

General	Specific
Applegate Apartments	Applegate Apartments
8500 Wordsworth Avenue	From $375 per month
Turn right at light	Model open 11–7 daily
	Turn right at light

considered. Records should be maintained on the manner in which each visiting prospect first learned about the property. Each type of advertising should be analyzed to determine where advertising dollars will be most productive.

Signs and Billboards

Signs and billboards can be a very effective form of advertising—more effective than newspaper advertising. A well-designed sign catches the attention of prospective residents and draws them into the rental office.

The logo should appear on all major signs. All signs on the property, whether promotional or informational, should be in a uniform style. Signs can be either general or specific (see exhibit 8.1). A general sign is a permanent sign identifying the property by name, logo, and perhaps exact address. A specific sign, used primarily for advertising purposes, contains more detailed information. No sign, however, should give out so much information that an actual visit to the property is unnecessary.

Signs next to major roads and highways should be fairly uncomplicated. If the sign is next to a road where the speed limit is more than 20 miles per hour, the prospective resident driving by will only be able to register two or three details before the sign is out of sight. Any directions given, therefore, should be easy to follow. Two-way signs should be used so that traffic in both directions can read the sign.

Billboards are larger and more expensive than signs on the property. Professional guidance should be sought if it is determined that a billboard would be a cost-effective method of advertising.

Contracts with billboard companies can be short- or long-term and can stipulate a fixed or a floating location. For example, the billboard might be leased for six months. For two months, it would appear in one location; for the next two months, at another location; and for the final two months, at a third location. This gives the appearance of the billboard being "everywhere," when in fact, it is one billboard used in three locations.

Newspaper Advertising

Newspaper advertising can be an effective marketing tool if properly handled, a waste of budgeted funds if not. The value of newspaper advertising may vary seasonally. The amount of signage the property displays may decrease the need for newspaper advertising. Newspapers will often provide marketing statistics which can assist the manager in determining the value of this medium.

Type of ad. There are two types of ads run in newspapers: *classified* and *display* (see exhibit 8.2). Classified ads are often arranged geographically and appear in the classified section; display ads are larger, often have a graphic design, and appear throughout the newspaper. The decision on the type of ad to be run should be made by determining which type of ad proves cost-effective. Classified ads are, of course, much less expensive than display ads, but in some cases, as in opening a new property, display ads will bring in more prospects.

If display ads are run, they should be professionally designed. Often the newspaper can provide a graphic designer or layout artist at a low cost. If an advertising agency is being used to prepare the property's brochures, the expense of preparation of several display ads for the newspaper can be included in the contract at a moderate increase in cost.

Information in the ad. There are two theories about the information that should be included in a rental ad. The first suggests that only enough information to make the prospect aware of the property should be included, and nothing more. The second theory suggests that the ad should create in the buyer not only an awareness of the property, but a desire to live there as well.

Exhibit 8.2   Classified and Display Ads

2 BEDROOMS, 2 BATHS
$450 includes heat. Garages avail.
Children, pets welcome. Office
open 12-6 daily. 336-4545.

INDIAN HILLS APARTMENTS
6440 W 18th (off Jefferson)

Indian Hills

2-bedroom, 2-bath apartments now available for immediate occupancy. Acres of landscaped walks and lawns, just minutes from downtown and convenient to public transportation. Fireplaces, garages, lovely views. Children and pets *are* welcome! Rentals from $450, includes heat, water, and gas.

Office hours are from noon to 6 P.M. daily. Phone 336-4545.

Indian Hills Apartments

6440 West 18th Street, just off Jefferson Parkway

During normal marketing conditions, the first approach will probably be effective. The following information should be included in a limited-information ad:

Location. Inclusion of this information will eliminate callers who are not interested in the neighborhood.

Availability. The number of bedrooms in the available units and approximate dates of availability.

Amenities. A partial list of amenities and recreational facilities.

Rental rates. A range should be given, so that prospects can eliminate themselves if the units are not in their desired price range.

Contact. Name of the person to call, the hours to call, and the telephone number.

In poor market conditions, a more elaborate ad is called for. This ad needs to create the desire to rent in addition to an awareness of the property. To the above list would be added further details on amenities and a schedule of rental office hours. Mention should be made of any policies welcoming children or pets.

Ads should be varied from week to week. A slightly different ad may attract a prospect who didn't find the first ad appealing. By comparing responses, the effectiveness of each ad can be determined.

Timing of the ad. The decision on when to run the ad is based on several factors. As we have mentioned, newspapers keep statistics on their readership. In some cities, prospective residents who intend to shop for an apartment will check the morning paper. In other cities, prospective residents may obtain the evening edition to use the next day. Learn which edition of the paper reaches the desired market segment.

The most profitable days to run the ads may be on weekends, when it is easier for most people to visit the rental office. To determine the days on which ads produce the best response, run daily ads during a test period and chart the number of calls and visitors received each day.

The newspaper's rate structure will also have an effect on the timing of the ad. Most newspapers have one rate for weekdays, another rate for Sundays, and a variety of contract rates. Say that the classified rates for a newspaper are $4 per line on weekdays and $4.50 on Sundays. One contract rate might be $2 per line on Sundays, provided that 5,000 lines are run per year. Another set of contract rates might offer discounts on shorter weekday ads (sometimes called *rate holder* ads) provided that ads are run seven days a week.

Brochures, Handbills, and Flyers

Brochures serve an advertising purpose as well as an informational purpose; therefore, they should be designed with the property's theme and overall graphic scheme in mind. A brochure should be very attractive, but not so fancy or elaborate that the manager hesitates to give it out. A brochure will do no good sitting in a box behind a manager's desk.

As part of the market survey, the manager will gather samples of brochures and promotional materials being used in the area. The manager can also obtain newspapers from other cities, note the most attractive display ads, and send away for brochures from those properties. By gathering many samples of brochures, flyers, and display ads, the manager can assist in planning the promotional materials for the property.

All brochures should answer both general and specific questions about the property. The current list of rates and/or availability of vacancies may be printed separately as an insert for the brochure. A business card should also be inserted or attached to every brochure, thereby enabling the prospect to make further contact easily. A brochure can be further personalized by jotting information on its cover for ready reference by the prospect.

Floor plans in brochures are sometimes too reduced to be of much use to the prospective resident. As the average apartment unit grows smaller, room dimensions are often omitted from the brochure. Some prospective residents, however, will insist on knowing room dimensions. Simple, clear floor plans with room dimensions should be displayed in the rental office, particularly if no model apartment exists.

If local ordinances permit, the distribution of handbills or flyers on cars parked at nearby shopping areas can attract prospective residents. Handbills and flyers should resemble the brochure, but should not contain so much information that the prospect can make a decision without seeing the property.

Direct Mail

Direct mail advertising consists of a letter or flyer that is sent to individuals in a target mailing area. Direct mail is a very expensive form of advertising, and is cost-effective only when great care is taken in the design and targeting of the mailing. One of the conditions necessary for "making a sale" is that the customer must have a need or desire for the product. A mailing targeted to every address in a 20-block by 20-block area will reach many people, but many of them may not be in the market for a new apartment. A better target would be a nearby apartment building where a condominium conversion is imminent. Many residents of this building would probably have need of a new apartment; by targeting the mailing to them, this portion of advertising money is being spent more efficiently.

White and Yellow Pages

Business telephone service includes a listing in both the white pages and the Yellow Pages of the directory. For a moderate fee, the listing may be printed in boldface type, which catches the eye more easily.

Display ads in the Yellow Pages of the telephone directory are often used when a new property is opened. Since Yellow Pages are updated only once a year, it is not a good idea to list rental rates. Office hours should be listed only if they are not likely to change. The telephone company can provide marketing statistics to assist in determining the effectiveness of the proposed display ad.

Advertising for Specific Market Segments

Several forms of advertising can be used to reach specific market segments. Display ads in magazines, in programs for cultural or sporting events, and in newsletters of local businesses will all reach a different type of person. Radio and TV ads are sometimes used during the opening of a new property. Displays ads in busses are effective in reaching those dependent upon public transportation, such as senior citizens. People who live and work in the property's neighborhood can be reached by display ads on the bulletin boards of supermarkets, churches, and community centers.

Promotional Materials

Balloons and other attention-getters work well, especially when opening a new property. A combination of a banner which says "Now Leasing" or "Renovated Units Available" with flags will draw the prospects to the main entrance. Other promotions might include giveaways, from a ride in a hot air balloon to a drawing for a prize. Drawing prizes should be selected to appeal to the type of resident you wish to attract.

Referrals

Many prospective residents can be brought to the property through referrals from other managers, current residents, former residents, and suppliers. A loyal relationship must be established with suppliers and other managers in the area. If you make a practice of referring business their way, they will refer business your way. Supply the other managers and suppliers with flyers and business cards to give to prospects. Checking with your contacts from time to time to make sure their supply of flyers is not exhausted will remind them of your interest in their referrals.

Any referral fees, bonuses, or rewards that are paid to your contacts must be in compliance with state law. Many states prohibit payment of such fees to unlicensed firms or individuals. If your contacts do refer a prospect to you, be sure to express your gratitude in the form of a note or phone call. This "thank you" will create good public relations and encourage your contacts to send more prospects your way.

Some prospects may be referred to the property by a referral service that specializes in locating apartments. Their fees come from two sources: a *listing fee*, paid by the property, which places complete information on the property in a file or on a database; and a *referral fee*, paid either by the property or by the prospective resident when a referral results in a signed lease. Some of these companies guarantee that a partial refund of the referral fee will be made if the resident does not fulfill a minimum lease. In either case, a written contract is necessary.

Property Preparation

The advertising and promotional campaign will be of little use if the "product" being advertised is not ready to be marketed. The rental office and model apartments must be furnished and equipped and the property's appearance maintained before the actual leasing efforts begin.

Curb Appeal

Earlier in the book we defined *curb appeal* as the property's ability to make a favorable first impression on the prospective resident. Maintaining the property's curb appeal is an important part of marketing. The prospect's first impression often becomes his or her final impression, and it is important that this first impression be as positive as possible. Lawns should look well cared for. No trash or pet litter should be apparent. Fencing should be well maintained. Patios and balconies should be neat and uncluttered. All paved areas should be free of litter. All storage areas in view should be neat. Areas around trash containers should be either landscaped or fenced. In summary, the property should be clean and well kept, presenting an appealing appearance. This will make a good impression on the current residents as well as the prospective residents.

In chapter 2 we mentioned that awareness and alertness were two of the qualities needed to be a successful on-site manager. It is very easy to become accustomed to gradual deterioration of the property, but it is this condition that the prospective resident will notice first. For example, say that there is a dirty welcome mat by the door of the rental office. The manager, who steps on the mat 60 times a day, may have nearly forgotten its existence. The prospective resident, however, is stepping on it for the first time, and will almost certainly notice how dirty it is.

Rental Office

A rental office need not be large, but it should be attractive and well organized. Some part of the rental office should be private, where rental applications can be completed. If it is customary for two staff members to be on duty at the same time, each work station should contain complete forms and materials for preparing a rental application.

Furnishings and carpeting should be durable: rental offices have heavy traffic, necessitating frequent cleaning. Good lighting is important. If the office has a view, draperies should be left open. Signage both inside and outside of the office should include the name of the property and the office hours.

As we mentioned earlier, a set of representative floor plans should be displayed in the rental offices. Other displays might include carpet samples and color schemes displayed in glass cases near the floor plans.

The rental office is often an apartment unit that has been converted. Since apartment units are not designed as office space, some structural changes may be necessary to make the office efficient. This might entail, for instance, knocking out a wall or installing an extra door.

Model Apartments

Model apartments can largely determine the success or failure of a community; they should be decorated as attractively as possible. Attractive furnishings can be leased in most large cities, with decorating services included in the rental fee. When a unit will only be used as model for a short time, steps can be taken to save money on decorating without sacrificing quality. For example, if a unit will only remain a model for six to twelve months, then decorative mirror walls might be attached with mirror clips rather than permanently installed. Special decorating features in the short-term models should only be considered when costs can be regained in higher rental rates after the model is rented.

Plants provide an affordable means of decorating a model. If large, hardy plants are chosen, they can fill a room while providing an airy look. When the model is closed, the plants can easily be sold, often for more than their original cost. Plants are quite inexpensive, considering the amount of space they can occupy.

Summary

Marketing rental properties consists of the advertising and "selling" of apartments plus the creation of a public image through efficient management. Good public relations should be pursued not only to draw in prospective residents, but to create good relationships among current residents, suppliers, and the surrounding neighborhood.

The first step in creating advertising and promotional materials is the establishment of a theme for the property that will appeal to the market segment the management wishes to attract. The property's name, logo, and graphics scheme will be part of the theme, and will be used in most advertising and promotional materials.

A careful study should be made to determine the most cost-effective forms of advertising. Types of advertising media include:

1. **Signs and billboards.** May be either general or specific in nature, but should not give out so much information that a visit to the property is unnecessary.

2. **Newspaper advertising.** There are two types: *classified* and *display.* Many different rate structures exist.

3. **Brochures, handbills, and flyers.** Should be designed in accordance with the property's theme and should answer both general and specific questions about the property.

4. **Direct mail.** A very expensive form of advertising, direct mail is cost-effective only when the mailing is carefully designed and targeted.

5. **Listings in the white and Yellow Pages.**

Other means of promotion include balloons, banners, giveaways, prize drawings, and referrals.

Before the actual leasing effort begins, the rental offices and model apartments must be equipped, furnished, and decorated. The property's curb appeal should also be maintained.

9

Opening the New Property

Opening a new property can be an exciting opportunity and an interesting challenge for the on-site manager. All of the skills acquired in day-to-day on-site management take on a new dimension; communication and marketing skills become crucial. Though the results of the manager's hard work will not be seen for many months, the final result—a thriving, new community where none existed before—will be very gratifying.

Opening a new property involves functions in three areas: (1) planning, (2) preopening, and (3) construction management. Planning—one of the five functions of management we discussed in chapter 2—becomes of prime importance in opening a new property. The management team is essentially working from scratch. Every detail of the property and its operation needs to be worked out as much as possible in advance, from the hours of the rental office to the doorknobs on the apartment doors. Preopening activities consist primarily of developing a marketing program for the new property. Construction management involves working with the contractor and dealing with the problems that occur when residents are living in a property still under construction.

Planning and Design

Units and Features

An on-site manager will often be involved with the opening of a new property from the very beginning, working with the property manager or developer on proposed plans to determine the sizes and types of units most in demand. The market survey from the management plan (see chapter 3) is consulted to determine the competition's strong and weak points. The manager can also conduct an informal survey as well.

For example, say that the market survey concludes that a second bathroom, a fireplace, and large master bedroom are popular amenities in the neighborhood. But several nearby managers have also stated informally that less than half of the residents in their properties actually use the fireplaces. It appears, then, that even though it might be seldom used, a fireplace would make a good marketing tool. On the basis of this information, the architect might decide that a smaller and less expensive fireplace be installed.

When preliminary plans are ready, the manager may be asked to review them from a marketing standpoint and suggest modifications. The manager is often in a position to recognize a serious design problem that will adversely affect not only the marketability of the property but the turnover rate as well. Perhaps the kitchen floor plan designed is unworkable. Perhaps there is too little closet space. Perhaps the fixtures and equipment need to be altered. The manager tries to contribute management and marketing expertise to the decision-making process.

Rental Office and Model Apartments

The location of the rental office and model apartment or apartments is an important matter to be planned carefully. The office and models must be located to take advantage of the *traffic flow*—the flow of prospective residents as they move through the property. There must be enough parking nearby for all prospective residents. Adequate parking is necessary for any property, but it is even more important when the property is new. During the opening or *rent-up* period, it will not be unusual for 10 to 15 cars at once to be parked in front of the rental office and model apartments.

Planning ahead to add an extra temporary parking lot can relieve the pressure.

New mid-rise and high-rise buildings are normally finished from the roof down; hence, the rental office and models are often on an upper story. In this case, at least one elevator needs to be set aside for rental use. This elevator may be geared to stop only on the rental floor. Upper stories, however, are usually the most desirable location in the building and should not be tied up indefinitely. Proper planning can provide for the rental office to eventually be moved to an area near the lobby, freeing the apartment unit.

In multibuilding complexes, it is usually possible to place the models and rental office in the first building completed, thereby allowing visits from prospective residents early in the construction process. Amenities, however, such as a swimming pool and tennis courts, are often located away from the entrance of the first building. Until such time as the rental office can be relocated near the completed amenities, a descriptive site plan or scale model can feature the recreational facilities.

The rental office may be located in a building or entrance with other units. It is often wise to delay leasing those units until leasing is well underway and the property's reputation is established. Prospective residents might be unfavorably impressed by the sight of a resident in a bathrobe doing laundry on a Saturday morning. Prospects visiting an adults-only property might look askance at the five grandchildren who happen to be visiting the delightful empty nester couple on a busy Sunday afternoon. The property needs to be presented in its best light. If this means leaving several units vacant, inexpensive sheer curtains may be installed in windows and temporary nameplates put on the mailbox. This will save countless explanations of the reasons the units are unoccupied.

In the beginning, several model apartments may be necessary. This does not mean furnishing a number of units in an expensive manner: If the bedrooms in a two-bedroom unit are identical to those in a three-bedroom unit, considering furnishing the bedrooms in only one unit. Empty bedrooms need not go to waste. Area maps, display boards with floor plans, and examples of decorating styles

can fill an empty room and encourage a prospective resident
to linger. When the rent-up period is over and most of the
units are leased, the models can be moved, rented, or closed
down.

Construction Site

During the rent-up period, prospective residents will
probably be visiting the property as construction is going
on, which makes security in the construction area very
difficult to maintain. Prospective residents who want to see
units before making a choice may not understand the
necessity of keeping the construction areas off-limits to
everyone except the workers.

Wherever possible, moveable fencing should be installed.
Signage should be professional and explicit. Prospective
residents may be discouraged from entering the
construction area by large, conspicuously posted signs
proclaiming "Hard Hat Area" at the points where finished
buildings adjoin unfinished buildings. An explanatory sign
in the rental office should state:

> For your safety and to comply with state regulations, we
> must ask that you not enter the construction area without
> a hard hat.

In working with the contractor it may be possible to "bend"
this rule on weekends. It is the on-site manager, however,
who bears the ultimate responsibility for safety. Prospective
residents should only be taken into the construction area
when it is completely safe.

Marketing

After design matters have been decided upon, attention
turns to the marketing program. The importance of
marketing in a new property need hardly be stressed. A
large volume of prospective residents must be drawn into
the property during the rent-up period. Promotional
programs and advertising are grander and more spectacular
than they will be after the property has been established.
Careful records should be maintained to determine which
advertising and promotional programs bring in the most

prospective residents. Advertising and promotional programs can be adjusted often to take advantage of the most cost-effective methods.

Appearance

The appearance of the property is crucial to the marketing effort of a new property. Money should be spent to keep the property fresh and clean to increase curb appeal. Extra landscaping may improve the appearance of those areas still under construction. Matching blazers for the staff will present a uniform appearance. Most managers feel that any funds spent to present an organized, smooth running property will return benefits many times over.

Advertising

If the owner, developer, or property management firm has successfully developed other properties, be sure to draw on that reputation in the advertising. A simple line in your advertising such as, "Another fine property developed by CDM," will suffice. A display for the rental office could be created that shows photographs of other properties developed and managed by the management firm.

Brochures

Brochures for the new property follow the same guidelines we discussed in chapter 8 with two exceptions:

1. A variety of rates are used when opening a new property (these are discussed later in the chapter); brochures, therefore, should be easily updated. It is best to have single sheets printed with the current rental rates to be inserted into the brochures.

2. It may be advisable to have two brochures printed: one for use during the preopening and grand opening stages, and a larger, more detailed brochure for use after the property is filled. If they are designed and printed at the same time, they may be less expensive.

Policies and Procedures

During the opening of a new property, many standard policies and procedures are altered while other special policies and procedures are established.

Rental Rates

In an established property, rental rates tend to be changed once or twice a year. In a new property, there will be several levels of rental rates. How the manager handles these levels and applies them to residents already in occupancy vitally affects the cash flow. For example, the levels of rental rates might be as follows:

	One-Bedroom Units
Pre-construction rate: Jan–Mar	$320/month
Grand opening rate: Apr–May	330/month
Current rate: June–Dec	350/month
Next year's rate:	360/month

When rental rates are increased, the rental rate of each resident must be increased to the new rental rate, regardless of the rate they began with. For instance, say that you have two residents, one who leased at the preconstruction rate of $320 per month and another who is paying the current rate of $350 per month. When rents are increased, the rates of both residents must be increased to $360 per month. Each time rents are increased, they must be increased to the prevailing standard. The incentive for leasing a unit early on in the rent-up period should be the advantage of the lower rate for the first year—not a permanent discount from prevailing rates. (See chapter 6 for further information on rental rates.)

Part-Time Rental Agents

Because of the large volume of prospective residents visiting a new property, a few extra part-time rental agents are often hired. Their training will in most cases be different from the training of the regular rental agent or agents. Since these extra agents will not be working regular hours, the responsibility for *follow-up*—following up on a prospective resident's interest in the property—cannot be delegated to them. A system of referral must be developed. The prospective residents who talked with the part-time agent, Bill, on Sunday may not feel comfortable starting all over with the full-time agent, Mary, on Tuesday. The apartment may still be leased, however, if Mary can tell the returning prospective residents that she has their card with Bill's notes, that Bill even asked her to help these prospects personally. In order for this to occur, the part-time rental agents must be carefully trained in recording such information and communicating it to the full-time rental agent.

The importance of the extra agents to the success of the property must be emphasized. If the part-time agents feel that they are only extra personnel and have no real responsibilities, poor work may result. A time should be arranged at the beginning of each shift where either the manager or regular agent catches up on what has happened during the part-time agent's duty. An enthusiastic attitude displayed by the regular staff can make the extra agents feel a part of the team.

Residents are occasionally hired as part-time rental agents. This practice has its advantages and disadvantages. Residents are readily accessible and know the property, but they also may find it difficult to be residents part of the day and staff members the rest of the day. Only after a careful interview and considerable thought can it be determined whether or not a resident will make a good rental agent. When training a resident as a rental agent, emphasis must be placed on the confidentiality of the work and the position of respect the agent will hold. It is important for the manager to check frequently on the performance of all part-time rental agents.

Extended Hours

Extended hours are necessary in a new property. Without the rental agent or manager present to display the premises properly, prospective residents visiting the property may only see the unfinished areas and, disappointed at not being able to visualize the finished product, may never return. The property's hours may be determined by the season and by the competition's hours. Hours need not be fixed week after week.

In a new property, there are often visitors entering the rental office from a minute after opening time to a minute before closing time. Prospective residents should not be made to wait 15 minutes after the scheduled opening time while the staff is getting organized; neither should they be turned away by a rental agent hurrying to lock the door at one minute after closing. If the property's hours during the opening period are advertised as 10 A.M. to 6 P.M., staff should be scheduled to cover the hours of 9 A.M. to 7 P.M.

In the hour before opening, the staff prepares for the day with the doors locked and the telephones on answering service. The guest book is updated; the lights are turned on; the telephone messages received overnight are returned. By opening time, the office is completely ready for visitors. In the hour after closing, the staff members clean up and reorganize after the day, and are prepared to assist any late visitors. It is appropriate to display the "closed" sign at the scheduled closing time and lock the doors 15 minutes later.

Registration and Traffic Report

In a new property, the management plan is often a management proposal. The discovery of which marketing techniques are effective and which are ineffective may dictate a revision in the management plan.

The first step in analyzing marketing techniques is the registration of all visitors to the property, using either a guest book or an individual registration card. If a card is used, list each type of advertising used by the property with a box for the visitor to check, in order to determine how the visitor discovered the property. Visitor registration also enables the rental agent to address the prospective resident by name.

Visitor registration facilitates the compilation of the *traffic report* (see exhibit 9.1), submitted to the management office weekly. This report is a record of the number of prospective residents visiting the property on a daily basis, along with other pertinent data such as the weather conditions that day and the type of advertising that drew the prospect to the property. The traffic reports are examined and analyzed to determine how well the property is achieving its goals.

Exhibit 9.1   Traffic Report

Week of _____

Prepared by _____

Property	Monday	Tuesday	Wednesday	Thursday	Friday	Saturday	Sunday	Total
Nature of Inquiry								
Telephone call								
Visitor								
Time of Inquiry								
Morning (before noon)								
Afternoon (noon to 5 p.m.)								
Evening (after 5 p.m.)								
Referred by								
Large display ad in newspaper								
Classified ad								
Billboard								
Drive-by								
Telephone directory								
Word-of-mouth								
Direct mail								
Apartment locator service								
Television								
Radio								
Unit Desired								
One-bedroom								
Two-bedroom								
Three-bedroom								
Efficiency								
Furnished								
Unfurnished								
Weather Conditions								
Comments								

Perhaps the traffic reports indicate that two-bedroom units are leasing at a faster rate than one-bedroom units. The immediate action taken might be to lower the rental rate on the one-bedroom unit, thereby creating a better value. If, however, the market survey and analysis shows that the one-bedroom rate compares well to the competition, it might be preferable to raise the two-bedroom rate rather than lowering the one-bedroom rate. As a long-range solution, the architect might adjust the unit mix in the next phase of construction. With carefully kept records, the on-site manager and the property manager or owner are in a position to analyze the results and make the necessary changes to the management plan.

Security

Some concerns are ongoing, beginning when the property is new and continuing through the useful life of the property. One of these concerns is security. In a property under construction, security is important for the staff, the residents in occupancy, the visitors, and the construction site itself.

The manager should visit several properties already under construction to see how security is handled. While the problems in other properties may not be the same ones the manager anticipates occurring in this property, an inspection will increase the manager's knowledge and awareness of security problems.

The contractor will arrange security for the construction area. The manager should be aware of these security measures and be alert for unlocked buildings and gates and unauthorized persons in the area.

During the rent-up period, the staff will most likely be keeping late hours and leaving at dusk or later. Use timer lights to keep the area well-lit during these hours. Anticipate a volume of checks and deposits, particularly on the weekends. Arrange for the funds to be taken to the main office or bank on a daily basis. The office and models should have secure locks on all doors and windows. As an extra security measure, install an alarm system on the rental office to further safeguard master keys stored there.

Residents should be educated in security measures. It is often recommended that a security patrol be engaged in the early stages of a new property as a preventive measure. Many of your residents will be living in this area for the first time and will be unfamiliar with how to reach the local

police and fire departments. Every staff member and
resident should know exactly how to summon emergency
assistance.

Maintenance

A new property may have more maintenance problems than
an established property; therefore, an efficient system to
receive after-hours service requests is essential. An
answering machine on the rental office telephone line
should be used only if it directs the caller to another number
for emergency assistance. The machine, however, cannot
screen calls. The recipient of the "emergency" calls may find
that many of them are prospective residents seeking rental
information during off hours. A telephone answering
service, though more expensive than an answering
machine, screens all calls and will direct all true
emergencies to emergency assistance. When possible, a
separate telephone number should be assigned for
maintenance calls to separate them from general inquiry
calls.

Residents should be provided with a list of the emergency
telephone numbers of the utilities subcontractors (plumbing,
heating, and electrical). The contractor usually guarantees
the work for up to a year after completion. The
subcontractors usually have on-call arrangements for
emergency assistance calls.

Working with the Contractor

Several months prior to opening, the buildings will begin to
take shape and a construction schedule will forecast the
completion dates. At this time the manager begins working
more closely with the contractor and construction
superintendent.

Communication

As with so many aspects of the on-site manager's position,
working with the contractor requires clear, concise

communication. Contractors and superintendents are unaccustomed to taking orders. While they recognize the importance of meeting a schedule that allows orderly leasing, their construction comes first. The manager must solve all conflicts between leasing and construction schedules in a way that does not slow down construction.

All construction superintendents have their own system of communication. It is important that the manager understands this system. Learn the best (and worst) times to telephone the construction office. Try to organize your calls so that several matters are handled on each call. When possible, agree upon a time each day for communication so that the superintendent can simply call you or stop by for messages. By establishing regular communication, you can keep the contractor informed of your needs and be posted on changes in the construction schedule which can affect your leasing efforts.

It is wise to actually meet with the construction superintendent on a regular basis—perhaps once a week—but the manager should not make a practice of continually stopping in at the construction office.

Leasing and Completion Dates

The majority of problems between manager and contractor will arise in the area of leasing and completion dates. The manager sometimes makes a promise to a prospective resident of a completed unit on a certain date—a promise the contractor cannot keep. Early in the construction process, the manager should meet with the construction superintendent and/or contractor and decide upon a system to avoid problems between leasing and construction.

While written communication with the superintendent is important, a steady stream of little notes into the construction office should be avoided. A weekly report form can be devised to keep track of scheduling and occupancy. This form is similar to the rent roll: it contains unit number and location, the scheduled completion date, and the scheduled occupancy date. At the end of the week, the manager gives the updated sheet to the construction superintendent, showing which units have been leased that week and when they are to be occupied. On the basis of this information, the superintendent may decide to hasten work on a particular unit. The superintendent then makes any necessary adjustments to the scheduled completion dates and hands the sheet back to the manager, who makes adjustments to the scheduled occupancy dates on the basis of the new information. In this manner, the manager, the superintendent, and the construction staff keep each other informed of current progress.

The target date for the completion of a unit should be decided upon by the 25th of each month, as most incoming residents who currently rent elsewhere will need to give notice to their present landlord. Allowing for a few day's leeway in the schedule is important. The schedule should not be cut so close as to be unworkable. It is far better to inform an incoming resident on the 1st that the unit will not be ready by the 25th than to wait until the 15th for such an announcement.

The earlier the property is in the construction process, the harder it is to promise a prospective resident a firm *completion date*, or date the unit will be ready for occupancy. Units which are scheduled to be ready within 60 days are referred to as *upcoming inventory*. When leasing units this far in advance, the manager walks a tightrope between scheduling occupancy for the earliest possible date to generate income and allowing for delays in the construction schedule. The manager avoids giving an absolute guarantee by the way in which the completion date is described.

If the completion date of a particular unit to be leased is more than 60 days away, the manager or rental agent should refer to a *projected completion date*. Prospective residents will be more willing to wait for a firm completion date if they realize and understand that pinpointing the construction schedule more than 60 days in advance is simply guesswork.

When a unit is within 60 days of completion, but still more than 30 days away, it is wise to refer to the completion date as *proposed*. When the unit is within 30 days of completion, the term used can be *scheduled*. Terms such as "projected," "proposed," and "scheduled" carry the implication that everyone will do the best they possibly can, but that no guarantee actually exists.

It may also prove helpful to inform incoming residents that status changes in completion dates are only received once a month. Emphasize to them that asking the superintendent or crew may result in inaccurate information. If all channels of communication go through the manager, there will be less likelihood of misunderstanding and disappointment.

Custom Finishing

In most new properties, all apartments are painted white or off-white. It is possible, however, to establish a system whereby incoming residents may specify their own preferences for decorator items such as carpet color, paint color, and wallpaper. The availability of these choices should be simplified and kept to a minimum. A cutoff date for color selections should be established well in advance of completion—usually 90 days before the scheduled completion date. This lead time is necessary so that the materials can be delivered from the manufacturer.

One method of simplifying color choices is to develop a limited number of color schemes and preassign them to individual units. If the unit the prospective resident wishes to rent is the wrong color, it may be possible to exchange that unit's color scheme with the color scheme of another unit in the building.

Completion and Final Inspection

When a unit is placed on the "completed" list by the construction superintendent, the final inspection is made. The arrangement for the final inspection is generally handled by the contractor, not by the on-site manager. To avoid any last-minute problems, carefully coordinate the contractor's completion schedule, the inspection schedule, and the occupancy schedule.

New buildings require an occupancy certification by the local building department. No unit may be occupied by residents or by their furniture until the final inspection is made and the certificate issued. As a building is occupied, it is necessary to notify the insurance company that the building is partially or completely occupied to validate the liability insurance coverage.

Exhibit 9.2   Letter to Incoming Resident

Dear Incoming Resident,

Thank you for choosing Oak Forest to be your new home. We anticipate that your unit will be completed during the month of _____. You will be given at least 30 days notice of the scheduled completion date.

Watching your unit and building being completed is exciting. However, for safety reasons we must ask that you not enter the construction area at any time without first obtaining permission from our rental office. The contractor does not permit visitors on the job site during working hours.

As the completion of your building and unit approaches, the superintendent will make the first of several inspections of your unit and will find many items that will need correcting. This work will be done during the last week of construction just prior to final cleaning. The crew works on a planned schedule in order to complete all of the units on time. We ask that you not alter the planned inspection procedure by bringing in reports of problems or requests for modifications.

About a week prior to completion, a staff member will inspect your unit with the superintendent. At that time, any problems which have not already been taken care of will be noted. We have found through experience that this method tends to produce the quality we expect and allows us to maintain our completion schedule.

Naturally, if you observe any dangerous situation, or a problem that you feel will be impossible to correct at a later date, please bring it to my attention personally.

Thank you again for choosing Oak Forest—we look forward to having you as a resident in our new community.

In order to maintain good public relations, incoming residents should receive a letter explaining the inspection process at the time the rental application is completed (see exhibit 9.2).

All keys to the unit should be collected at the time of the final inspection. If temporary locks are being used during the construction stage, the permanent locks should now be installed. Most lock companies supply locks which work on a construction master key system. Once the individual key is used in the lock, the mechanism is "tripped" and the construction key will no longer work—only the master key and the individual keys will work.

The security of the master keys is important; however, once the master keys have been distributed on the construction site, they will probably be copied for the convenience of each subcontractor. The best way to

maintain security is through the following method: After
the unit is completed and the lock is tripped to void the
construction keys, one individual key from the set should be
tagged and placed on a key board. It is this key—and only
this key—which should be given out to workers for further
access to the individual units. If the key is missing at the
time occupancy is scheduled, it is a simple matter to
exchange the lock of that unit with the lock of another unit.

Move-In Problems

Partially Completed Buildings

The move-in process, discussed in chapter 5, has its own
special problems when the property is new. In spite of your
best efforts, it may be necessary to move residents into a
partially completed building. In this situation, the manager
should walk through the building with the resident, noting
anything which could affect the resident's safety—for
instance, an unfinished lobby, lack of a permanent stair rail,
or incomplete lighting. Counsel the resident to be alert to
these situations. Under no circumstances should you permit
a resident to move into a building where you cannot provide
safe access.

If any of the services to the building are temporary
because of construction, explain the particular limitations or
modifications. For example, perhaps the building is on a
temporary electrical line and it is not possible for the
resident to operate major appliances while the workers are
drawing on the power during the day. The potential
overload situation should be explained in writing so that no
misuse will occur. If tap water will not be available at
certain times of the day or week, inform the resident of this
situation.

Incomplete Amenities

As residents begin to occupy the new property, the
amenities may be incomplete. It is not unusual for a resident
to object to paying the full rent when the swimming pool
and other facilities are not yet in use. In leasing the
apartment, the manager should never promise or imply that
the facilities will be ready when the first building is ready. If

the amenities are to be located in a section scheduled for a later completion for which construction has not yet started, no commitment to a completion date should be made. Instead, explain to the residents that the amenities are scheduled to be completed during the second construction phase; and that when the completion date for that section is projected, the residents will be informed.

Emphasis of this point should be made in writing at three stages: (1) when the rental application is signed, (2) when the lease is signed, and (3) when the resident takes occupancy.

Residents in Occupancy

There will be times during the opening of the property when the contractor will be unable to give adequate advance notice of the interruption of services to residents already in occupancy. Whenever possible, give the residents notice by using a preprinted form with "Alert" at the top in large letters and a space to describe the problem. For example:

> ALERT! Water will be off from 8 A.M. to 4 P.M. Tuesday the 10th so that the next building may be hooked to the main.

Notices should be dated and, whenever possible, the reason for the interruption given. By working with the contractor and your residents, it may be possible to select a time that will cause the least amount of inconvenience for all.

Residents Awaiting Occupancy

Prospective residents who have signed leases and are awaiting occupancy are likely to be very excited about moving into the new property. Their enthusiasm, though in itself an asset, can put them underfoot constantly. By providing the future residents with the same newsletter the other residents are given, the manager promotes a feeling of belonging. Occasionally, a newsletter can be specifically designed for future residents, which gives information on their new neighbors and progress reports on their own building and the entire property.

Summary

The on-site manager often works with the property manager or developer in the planning and design of a new property. The rental office and models must be carefully located to take advantage of the traffic flow. Arrangements must also be made in the planning stage for the security and safety of prospective residents visiting the construction site.

The marketing program must draw a large number of prospective residents into the property during the rent-up period. Advertising is on a grander scale. Brochures should be easily updated. The appearance of the property must be carefully maintained.

During the opening of a new property, many standard policies and procedures are altered while other special policies and procedures are established. There will be several different levels of rental rates in a new property. Part-time rental agents will be hired; care must be taken in training them to refer prospects to the full-time agents. Hours are often extended; allowances should be made for prospective residents arriving slightly early or late. All prospective residents should individually register. The weekly traffic report is compiled from this registration.

Special arrangements must be made for the security of the construction area and rental office. An efficient system must be set up to receive after-hours service requests.

The manager must solve all conflicts between leasing and construction schedules. One way to reduce these conflicts is to refer to the completion date given to the resident as a *projected*, *proposed*, or *scheduled completion date*, depending on how far the unit is from completion. Some arrangements may be made for custom finishing of the incoming resident's unit. When a unit is complete, the final inspection is made. The lock will be tripped to void construction keys.

Some residents may be moving into partially completed buildings. The resident must be made fully aware of any limitations this will cause, such as temporary electrical outages or unfinished recreational facilities.

10

Leasing the Apartment

Leasing the apartment units is a prime responsibility of the on-site manager. The manager's skills in leasing—or lack of them—directly affect the vacancy and turnover rates, which translates into increased or decreased profits for the owner. Successful leasing of apartments requires careful resident selection and effective salesmanship.

Resident Selection

To better understand the importance of resident selection in the leasing process, let us look at two hypothetical apartment properties, Birch Bay and Maple Ridge. These two properties are similar in construction and design, but there the similarity ends.

Joan, the on-site manager of the Birch Bay property, carefully selects and diligently educates her residents. She screens potential applicants and places new residents in buildings where she believes they will fit in. She has a complete set of resident selection guidelines that suggests the best type of resident for each unit. The resident handbook emphasizes courtesy, mutual respect, and cooperation; no detail of policy is left unmentioned. An open-door policy exists at Birch Bay. Small problems are solved before they become large issues.

The result is that Birch Bay enjoys full occupancy with a long waiting list. Turnover is moderate, morale high, the atmosphere friendly. Singles, young families, and empty nesters live side-by-side with a minimum of problems.

Maple Ridge offers features, amenities, and rental rates very similar to those of Birch Bay. But Jean, the manager at Maple Ridge, firmly believes that any sort of selection process is discriminatory. No system of resident selection and placement exists. Jean feels that as long as a prospect has satisfactory credit, the unit should be available to them. She feels her empty nesters should be more tolerant of the children on the property, and therefore refuses to listen to any of their complaints. Her residents, she believes, are perfectly capable of working out their differences among themselves without bothering the management.

As a result, the turnover rate at Maple Ridge is very high. No counseling or arbitration is available for settling resident disputes under Jean's "hands off" policy, such as conflicts between the empty-nester couple who go to bed at 8 P.M. and the students living above them who party until 1 A.M. An angry atmosphere exists in this property, which could have been easily avoided through careful resident selection.

Resident Profiles

To succeed in resident selection, the manager must have an understanding of the different types of people who reside in apartments.

Empty nesters. The mainstay of many an apartment property is the *empty nester*, a name coined to describe the retiree whose family is raised and who is ready to give up the responsibility of a large home. Empty nesters usually enjoy retirement. They may be inclined to "oversee" the building, reporting even the smallest problem to the manager. They often take as much pride in the building as they did in their own home.

Professionals. Professional, career-oriented singles and couples are primarily interested in their field of employment; where they live may be of secondary importance. They expect the property to be managed with the same high standards of their own profession.

Families. Families often lease apartments because they cannot afford a home; an apartment is often not an ideal environment for them. Special attention, therefore, is necessary in meeting their housing needs. If both parents work, their children may be unsupervised at home for several hours a day. If the family's financial position necessitates their occupying smaller quarters than would be desirable, excess friction and noise may exist. A family may consist of a single parent with a child or children. This parent carries the extra burden of raising the children alone, which may add to the tension of the living situation. Well-defined policies regarding families can ease the tension in buildings where families live.

Singles. Young, single residents are highly transient; consequently, they may not often think of their apartments as "home." If they are not career-oriented people, their financial situation may be somewhat unstable. Noise, late hours, and lack of proper upkeep are problems often associated with singles. At the worst, their apartments become simply places for meeting and partying. Their overall lack of interest in the property creates different management needs.

Students. If your property is within convenient commuting distance of a university or community college, students may be prospective residents. College students are often away from home and restrictions for the first time, and managers may find themselves in the role of authority figure. Students' recreation is often loud and boisterous. The wear and tear on a building with a large student population can be excessive. Students tend to group together to economize on expenses, and are notoriously vague about the specific terms of the lease. Renting to one or two students in a unit does not guarantee that more will not occupy the apartment. Student applicants must be screened carefully to determine their ability to pay rent and their willingness to accept responsibility.

Graduate students are generally more responsible than undergraduate students. Graduate students have often left well-paying jobs to obtain a master's or doctorate degree. They need much privacy and quiet and are likely to insist on attentive management to provide the proper environment for their studies.

Students from foreign countries often attend American universities and schools, especially for graduate studies. Special attention must be given at the time of their application to ensure that they have a clear understanding of all that is expected of them.

Blue collar. In larger cities, properties located near large industries attract tradesmen or blue-collar workers. The work schedules of these residents are often earlier than a normal working day. Their early morning departures may upset late sleepers in the building.

Resident Selection Guidelines

Before actual leasing begins, guidelines must be drawn up for resident selection. These guidelines show the resident profile or profiles best suited to the property, as well as all other factors figuring in resident selection.

Looking at the resident profiles listed earlier, the manager may wonder why the resident selection guidelines should not simply call primarily for empty nesters, with a few professional couples thrown in for good measure, thereby avoiding many management problems. Resident selection, however, is not this simple. In preparing guidelines for resident selection, the manager will answer these questions:

1. What is the typical profile in my marketing area?
2. What resident profile will best fit my property?
3. If it is not feasible to completely fill my property with that profile, what alternative profiles should be sought?
4. What are the next best choices? What mix of profiles might be suitable?
5. Is there a particular profile that will not fit my property?

6. Having created a composite group of profiles, can I offer the services and facilities that each will expect?

7. Will we accept pets? What types and size? Will we have a pet section in the property? Or will we have a section where pets are not permitted? Will we have a limit on the total number of pets in the property?

8. Will we charge "head" rent (see chapter 6)?

9. What is my competition doing about items 1 through 8?

10. Are any of my policies discriminatory?

11. What does the marketplace dictate as being the best mix of profiles?

12. What does the ownership prefer?

Resident selection guidelines are categorized by type of unit. For example, the guidelines might set a maximum of two people in a one-bedroom unit, provided both are adults, or a maximum of three occupants in a two-bedroom unit. Other typical guidelines might stipulate that up to three people may occupy a two bedroom unit provided there are no more than two vehicles, or that all children of opposite sex over age six must have their own bedrooms. The rationale for all restrictions must be clear. If the restrictions are both workable and logical to the manager, the policies will probably be acceptable to the prospective residents.

The Selection Process

When the resident selection guidelines have been made final, the selection process can begin. By carefully screening all prospects at the rental office, the manager can determine which prospective residents shall receive a sales effort at the outset, and should thereby have few surprises when the prospect reaches the written application stage.

Qualifying the prospects—determining how well qualified the prospects are to become residents of the property—

requires skills that are acquired through experience, trial and error, training, and continued education.

In qualifying the prospect, the manager is seeking answers to the following questions:

Does the prospect's profile fit the available units?

Does the prospect seem to fit the rental and lease structure we offer?

Does the prospect seem to be sincere about leasing?

If the prospect plans to move in with a family, what is the size of the family?

Does the prospect have any pets?

Is the prospect financially responsible?

What lease and rental terms does the prospect prefer?

It is not unprofessional to ask prospective residents about their circumstances and needs before beginning the sales effort. If you do not accept pets, it is much better to uncover the existence of a pet at this stage than at the application stage.

One technique for discreetly obtaining the necessary information from the applicant is called *trading*, a process of exchanging information. While giving out information, always pose a question in return. For example, when you greet a resident, give your name, then add, "And your name is?" You can then call the visitor by name when asking him or her to register. When the prospect asks, "How much are your two bedroom units?" answer, "They range from $350 to $400 per month and are about 800 square feet. How does that compare to your present home?" By exchanging or "trading" information, the manager is assimilating oral and inferred information, creating a level of comfort and confidence, and obtaining the necessary data to qualify the prospect *before* the prospect expresses serious interest.

For example, in your property there might be a policy requiring one year leases, when it is typical in the area to require only a six month's lease. You will need to know if the prospective resident is willing to sign a one-year lease. Therefore, in answering a question about the length of the lease, you might add, "Are you accustomed to the advantages of an annual lease?" If the answer you receive is unsatisfactory, you know that there is a possibility the prospect is not suited for your property.

When the manager does not screen prospects correctly, the appraisal of the prospect may be based on the personality, dress, or physical appearance of the prospect. Measuring a prospect up to the manager's subjective yardstick is not a selection process. Not only is it unfair and unprofessional, but it may also be discriminatory. Without qualifying the prospect first, the manager may unfairly encourage a prospect to apply for a unit when both the property's and the prospect's needs cannot be met.

We have already mentioned the value of reciprocal referrals in creating and maintaining good public relations. In the market study of the neighborhood, you have already become familiar with the features, rental prices, and resident mix in other nearby apartment properties. When it is apparent that prospective residents are not suited to the property, you should be prepared to refer them to properties to which they will be suited, thereby creating good public relations.

Salesmanship

In rental housing, the manager is not selling the apartment to the prospect, but selling the prospect *on* the apartment. To convince potential residents to become applicants, good sales techniques must be used, even though no "sale" actually occurs.

Appearance and Approach

Before the sales effort begins, you must make certain that you are presenting yourself in the best possible light, and that your approach is friendly but businesslike. A professional appearance and approach include the following:

Stand up when the visitor enters the rental office.

Greet the visitor immediately. If you are on the telephone, ask your caller to hold a moment, then tell the visitor, "Hello! I'll be right with you!"

Look like a professional. Do not smoke, eat, or shuffle papers while you are talking with the prospect.

Maintain eye contact. By looking the visitor in the eyes, you are communicating that your attention is focused on the conversation, not on other matters.

Share the conversation. Avoid dominating or continually interrupting the conversation. Do not ask questions that require only a yes-or-no reply.

Dress professionally. Blue jeans have no place in the office, but neither does the on-site manager need the wardrobe of a model or a closet of three-piece suits. The manager's wardrobe should consist of well-fitted, attractive separates or suits appropriate to the marketplace.

Any makeup used by women should not be theatrical. The use of heavily scented perfume or aftershave lotion is discouraged.

Neighborhood, Property, and Competition

While still in the rental office, before showing the unit, the manager must create a good overall impression of the property, the neighborhood in which the property is located, and how well the property compares with the competition. At the same time, the manager has an opportunity to establish an atmosphere of trust in which the "sale" can take place. In preparation, you must have all the information on the neighborhood and competition gathered in the market survey at your fingertips. You must also be able to tell prospective residents everything they want and need to know about the available units, from location to view to decor.

In many cases, the prospect will be entirely new to the neighborhood—perhaps to the city as well. This provides you with a good opportunity to discuss the location and availability of shopping, schools, churches, libraries, public and private transportation, recreational facilities, and other desirable features of the neighborhood.

Next, emphasize the features or policies that set your property apart from the competition. For example, if your pool is open until 10 P.M., while your competition's pool is open only until 7 P.M., emphasize the additional pool hours of your property. If you are talking with a prospect who has a pet, and your pet policy is more liberal than the competition's, make sure the prospect feels his or her pet is welcome. You will be shopping your competition regularly to update your knowledge of the competition's policies and features: use that knowledge to "sell" your property. It is important, however, to present your property's features and advantages without appearing to unduly criticize the competition.

Showing the Unit

The next step in leasing the apartment is actually showing the unit to the prospect. The manager or staff member should always accompany the prospect to the unit in person. If the property uses a model apartment, be prepared to explain the differences between the model and the unit or units available to the prospect.

If the unit is currently unoccupied, it should be in perfect condition, completely ready to be occupied. On the walk from the rental office to the units, use the time to reinforce the image of the property as a desirable place to live. (Your dialogue should not be so detailed, however, that the prospective resident cannot take time to observe the area.)

When you arrive at the unit, point out the unit's best or most unusual features, such as an excellent view or new carpeting, and then let the prospective resident wander through the unit undisturbed. It may even be appropriate to leave the prospect alone in the unit for a brief time. By allowing prospects free rein of the apartment, they are made to feel at home.

If you are showing the prospective resident more than one unit, directly compare them in the following manner: "Do you prefer the earthtone color scheme of this unit or the green color scheme of unit 207?" By asking a question about the units that cannot be answered "yes" or "no", you are offering the prospect a choice not between leasing and not leasing, but between leasing one unit or another unit.

After the units have been shown, it is helpful to tour the amenities with the prospect on the return to the rental office.

Closing the Sale

That part of salesmanship called *closing*—actually
persuading the customer to buy—is an art unto itself. If no
attempt is made at closing, the sale will probably not be
made. The salesperson walks a thin line between too much
pressure for a sale and too little. New on-site managers, not
being primarily in sales, often cripple their sales effort by
saying a mere "thank you" to the prospective resident after
the units have been shown.

One technique salespeople use in closing a sale is asking
for a smaller order when their request for a larger order is
refused. In the case of leasing apartments, asking for the
"larger order" might be asking the prospect to complete a
application. Say that you, the on-site manager, have just
shown a unit to a prospective resident named Brown. You
ask, "Mr. Brown, why don't we complete the application so
that unit 203 is yours? It will only take a few minutes."

If the prospect responds, "I need to do more looking," or,
"I'm not ready to make a decision—I'll let you know if I'm
interested," ask for the "smaller order"—in this case, asking
the prospect to place a small deposit would be appropriate:

"Mr. Brown, I can understand that you might not be ready
to lease the unit today. If you'd like to make sure that your
unit will still be available, you could put a small deposit
down to hold the unit until Saturday."

You have accomplished three things by asking for the
"smaller order":

1. If Mr. Brown accepts your proposal, a psychological
   bond is created. Now he will probably compare any
   units he looks at with "his" unit in your property.

2. You have something of a commitment from him
   that if he does not find another suitable unit in the
   next few days, he will lease your unit.

3. You have made it easy for him to choose to lease
   the unit. Leasing an apartment is a considerable
   commitment. The prospective resident may find the
   commitment easier to make if it is split up into
   parts, such as placing a small deposit down one
   day and completing the application a day or two
   later. Having placed a deposit down, Mr. Brown
   will also probably feel a sense of relief. The
   pressure to find a place to lease is over. Now he

can comfortably look around and confirm his
selection. He knows that he likes this unit well
enough to have given you a deposit.

If Mr. Brown agrees to leave a deposit, the necessary papers
should be on hand. The receipt for the deposit should be
brief but complete. It should indicate the purpose, the
amount, the date paid, the unit, and the application
appointment time set. It will be helpful to include your
telephone number and brief instructions on how the
prospect can complete the transaction.

Rental Applications

A typical rental application is shown in exhibit 10.1. The
application should provide three types of information:

1. Facts needed to process and approve the applicant,
   such as current employment and credit references.
2. Facts needed to set up files and prepare the lease,
   such as the complete names of applicants and
   number of dependents.
3. Facts which the applicant must acknowledge with
   a signature, such as the nature of the investigative
   process.

Space for other information may need to be added to the
rental application form. For example, credit bureaus in many
areas cannot process a credit report without the applicant's
social security number. In a new property with units still
under construction, a paragraph covering anticipated
completion dates might be added. Pet agreements may also
be included as part of the application.

Once the applicant has completed the application, the
manager should take time to review it with the applicant,
making sure that any missing information is noted and that
any questions which do not apply are marked "not
applicable."

Applicants will often be reluctant to give out information
they feel is personal and, in their eyes, unnecessary for
approving the application. This reaction is normal and

Exhibit 10.1 Rental Application

Date _____   Property _____

Unit _____   Monthly Rental $_____

The undersigned hereby makes application to rent unit number ____

located at _____

beginning on _____, 19_____,

at a monthly rental of $_____,

and submits the following information:

Name of Applicant _____

Name of Co-Applicant _____

Number of Dependents _____ Ages _____

Other Occupants and Their Relationship _____

Pets (Number and Kind) _____

Current Address _____ Phone _____

    How Long? _____ Reason for Leaving _____

    Owner or Agent _____ Phone _____

Previous Address _____

    How Long? _____ Reason for Leaving _____

    Owner or Agent _____ Phone _____

Current Employer _____

    How Long? _____ Employed as _____

    Supervisor _____ Phone _____

    Address _____

    Social Security Number _____

    Salary $ _____ per _____

Name of Bank _____

    Checking Account Number _____

    Savings Account Number _____

Credit References:

    Name   Account Number

_____   _____

_____   _____

Automobile License Number _____

    State of Registry _____

    Automobile Make, Model, Year _____

    Driver's License Number _____

Have you ever: filed for bankruptcy? (   ) Yes   (   ) No

                  been evicted from tenancy? (   ) Yes   (   ) No

                  willfully or intentionally refused to pay rent when

                  due?

                      (   ) Yes   (   ) No

Exhibit 10.1 (Continued)

I hereby apply to lease the above described premises for the term and upon the conditions above set forth and agree that the rental is to be payable the _____ day of each month in advance. As an inducement to the owner of the property and to the agent to accept this application, I warrant that all statements above set forth are true; however, should any statement made above be a misrepresentation or not a true statement of facts, $_____ of the deposit will be retained to offset the agent's cost, time, and effort in processing my application.

I hereby deposit $_____ as earnest money to be refunded to me if this application is not accepted within _____ business banking days. Upon acceptance of this application, this deposit shall be retained as part of the security deposit. When so approved and accepted I agree to execute a lease for _____ months before possession is given and to pay the balance of the security deposit within _____ business banking days after being notified of acceptance, or the deposit will be forfeited as liquidated damages in payment for the agent's time and effort in processing my inquiry and application, including making necessary investigation of my credit, character, and reputation. If this application is not approved and accepted by the owner or agent, the deposit will be refunded, the applicant hereby waiving any claim for damages by reason of nonacceptance which the owner or his agent may reject without stating any reason for so doing.

I RECOGNIZE THAT AS A PART OF YOUR PROCEDURE FOR PROCESSING MY APPLICATION, AN INVESTIGATIVE CONSUMER REPORT MAY BE PREPARED WHEREBY INFORMATION IS OBTAINED THROUGH PERSONAL INTERVIEWS WITH MY NEIGHBORS, FRIENDS, AND OTHERS WITH WHOM I MAY BE ACQUAINTED. THIS INQUIRY INCLUDES INFORMATION AS TO MY CHARACTER, GENERAL REPUTATION, PERSONAL CHARACTERISTICS, AND MODE OF LIVING. I UNDERSTAND THAT I MAY HAVE THE RIGHT TO MAKE A WRITTEN REQUEST WITHIN A REASONABLE PERIOD OF TIME TO RECEIVE ADDITIONAL, DETAILED INFORMATION ABOUT THE NATURE AND SCOPE OF THIS INVESTIGATION.

The above information, to the best of my knowledge, is true and correct.

Signature of Applicant _____

_____

Application and Deposit of $_____

Date Received _____

Received by _____

Co-applicants must file separate applications.

understandable. The information may be obtained
diplomatically by saying, "The office requires that we
include this information on all applications to avoid
discrimination. I can tell you that the information in your
application will be treated confidentially." If the applicant
still declines to supply the information, and the information
is not critical to processing the application, have the
applicant mark "confidential" in the space for that
information.

The deposit and the form of payment (check and check
number, cash and receipt number, etc.) should be noted. If
your state laws require that each applicant be given a copy
of the application, obtain acknowledgement that one has
been received; it is often practical and professional to give
each applicant a copy of the application regardless of
whether or not it is required by law.

Briefly review the completed application. In cases where it
is obvious that the application will not be approved—for
instance, if you discover at this late stage that the resident
has a pet and your property is restricted to residents
without pets—it is both professional and courteous to
disclose the problem immediately and resolve the situation,
even if it means voiding the application.

As the interview ends, you should reiterate the process
through which the application will go: "Mr. Brown,
everything appears to be fine. Our office usually needs two
or three working days to process an application. As soon as
I have the approval back from the office I will telephone
you." Try to send the applicant away with the idea that the
processing of the application is merely routine paperwork. If
you have practiced good resident selection and
salesmanship, it should be routine.

Summary

The on-site manager's skills in leasing directly affect the
vacancy and turnover rate of the property. Successful
leasing of apartments requires careful resident selection and
effective salesmanship.

Resident selection is the art of determining which
resident profiles will fit the units available in the property.
Typical resident profiles include retired "empty nesters,"

career-oriented professionals, families, singles, students, and blue-collar workers. Each profile has its own set of needs and problems. The apartment property and its competition are studied and a set of resident selection guidelines drawn up. These guidelines suggest the combination of resident profiles that will be best suited for the property.

All prospects are qualified to determine their suitability as residents. The qualifying process seeks to determine the prospects' ability to pay, the degree of their interest, their needs and wants, and anything about the prospects that would make them immediately unsuitable. By qualifying prospects before they have expressed an interest in the apartment, the manager determines how much effort should be put into the sales presentation.

Effective salesmanship begins with the manager's professional appearance and approach. The manager should be dressed appropriately, should greet the visitor cordially, and should never dominate the conversation. The manager begins the sales effort by discussing the merits of the property and neighborhood, then leads the prospect to the unit.

The manager then attempts to "close the sale" by getting a commitment to lease from the prospect. If the prospect does not wish to fill out an application, the manager may suggest that the prospect place a deposit on the unit.

The rental application should contain blanks for financial information needed to approve the applicant, personal information needed to prepare the lease, and information which the applicant must acknowledge with a signature. The completed application is double-checked for completeness, and the approval process is reviewed before the applicant leaves.

11

Maintenance Management

It is easy to overlook the importance of maintenance in on-site management. In the rush to acquire management skills, maintain proper occupancy, minimize turnover, and increase rents, the on-site manager can forget that without proper maintenance, the property will fail to succeed. A resident's call for maintenance is not necessarily a complaint, but should be considered a request for service. The maintenance worker is often considered to be at a lower level than other management personnel, but in fact is an indespensible member of the management team. It is the maintenance worker who readies the unit for occupancy and maintains it, thus creating the most valuable tool the manager has in "selling" the property—an attractive, desirable product.

Good maintenance service reduces turnover, develops resident satisfaction, and contributes to the financial success of the property. Poor maintenance creates vacancies, high turnover, and affects the value of the property adversely. It is the result of disorganization, poor communication and judgement, and a lack of adequate systems, controls, and employee training.

The responsibilities of a maintenance worker vary from property to property. In some properties, the worker may be directly responsible for interior and exterior repairs, inventory control, ordering, and scheduling. In others, the worker might simply keep up with routine repairs. A qualified maintenance worker will provide expert skills, experience, and common sense, and will work to create good will between the management team and residents. To the resident, in many cases, the maintenance worker may be the most important member of the staff.

Types of Maintenance

There are six basic types of maintenance: (1) preventive, (2) corrective (3) deferred, (4) routine, (5) emergency, and (6) cosmetic. The manager should clearly understand the differences between these types.

Preventive

Preventive maintenance decreases the number of breakdowns or failures and helps to avoid interruptions of services. Preventive maintenance is of two types: (1) normal, scheduled upkeep on equipment, and (2) treatment of problems in their early stages in order to prevent them from becoming serious problems.

An example of the first type is a service contract for major equipment which provides for regular inspections and repairs when necessary. When the elevator contractor oils the elevator motors and pumps, preventive maintenance is being performed. No problems exist, but if the elevator were not regularly oiled, serious problems would arise. Another example would be draining a few buckets of water from a water heater each month. There may be nothing wrong with the heater. If the water is not drained regularly, however, scale and lime deposits will build up on the inside of the tank, eventually causing failure and necessitating replacement.

An example of the second type of preventive maintenance would be patching a small hole in the asphalt driveway before it *alligators* (breaks apart into small pieces) and eventually becomes a large chuckhole.

Corrective

Despite the manager's efforts at preventive maintenance, trouble will develop and equipment malfunctions will occur.

Corrective maintenance consists of repairs to the building and equipment due to natural wear and tear or faulty preventive maintenance. A specialist, such as a plumber or electrician, is often called in for corrective maintenance.

With equipment problems, there may be a question as to whether the particular item should be repaired or replaced. If the item is of major importance, such as a boiler, the matter should be brought to the attention of the property manager. For less expensive items, a good rule of thumb is to replace the item if the cost to repair is more than half the cost to replace—although this guideline cannot be followed in every situation.

Routine

Routine maintenance consists of custodial maintenance, basic lawn care, and responding to service requests from residents. Like preventive maintenance, consistent and careful routine maintenance may help to prevent more serious problems from occuring.

Deferred

Occasionally, necessary maintenance is put off until a later date; this maintenance is called *deferred maintenance*. Contributing to the delay might be budget limitations, owner preference, the availability of parts, or inclement weather. Deferred maintenance should be avoided when possible. Further damage may occur, lowering the value of the property. If the situation is allowed to deteriorate long enough, it may become an actual emergency.

Deferring certain maintenance tasks, however, is sometimes necessary. For example, the repair of a small roof leak discovered in the middle of winter might be deferred until the temperature would permit a repair. Necessary steps would be taken to prevent further damage until the deferred repair could be made. Perhaps carpet cleaning must be deferred until the unit can be painted, or until the carpet repair worker fixes a damaged area. These are all examples of properly deferred maintenance.

Emergency

Emergency maintenance is nonscheduled repair that must be performed immediately. The situation is usually a crisis. We have seen that the failure to perform preventive, routine, or deferred maintenance can create more serious problems: those problems may eventually become emergencies.

An emergency can be defined as a situation where life, property, or both will be endangered if repairs are not made promptly. Examples of true emergencies might be a broken water line where water is flowing, a fire, or an inoperative elevator in a high-rise building. An emergency maintenance phone number should be provided to all residents.

Other less serious situations are often perceived as emergencies, but in fact are not emergencies. In these situations great distress and discomfort may occur, but there is no endangerment of life or property. A broken lock, for example, would only be an emergency if the lack of this particular lock would completely breach security; if there were other locks, there would be no emergency. Many inexperienced managers might routinely classify lack of heat as an emergency, but lack of heat is only an emergency when the outside temperature is low enough to cause property damage or harm health without heat.

Cosmetic

Cosmetic maintenance involves those repairs which do not affect the function of the item but make the item or area more appealing. The manager must carefully weigh the benefits of cosmetic maintenance against the effect on the cash flow, determining whether or not the cost of the cosmetic maintenance will bring in high enough rental increases to offset the cost.

Wallpapering a bathroom is an example of cosmetic maintenance. Wallpaper makes the bathroom more appealing; therefore, the maintenance is cosmetic. Likewise, replacing a single-door refrigerator with a two-door refrigerator containing an icemaker might be a form of cosmetic maintenance: the older refrigerator worked fine, but the new refrigerator contains features which will attract a resident to lease the unit.

Obsolescence. Some cosmetic repairs are related to obsolescence. For example, the single-door refrigerator we mentioned was *functionally obsolete*. Because it was less desirable than newer styles of refrigerators, the unit was not as easy to lease. Functional obsolescence often occurs in older buildings where fixtures and appliances were installed before modern innovations. For example, in apartments built in the mid-1930s, it was popular to place the bathroom off the kitchen for the convenience of the plumber. In today's rental market, residents prefer to have the bathroom located near bedrooms.

Fortunately, the old refrigerator was also *curably obsolete*. The functional obsolescence could become curable obsolescence by replacing the old refrigerator with a new model. Some functional obsolescence may be part of the structure itself and not curable, such as a lack of closets.

Economic obsolescence is caused by factors in the neighborhood. For example, say that a small apartment building built in the 1950s, located in a quiet, older neighborhood, is now surrounded by light industrial business instead of homes. The change of the neighborhood has created a condition that adversely affects the value of the units.

Establishing a Maintenance Program

In chapter 3, we discussed the five functions of management that need to occur in the performance of every management task. These five functions are (1) planning, (2) decision making, (3) organizing, (4) directing, and (5) controlling. These functions will serve as a guide in discussing the policies and procedures that must be devised in establishing a maintenance program.

Planning

Planning is the first step in any successful operation. As it applies to maintenance management, planning includes writing the maintenance portion of the operations manual, property inspections, and budgeting.

Operations Manual

One of the most overlooked aids in operating a property today is the operations manual, the creation of which is discussed in chapter 3. The operations manual is divided into sections on staff and employment policies, resident policies, rental collection and record keeping, legal procedures, marketing and leasing, and maintenance. The maintenance section is broken down by categories into the six types of maintenance already discussed: preventive, corrective, deferred, routine, emergency, and cosmetic. There is also information on inspections, purchasing, and control procedures.

Inspections

In order to efficiently plan maintenance, the manager must be aware of the problems needing maintenance. As we have mentioned in previous chapters, the on-site manager must develop and maintain a keen sense of observation. It is easy to spot flaws and problems in an unfamiliar building, but it is also easy to overlook problems in a building you see every day. This tendency can be avoided through the use of inspection forms, which serve as reminders to look carefully at specific details of the property that often may be overlooked.

By using written inspection forms, the manager has an opportunity to note corrections needed. As many noted problems as possible should be corrected by the on-site staff as routine maintenance; problems identified as an area of major concern should be summarized and included in the on-site manager's periodic report to the property manager.

Regularly scheduled, routine inspections should be performed at least monthly in small properties, bimonthly in larger properties, to observe the overall picture of the property and keep up with scheduled repairs. Occasional impromptu inspections allow the manager to view the property as it actually exists, not as it would be on the day of a scheduled inspection. Impromptu inspections remind employees that the property needs to be orderly and clean at all times, not just when an inspection is anticipated.

Evening inspections can bring security problems to light that might go unnoticed during the day. The lighting of the parking areas and buildings should be sufficient to discourage prowlers and wanderers. Most lawsuits against management companies and owners regarding evening crimes claim that there was insufficient lighting. If there is a patrol or guard service, an evening inspection will check its effectiveness.

Daytime inspections give the manager the opportunity to talk informally with most of the employees. The manager can also observe how the employees interact with the residents. Is the staff courteous, helpful, and representative of the image the company wishes to project? Is efficiency and concern being displayed? Or are coffee breaks longer than the work periods? These potential sources of problems can be explored during a routine daytime inspection. The manager must take care that the inspection does not disrupt the work routine.

There are three basic types of inspections: exterior, interior, and unit.

Exterior inspection. An exterior inspection (see exhibit 11.1 for an exterior inspection form) should begin at the entrance to the property, viewing the property as a prospective resident would see it. Resident common areas, such as the swimming pool and recreational areas, should especially be inspected for curb appeal.

Several structural details demand inspection. Gutters and downspouts must be checked to make sure none are blocked and all are properly joined and free from leaks. The *splashblocks* (concrete blocks which guide water away from the building at the bottom of downspouts) should be inspected to make sure the water is draining away from the building instead of towards it. Cracks in the exterior surface of the buildings may indicate serious structural problems and should be noted and reported to the property manager. The parking areas should be inspected for litter, improper drainage, clearness of markings, and alligatoring of the asphalt. The trash or dumpster area needs frequent inspection to ensure that it is clean, landscaped or concealed to provide an attractive appearance, and adequate for the property's needs.

Roofs are usually inspected twice a year. If any problems are found, inspections should take place more frequently. An

Exhibit 11.1   Building Exterior Inspection

Property _____ Date _____

Inspected by _____

Area	Condition			Maintenance Required	Estimated Cost
	Good	Fair	Poor		
Front Wall					
Base					
Top					
Surface					
Cleanliness					
Side Walls					
Base					
Top					
Surface					
Cleanliness					
Rear Wall					
Base					
Top					
Surface					
Cleanliness					
Roof					
Flashing					
Surface					
Gutters/Downspouts					
Chimney					
Vents					
Light Fixtures					
Fixtures					
Bulbs					
Switch/Timer					

excellent time to inspect a roof is just after a rainstorm, where puddling can be observed or loose shingles noted before damage occurs to the interior of the building.

As we have already discovered, signage is an important part of the property's marketing effort. Particular attention should be paid to signage: Are street signs visible? Are directional signs to various areas of the property well presented and consistent in theme? Are all signs freshly painted? Much rental traffic is brought into the property through signage.

Another item to consider in an exterior inspection is safety. Local fire safety laws should be consulted (these are discussed later in the chapter). Expanding fire escapes, if they exist, should be checked several times a year to ensure proper operation. Panic bars and all fire doors should all be operable. Fences should be checked for damage or openings.

The manager's best method of completing an exterior inspection is to walk around the entire area. In large properties, golf carts may be used for exterior inspections. The manager might also take the maintenance worker along on the inspection tour, and together decide on a plan of action for each problem found.

Interior inspection. (For an example of an interior inspection checklist, see exhibit 11.2.) Cleanliness of the common interior areas (lobbies, hallways, etc.) is often more important to residents than exterior cleanliness. A resident might be inclined to overlook debris in the parking lot, but will complain (and rightly so) that the lobby is untidy. Much of the interior inspection, then, is for cleanliness. The lobby should be spotless. Elevators should be cleaned regularly and should be well lighted and appealing. The hallways and stairways often contain light fixtures which are rarely dusted. Small spots on carpeting should be removed weekly. If they are neglected, a buildup of spots can necessitate a complete shampooing before one is scheduled. Particular attention should be paid to the areas that must withstand heavy resident and visitor traffic wear and tear, such as a clubhouse or rental office.

Interior areas must also be inspected for safety. Many local fire departments will welcome an invitation to visit and inspect the property annually to offer professional suggestions on fire safety. While most states have particular laws regarding the inspection of fire extinguishers, smoke detectors, and emergency exit lights, it is an excellent idea to check these items more frequently than the code requires.

An area not to be overlooked is the storage room. Inflammable materials unknowingly stored by a resident or maintenance worker may prove to be the cause of a destructive fire. One manager found a case of dynamite in an unassigned storage locker during a routine inspection.

Exhibit 11.2   Building Interior Inspection

Property _____   Date _____

Inspected by _____

Area	Condition			Maintenance Required	Estimated Cost
	Good	Fair	Poor		
Entry Door					
Glass					
Transom					
Hinges					
Knobs and Locks					
Door Check					
Door Finish					
Kick Plate					
Entryway/Vestibule					
Walls					
Ceilings					
Floors					
Door Mats					
Mailboxes					
Doors					
Locks					
Name Plates					
Intercom					
Signal Buttons					
Hallway, Front					
Risers					
Steps					
Landings					
Handrails					
Walls					
Ceilings					
Floors					
Windows					
Window Covering					
Hallway, Rear					
Risers					
Steps					
Landings					
Handrails					
Walls					
Ceilings					
Floors					
Windows					
Window Coverings					

Unit inspection. (For an example of a unit inspection
checklist, see exhibit 11.3.) Although today's emphasis on
resident privacy may cause managers to hesitate to inspect
individual apartment units, an annual inspection should not
be considered an intrusion on the rights of the resident. The
inspection can often be combined with a routine service
call. For example, in properties where each apartment has
individual heating or air conditioning units, the unit can be
inspected as the filters are changed.

Exhibit 11.2   (Continued)

Area	Condition			Maintenance Required	Estimated Cost
	Good	Fair	Poor		
Elevators					
Signal Buttons					
Doors					
Cab Floor					
Cab Walls					
Cab Ceiling					
Floor Numbers					
Light Fixtures					
Entryway					
Fixtures					
Bulbs					
Switch/Timer					
Entrance					
Fixtures					
Bulbs					
Switch/Timer					
Hallways					
Fixtures					
Bulbs					
Switch/Timer					
Laundry					
Walls					
Ceilings					
Floors					
Washers					
Dryers					
Vending Machines					
Tubs and Faucets					
Windows					
Window Coverings					
Doors					
Furnance Room					
Walls					
Ceilings					
Floors					
Pipes					
Doors					

Residents should be notified in advance that a general inspection is pending. If the situation makes it inappropriate to notify the residents in advance, an information card indicating you were in the unit that day should be left in an obvious place (see exhibit 11.4). With advance warning or with a followup card, residents should feel that their rights to privacy are being respected.

Exhibit 11.2 (Continued)

Area	Condition			Maintenance Required	Estimated Cost
	Good	Fair	Poor		
Hot Water Heater					
Tank					
Insulation					
Controls					
Pipes					
Water Temperature					
Cleaniness					
A/C Compressors					
Motors					
Mounting					
Cleanliness					

Most residents will keep their units in reasonable shape. Unit inspections are necessary, however, to identify those residents who do not use their units properly. You may find, for instance, that a resident is keeping a motorcycle inside the unit, ostensibly to protect it from theft. In the meantime, the carpeting is being destroyed by grease, oil, and dirt, and the kitchen sink is being used for soaking parts in acid solutions. Another resident might save newspapers for months, which could create a potential fire hazard.

Exhibit 11.3   Unit Inspection Report

Property _____ Unit _____

Date _____ Inspected by _____

Area/Item	Condition			Remarks
	Good	Fair	Poor	
Living Room and Dining Room				
Doors and Locks				
Floors and Baseboards				
Walls and Ceilings				
Windows and Drapes				
Electrical Fixtures				
Electrical Switches, Outlets				
Closets				
Kitchen				
Doors and Locks				
Floors and Baseboards				
Walls and Ceilings				
Electrical Fixtures				
Electrical Switches, Outlets				
Range and Refrigerator				
Sink				
Cabinets				
Bedroom(s)				
Doors and Locks				
Floors and Baseboards				
Walls and Ceilings				
Electrical Fixtures				
Electrical Switches, Outlets				
Windows and Drapes				
Closets				
Bathroom(s)				
Doors and Locks				
Floors and Baseboards				
Walls and Ceilings				
Windows and Drapes				
Shower				
Lavatory and Tub				
Faucets				
Toilet				
Electrical Fixtures				
Electrical Switches, Outlets				
Closet				
Towel Rack				

Budgeting

While maintenance expenses are an integral part of the
overall budget, as discussed in chapter 3, the maintenance
portion of the budget has several unique characteristics.
First, it must budget adequately for personnel as well as for
materials and supplies. Second, it must accumulate funds for
the purchase of major equipment and tools over several

Exhibit 11.4   Unit Entry Notice

Someone was in your apartment today to:

☐   Check heating or air conditioning.

☐   Check plumbing.

☐   Check electrical.

☐   Other _____

_____

Date _____

Time _____   Signed _____

years. Finally, it must provide for the cost of major expenditures such as appliance or carpet replacement. In order to accomplish these goals, as well as to understand the budget, work within its boundaries, and provide input for next year's budget, the manager must maintain accurate records of monies spent within the property and categorize each expenditure.

When analyzing the budget and actual expenses, the manager should keep in mind such questions as the following:

Where can costs be cut without decreasing service to the residents and/or decreasing the income to the property?

Should major changes such as redecorating be made in order to attract more residents?

How will the owner's objectives affect maintenance?

Do the owner's objectives need to be modified in order to provide reasonable services and maintain a realistic cash flow?

The manager's answers to these questions should be passed on to the property manager and/or owner.

Decision Making

Decision making is the second function of management. An on-site manager makes decisions on a daily basis and is responsible for their results. In making any decision, four steps must be followed: (1) the problem is identified, (2) the available alternatives are analyzed, (3) the decision is made and (4) the decision is implemented.

Areas that involve decision making for the manager include purchasing, making major changes or alterations to the property, deciding whether to use contract maintenance services or in-house personnel, and staffing.

Purchasing

The primary rules of purchasing are (1) never order anything without prior authorization, and (2) never exceed your level of purchasing authority. Avoiding these two pitfalls will keep you in good stead with the property manager and/or owner.

Once you have been authorized to make a purchase, a purchase order is filled out. A purchase order is a written communication to the vendor giving detailed information on the purchase. The order is written down to keep an exact record to which you may refer should problems arise.

A purchase order (or P.O., as it is called) should contain the following information:

Name, location, and phone number of the property.

Date of the order.

Detailed description of the parts or materials ordered.

Quantity requested.

Unit price and total price of order.

Expected date of delivery.

Terms of payment.

Signature of person ordering.

Depending on the policies of the management company, purchase orders may be in duplicate, triplicate or quadruplicate. The vendor, manager, and accounting department each need a copy. Purchase orders, like receipts, should be numbered consecutively so that the on-site manager can be assured that none have been lost or stolen.

Upon delivery of the materials or parts, the manager should
check price, quantity, and quality to make sure the delivery
corresponds with the purchase order. Then, and only then,
should authorization be given to pay the bill. It is often
easier to correct problems with vendors before the bill has
been paid rather than after.

Another advantage of the written P.O. system is that
order and delivery dates are specific. If the vendor is late in
filling the order, it is much more professional and effective to
say, "The part was ordered on the 10th with delivery
scheduled for the 15th," than it is to say, "It was ordered a
week or so ago and scheduled to be delivered sometime this
week."

In certain situations, it is sometimes necessary to order
materials over the phone. Many suppliers have special order
desks to facilitate placing orders by telephone. The manager
should complete a written purchase order, read it over the
telephone, and mail a confirming copy if the order is lengthy.
Checking the delivered order for completeness and accuracy
is especially important if the order was placed by telephone.

The level of purchasing authority extended to an on-site
manager will depend on the size of the property and the
policies of the management company. In some cases the
manager may have to clear every purchase through the
management company, while in others the manager may be
making purchases of hundreds of dollars. Either system
involves decision making on the part of the manager.
Maintenance costs are the largest single item of operating
expense over which management has control; consequently,
the decisions made by the on-site manager are crucial to the
profitability of the property.

In order to make a purchasing decision, you must identify
the problem—the first step in the decision-making process.
The needs of the property are identified from two sources:
inspections and resident service requests. You then must
analyze what alternatives are available.

Say that a refrigerator breaks down in a unit. You must
determine whether or not the refrigerator can be repaired
and whether or not the cost of repair makes monetary
sense. If the refrigerator is only 2 years old and the cost to
repair it would be $75, as opposed to a cost of $400 for a
new refrigerator, your decision should be to repair the unit.
However, if the cost of repairs is estimated at $300 and the

refrigerator is 10 years old, it would be wisest to purchase a new refrigerator.

If you decide to purchase a new refrigerator, you must also decide on what type of new refrigerator to purchase. It is best to upgrade the property whenever possible. You might decide to purchase a self-defrosting refrigerator rather than merely replacing the 10-year-old model that must be defrosted by the resident. In most areas of the country, the market is now demanding the convenience of a self-defrosting model. Therefore, the purchase of the refrigerator would be justified.

You must be ready to justify the purchase of the more expensive model to the property manager and/or owner. Be prepared to back up your decision with facts and figures. Not only should you be able to cite the advantages of the self-defrosting model, but you should have bids on the cost of supplying the self-defrosting model from two or three companies in hand for the property manager to analyze.

Major Changes and Alterations

The decision-making ability of the manager is tested when major alterations or changes within the property are being considered. Major changes and alterations would include repainting the exteriors of buildings, redecorating lobbies or hallways, resurfacing parking lots and driveways, or adding such amenities as saunas or volleyball courts. Each of these projects would involve large sums of money. Through competitive bidding, you must carefully obtain the best quality, services, and materials for each project based on the funds available.

To ensure competitive prices and bids, invite at least three bids or firm quotations from licensed contractors or suppliers. If equipment is to be supplied, it is often helpful to have any supplier interested in bidding to come to the property and examine the equipment now being used. By looking at the current installation, the supplier will be better able to make recommendations as to what new equipment would best meet the property's needs.

You must provide each bidder with written specifications for the project, detailing exactly what is wanted and any possible alternates. For purchases of equipment, the quotation or bid from the vendor should include the following information:

1. Description of the goods to be supplied.
2. Cost of goods, including delivery.
3. Cost of installation, including any modification necessary.
4. Warranties included, whether factory or supplier.
5. Trade-in options.
6. Deadline for receipt of bid or quotation.
7. Method and term of payment, including any discount privileges.
8. Any alternate bid.
9. Availability and delivery date.

Bids or quotations for contracted services, such as painting, parking lot resurfacing, or other major jobs, should include the previous information plus the following:

1. Estimated commencement and completion dates.
2. Licenses, permits, and insurance supplied by the vendor.
3. A lien waiver approved by the state.
4. Quality and quantity of supplies.

The lowest bid is not necessarily the one that should be accepted. For example, say that you have received bids for repainting one-third of the property's exterior walls. Of the five bids, four are very close to each other, but one is quite a bit lower. Before taking the low bid, examine the costs in detail, paying particular attention to the quality and quantity of paint to be used. This examination might show that the low bidder plans to use only two-thirds as much paint as the others, will air-spray it on, and will use a lower grade of paint than the other bidders plan to use, which will make repainting necessary much sooner. This bid might not be the best alternative. Many management companies supply the paint and get bids for the labor only, thereby controlling the quality of the paint used by the contractor.

The estimated commencement and completion dates also have a bearing on which bid to accept. Say that one of the painting bids is for $8,000, but the bidder could not start on the job for several months. Another bidder bid at $9,000 and can start immediately. You might decide to accept the higher bid because of the commencement date.

Stating an estimated completion date ensures that the contractor will complete the job in a timely manner. If the estimated completion date is not in the contract, you may find that the contractor starts the job but then pulls most of the men off of your job to start another job, leaving just a few men to complete the work over a longer period of time, delaying the completion date. Penalties for not maintaining the approved timetable, subject to acts of God, should be included in the final contract.

Specifying the arrangements regarding permits, licenses, and insurance will improve communication between contractor and management. Both parties know at the outset who will pay for and who will be responsible for obtaining the necessary documentation. These arrangements may also be a determining factor in deciding which bid to accept. If the bids are roughly equal, for example, the bid including the costs of licenses and permits would, in fact, actually be the lower bid.

It is very necessary to make sure the contractor has both liability and workers' compensation insurance. Obtain copies of both policies so that in the event an accident occurs, the property is protected against liability. In many states, the management may be held responsible for injury or damage without written proof of such insurance coverage.

Specifying the method and terms of payment will help to avoid misunderstandings regarding the final payment. Without such an agreement, the contractor may anticipate being paid in full as soon as the job is completed. With remodeling and new construction, it is customary to withhold 10 percent of the payment to make sure the work was done properly. Any such terms should be spelled out in the contract.

Warranties and guarantees may be incorporated in the contract and specified in separate documents. Both the contractor and the manufacturer of the equipment or materials used may guarantee the reliability of the work and product. For the sake of simplicity, many contracts spell out the contractor's or supplier's warranty and also recite the terms of the factory warranty. In any event, it is imperative that the warranty or guarantee be in writing. Oral warranties may be difficult to enforce.

A *lien waiver* stipulates that the contractor guarantees that no liens will be placed against the property. It is enforced by having the contractor, subcontractor, and major suppliers sign an acknowledgement of payment and completion each time funds are to be disbursed. A typical situation in which this might happen is a contract arranged for mechanical work—perhaps a boiler replacement. In this example, the general contractor might be a plumbing firm which subcontracts a portion of the job to a small firm specializing in work relating to boilers. The work is completed, and the manager pays the plumbing firm in full. But the plumbing firm fails to pay the subcontractor for the work they agreed upon. The subcontractor would then be able to place a lien against the property, putting the management in the legal position of having to pay twice for the same work. While a lien waiver does not guarantee security in this situation, it provides the framework for legal action against the contractor. Careful monitoring of bill payments is the most effective tool in preventing liens.

In summary, major alterations and changes involve large sums of money. When considering them, the manager must be able to demonstrate to the property owner or manager the justification for the expense. Questions such as these must be answered: Will the change increase marketability? Will the income be increased because of the change? Will the economic life of the property increase? Will the alteration or change provide higher resident satisfaction and hence less turnover? The answers to these questions can come only after the manager has identified the problem, analyzed the alternatives available, and reviewed the potential results from the change. Finally, the manager, selects the contractor, supervises the work, and completes the project.

Contract Services
vs. In-House Maintenance

Another maintenance decision the manager must make is whether to use contract services or in-house maintenance for various tasks. There are advantages and disadvantages to each system, and the advantages of each method of maintenance service for each assignment must be weighed carefully.

Services provided by contract might include landscape maintenance, pest control, plumbing, heating repairs, janitorial services for common areas, and even the readying of units for new residents. Service companies have certain advantages over in-house maintenance, as follows:

1. **Expertise.** A service company generally specializes in one field and should therefore possess more expertise than the maintenance worker with average skills.

2. **Quality of work.** The company generally has more personnel available than does the on-site staff. The company's expertise should reduce the amount of time necessary to perform the services.

3. **Specialized tools.** The contractor already possesses whatever specialized tools are necessary.

4. **Insurance.** The service company carries its own liability and worker's compensation insurance, thereby eliminating the necessity for the property to purchase this insurance coverage.

5. **Own supervision.** The service company will need less direct supervision, and will be able to perform a variety of assignments at once.

Hiring and training in-house personnel to perform maintenance functions also has its advantages:

1. **Supervision.** It is often easier to direct workers in your employ than to supervise those who work for a contractor.

2. **Scheduling.** The manager controls maintenance scheduling, providing flexibility and mobility of staff. Service companies, for instance, may not be able to reach your property rapidly in the event of an emergency.

3. **Training.** The service company will train its staff to perform work acceptable to the majority of its customers. The manager, on the other hand, can tailor the performance of the in-house staff to the property's needs.

4. **Familiarity with building.** An in-house staff is already familiar with the building. Each member of the staff knows the location of the mechanical rooms, shutoff valves, etc. Each new employee from the service company would have to relearn this information.

5. **Lower labor cost.** Since the apartment property is not in business to make a profit on service calls, labor costs are often substantially less for in-house personnel.

If the decision is made to contract for services, the manager's next responsibility is to establish a good working relationship with the various service contractors involved. A good relationship means establishing effective channels of communication. The company's response in an emergency will be better, since they know what is to be expected. The best way to gain the service company's respect is to pay all bills promptly, as specified and when due.

A reference card should be created for each contractor or service company. This card should identify the company, its address and location, name of the contact person for ordering or reporting, names of the usual service workers sent, hourly rate, overtime rate, hours, and other details. By having this information on hand, a knowledgeable order can be placed if it becomes necessary that someone other than the on-site manager request service.

Staffing

The number of employees placed on the maintenance staff will depend on the size of the property and on which services will be provided in-house and which will be provided through a service contractor. Depending on the management company policies, the on-site manager may be responsible for hiring the entire staff or simply providing initial interviews and input. In either case, the basic guidelines for selecting employees include investigating references, interviewing qualified applicants, and judging the appropriateness of the applicant's skills for the job opening. (The employee selection process is discussed thoroughly in chapter 4.)

While interviewing a prospective maintenance worker, it is important to review any paperwork that will be expected of them. Many maintenance staff members are excellent at hands-on work but are totally unprepared to do the necessary supporting paperwork. An employee who does not intend to complete paperwork under any circumstances is better off working in a position where none is required. Most applicants have clear ideas about the paperwork responsibilities they are capable of handling.

If you plan to give any tests to a prospective maintenance worker, be sure that the tests are related to the job assignment. It would probably be inappropriate to give a maintenance applicant a math test; it would, however, be appropriate to ask a maintenance applicant to demonstrate various repairs.

Organizing

The third function of management, organizing, is especially important in the area of maintenance. A lack of organization may cause certain important maintenance tasks to be neglected, which could lead to emergencies later on.

Lists

Lists are often overlooked as an important tool in organization. Making lists is a simple, efficient way to get things done. At the start of each day, make up a list of everything that needs to be done that day. Cross off the tasks on the list as they are accomplished. At the end of the day, recopy the remaining items onto the list for tomorrow. Keep a small tablet by each telephone, so that notes can be taken and promptly transferred to your main list. The satisfaction received from having completed every assignment on the list for the day is gratifying.

Maintenance Office

Operating the maintenance office, shop, and storage area is a problem in many properties. Attention to paperwork may be poor, facilities may be poorly arranged and inadequate, and security may be lacking. Special care must be taken in organizing the maintenance office.

An official maintenance office should be established, whether it is a partitioned area in a storage room or a formal office located near the management office. The maintenance office should be equipped with telephone, organizing systems such as pegboards, time clocks or time sheets, and office supplies necessary for purchasing, record keeping, and servicing. A file cabinet should contain records of service calls, maintenance schedules, warranties for equipment, a complete inventory of tools, supplies, and equipment, and other reports that are not kept in the management office.

The maintenance office should be off-limits to everyone except staff. A supply room for the storage of small parts and supplies should be near or adjoining the maintenance office. A second storage area is for larger equipment and supplies. Both areas should be well secured.

When ordered supplies and equipment are received, they are checked in and the packing slips validated. Any item removed from the storage area should be signed out or recorded on an inventory control card. In a large property, a weekly check should be made for any restocking needs. A more thorough inventory is taken monthly, so that items which require a longer time to obtain can be ordered. In a small or medium-sized property, a monthly inventory may suffice. A complete physical inventory of all parts, tools, and equipment should be taken at least twice each year and verified with the accounting records. If shortages are discovered, the cause should be investigated and identified. It may be faulty record keeping, poor inventory control, theft, or a combination of all of these causes. In any case, the cause or causes should be corrected.

An excellent plan for a large or small property is to have a maintenance workshop area, either as part of the storage room or as a separate building. Here major tools can be operated and repairs made easily. For example, many screens will be damaged and will need to be replaced by late fall. The frames can be brought to the maintenance shop and rescreened with a simple tool during spare time over the winter. If a general work area is not set aside for this type of maintenance, it might be necessary to either make repairs in an area unsuited for such work or dispose of the screen frames and purchase new ones.

Scheduling

Preventive and routine maintenance work is always going on in the apartment property and must be carefully scheduled. Seasonal tasks must be planned for their particular season; periodic tasks must occur at their regular interval.

To begin preparation of a schedule, make a list of every maintenance function, no matter how large or how small, that will need to be scheduled. Keep reviewing this list until you are sure it is complete. A look through last year's paid bills will often trigger reminders of small but important routine service items.

The next step is to fill out a card for each item on the list. The card will list (1) the materials and equipment needed, (2) the amount of time which needs to be allotted, (3) the quality and skill of labor needed, (4) any seasonal restrictions, and (5) any other tasks that must be performed in conjunction with this one.

The cards can be sorted using a color coding system. When you come across a task where timing is critical— such as pool maintenance in preparation for the season opening—label that task with red. Tasks that need to be completed in conjunction with another may be labelled with yellow. For example, if carpet cleaning must follow washing the lobby walls, then cards for both tasks would be coded with yellow.

Repetitive tasks are those which must be done more than once a year; changing furnace filters is an example of a repetitive task. Mark the cards for these tasks with blue. All other tasks which must be performed on a regular basis may be marked green.

The next step is to place the tasks on an annual calendar. The best type of calendar to use is a notebook-style calendar or datebook with a separate page for each day. You could also create your own daily or weekly forms to be placed in a loose-leaf notebook. The calendar should be clearly labeled and kept in an easily accessible location.

Sort the marked task cards by color. Now begin sorting the assignments by month, beginning with those tasks coded red, then yellow, blue, and finally green. Tasks should be as evenly distributed throughout the year as is possible. Try to avoid putting critical tasks back to back. If critical tasks are spaced apart, emergencies should not upset the schedule too greatly.

You may discover that too many seasonal tasks fall in one month. For example, you might see that no matter how you juggle the tasks, it will be impossible for the regular staff to handle the April assignments. Consideration should be given to hiring temporary workers or contracting with a service company, depending upon the size of the assignment.

After you have balanced between months, assign the tasks to individual days of the month until every task is accounted for. As you assign each task, note any tasks for which supplies and materials must be ordered. Estimate the amount of time needed to complete the order. Some items, such as furnace filters, might only take a week or two from order to delivery. Others, such as paint, may require several weeks in order to obtain quality bids, compare the bids, and make a decision. After assigning the task to a particular day or days, go back in the calendar the amount of time it will take to order and receive supplies and insert a cross-reference, such as, "Order paint for June painting."

Requested maintenance. Another factor to consider at this point is balancing scheduled routine maintenance with requested maintenance. All service requests should be handled within 24 hours of receiving the request from the resident, if possible. Optimum performance would be same-day service. Same-day service on maintenance requests can be your competitive edge in retaining good residents.

Service calls should not have to be postponed because of routine maintenance. For example, say that you have allotted 20 hours this week for routine landscaping. You have assigned this work to a maintenance worker who also handles plumbing repairs. By spreading the routine maintenance out over 4 days or 32 hours, rather than over

20 hours, you provide enough time for your worker to take care of whatever plumbing service requests arise. If you schedule the 20 hours of work for only 20 hours, or 2½ days, many service calls may have to be delayed.

Emergency maintenance. After routine maintenance has been balanced with requested maintenance, the main interruption to the maintenance schedule will come from emergency situations. To adjust the calendar in cases of emergency, complete the following three steps:

1. Estimate the amount of time needed to complete the emergency repairs.

2. Determine whether or not the emergency repairs will create a time shortage in this week's schedule that might cause scheduled routine maintenance to be delayed until next week.

3. If the emergency does create a time shortage, consider the following solutions individually and choose the best for the circumstances: (a) give either the emergency or routine repair to a contractor; (b) schedule staff to work overtime; (c) obtain extra temporary labor to assist or finish either repair; (d) rearrange the calendar, placing the routine maintenance in an upcoming opening; (e) rearrange several projects over several weeks until an opening is created to finish the project already started. Unless the solution is clear-cut, plan to confirm the rearrangement with the property manager.

Review. At the end of each day, the next day's planned schedule should be reviewed to make certain that all materials and staff are available, and that there are no leftover tasks that will require rearrangement. About the third week of each month, the next month's schedule should be reviewed and any necessary adjustments made.

Directing

Directing is the fourth function of management. Directing maintenance employees involves communication, supervision, and motivation.

Communication

Effective communication is very important to a maintenance program. Miscommunicating maintenance assignments and procedures can cost not only time but money. Here are five pointers on effective communication:

1. Organize what you have to say. Make written notes if necessary.

2. Catch people in an open frame of mind, at a time when they aren't preoccupied with other matters.

3. Give sufficient explanation. Repeat the instructions until you receive feedback indicating the message was received and understood.

4. Listen to what your staff tells you. It is sometimes easier to talk than it is to listen, but communication includes both.

5. Use written communication. Just as you can be overburdened with your own mental lists, so can your employees be overburdened with tasks to remember.

Not only must you make certain that you are communicating effectively, but you must make sure that your employees are communicating effectively with each other. All personnel must be aware of correct systems and procedures.

If at all possible, do not break the chain of command you have established. Perhaps Frank, your maintenance worker, always distributes work assignments to Stan, his helper. If you bypass Frank and assign Stan to handle a service call, you have left Frank out of the communication chain. If you fail to inform Frank of your action, he may become angry at Stan, thinking that Stan has gone off to do something on his own. Stan is caught in the middle of this situation—you are the on-site manager, and yet he usually gets orders from Frank. Following the chain of command, and communicating clearly when it needs to be bypassed, will help to avoid ill feelings.

Supervision

The degree to which the manager must directly supervise employees is sometimes difficult to determine. Too much supervision, and employees will feel that they are being spied upon or treated as children; too little supervision, and goals are not accomplished. Inspections, discussed earlier in the chapter, are important in supervising maintenance employees. Other effective forms of maintenance supervision are (1) reviewing daily assignments each morning, (2) observing the flow of work orders, and (3) spot checks on progress. The best form of supervision provides an atmosphere in which the employees will be motivated to do the correct job.

Motivation

Maintenance employees tend to be mobile and are often difficult to retain if they do not feel motivated. One of the best motivators for employees is appreciation. Frequent compliments on work well done are a necessity if employees are to feel that they are making an important contribution to the property. Whenever possible, input from employees should be sought on both small and large maintenance decisions. Compensation is also a motivator: small, frequent raises tend to increase morale. In many cases, the cost of hiring and training a new employee is far more than retaining a current one. The training of a maintenance worker represents a significant investment, and every effort should be made to motivate and retain the worker.

Controlling

Controlling is the fifth function of management. Controlling maintenance operations primarily involves handling service requests and record keeping.

Service Requests

All service requests should be put into writing as soon as received. The employee who receives the request should get as much information as possible from the resident describing the problem. In some properties, the resident is responsible for putting the service request in writing. All requests are put onto work order forms (see exhibit 11.5).

Work orders are arranged by priority to facilitate scheduling. There are several popular methods of organizing service requests. One system uses a pegboard with hooks. Each hook is for a different type of maintenance: plumbing, heating, electrical, etc. Each order is hung on the appropriate hook. The manager or a maintenance staff member reviews the orders and schedules the maintenance. By arranging the orders by type of maintenance, service calls requiring similar skills and tools can be grouped, thereby saving time.

Another system is to color-code orders by priority. Red would mean, "immediate/critical"; blue, "today for sure"; green, "check first and then schedule"; and yellow, "as soon as possible." At a glance, the maintenance worker can tell which ones are most important.

Both of these systems have one drawback: less important service requests may be continually pushed back, and the residents making those requests may come to feel that their needs are unimportant to the management.

As each service call is completed, the cause of the problem, its solution, and/or any parts needed should be noted on the work order form. A unit entry notice (mentioned earlier in the chapter; see exhibit 11.4) or a copy of the work order marked complete may be left in the unit, stating what repairs were made. The manager should check with each resident scheduled for service to make sure that the problems were handled satisfactorily.

The work order forms are returned to the office for sorting. If the problem was caused by the resident (for example, a child's toy was dropped in the toilet, causing it to stop up), the resident should be billed for the cost of the repair. All completed orders should be filed in the unit's folder for future reference.

Exhibit 11.5   Work Order

Work Order Number _____

Property _____ Date _____

Location _____

Maintenance Required

_____
_____
_____
_____

Maintenance Performed

_____
_____
_____

Materials Used

_____
_____
_____

Time Required _____

Cost of Labor	S
Cost of Materials	
Total	**S**

Maintenance Performed by _____

Unable to Complete Because of _____

_____
_____

Record Keeping

Besides records of service calls, maintenance records which must be kept include tool and equipment records, furniture and inventory records, and major periodic maintenance records.

Tool/equipment records. Proper tools and equipment are essential to the operation of the property. In some areas of the country, it may be customary for your employees to supply their own hand tools. In others, all tools are supplied and maintained by the property. The two main purposes of maintaining tool/equipment records are (1) to record any preventive maintenance needed, and (2) to retain warranty information along with model numbers, serial numbers, and brand names. Having this information is very helpful when a breakdown occurs. The equipment or tool may need to go to a particular repair shop specializing in that brand. If the maintenance staff plans to make the repair, the model and/or serial number may be necessary to obtain the correct part or parts.

All preventive maintenance on equipment or tools should be recorded—the scheduled maintenance and the maintenance actually performed. These records will indicate when a piece of equipment needs replacing.

Furniture and inventory records. Records of furnishings should be divided into five categories: (1) office, (2) models, (3) units, (4) recreational areas, and (5) common areas. The value of furnishings and fixtures is often depreciated or capitalized by the owner for tax purposes. If a piece of furniture is no longer useful, that information should be noted on the inventory and communicated to the owner.

If your property provides furnished units, exact records of furnishings become very important. If they are not carefully maintained, problems will occur when the resident vacates and furnishings are missing. The most common error occurs when furniture is moved from one unit to another, or in and out of storage, without it being noted on the records. One effective system is photographing the unit every time furnishings are switched. The camera will also record the condition of the furnishings.

Major periodic maintenance records. A file should be kept for each area of the property that requires major periodic maintenance. A swimming pool, for example, requires certain repairs every two to three years. Without a file it would be impossible to keep track, for instance, of when pumps were last replaced, or the pool interior was last repainted. It would be quite difficult in this case to schedule and budget for preventive maintenance.

Governmental Safety Regulations

An area of maintenance management that does not fall under one of the five functions of management, but which is very important nonetheless, is the area of governmental safety regulations. Annual inspections by government officials, fire departments, and insurance companies are required in many areas of the country. Advance warning is usually given, and the manager accompanies the inspector. If problems of a noncritical nature are noted, the property is allowed a certain amount of time to effect repairs. If serious problems are noted, the building may be closed down for emergency repairs.

Building codes have become increasingly stringent over the years, and many apartment buildings are now out of date. Older buildings are sometimes omitted from these new requirements if they were built before a certain date; this procedure is contained in a *grandfather clause*. (Some crucial requirements, such as smoke detectors or fire extinguishers, may not be "grandfathered.") When any remodeling or major repair work is anticipated, care should be taken to ensure that the completed project will meet current building codes. In most cases, a building permit is necessary and inspection at critical stages required before the work can continue, to ensure that safety and building code requirements are being met.

Summary

There are six basic types of maintenance: preventive, corrective, routine, deferred, emergency, and cosmetic. *Deferred* maintenance is necessary service or repair that is put off, for a variety of reasons, until a later date. *Cosmetic* maintenance involves those repairs which do not affect the function of the item but which make the item more appealing.

The five functions of management must occur in the performance of every management task: (1) planning, (2) decision making, (3) organizing, (4) directing, and (5) controlling.

Planning, as it applies to maintenance management, includes the following:

1. **Writing the maintenance section** of the operations manual.
2. **Property inspections.** There are three basic types of inspections: exterior, interior, and unit.
3. **Budgeting.** Accurate records of monies spent within the property must be kept, with each expenditure categorized.

Decision making is the second function of management. Maintenance areas that involve decision making for the on-site manager include:

1. **Purchasing.** Written purchase orders should be used whenever possible.
2. **Major changes and alterations** to the property. At least three competitive bids should be obtained.
3. **Contract services vs. in-house maintenance.** There are advantages to both.
4. **Staffing.**

Organizing, the third function of management, includes the following:

1. **Establishing a maintenance office,** supply room, storage area, and, if possible, a workshop area.
2. **Scheduling.** All routine and preventive maintenance work must be carefully scheduled.

Directing maintenance employees involves (1) effective communication, (2) supervision, and (3) motivation. Controlling maintenance operations includes:

1. **Service requests.** Work orders should be used.
2. **Record keeping.** Records which must be kept include tool and equipment records, furniture and inventory records, and major periodic maintenance records.

Annual inspections by government officials, fire departments, and insurance companies are required in many areas of the country. If serious problems are noted, the building may be closed down for emergency repairs.

12
Maintenance Procedures

In the last chapter we discussed the management aspects of maintenance—how to establish and administrate a maintenance program. In this chapter we will discuss the procedures and techniques involved in actual maintenance. These procedures may be divided into six areas: (1) grounds, (2) exterior structure, (3) interior common areas, (4) unit interior, (5) facilities and amenities, and (6) mechanical equipment. While many articles and texts can be written on each subject, the overview this chapter provides should serve as a guide for the on-site manager in planning some of the more common maintenance and repairs in the apartment property.

Grounds
Landscaping and Lawn Care
The variation in landscaping care throughout the country is extremely wide. In the northeastern states, the growing season is short and watering rarely a problem. In the dry areas of the Rocky Mountains, aeration of the soil is commonplace. Vegetation in the southern states is remarkably different due to high humidity. In the far west, still another type of landscaping exists. Each individual state has its own needs. A county agency or horticultural

school that specializes in lawn and landscaping care should be consulted for specific instructions for the area. Various publications detail types of landscaping and care recommended for various climates.

Emphasis must be placed on landscaping because of its importance to curb appeal and property value. There is no second chance for a good first impression. If the property is attractively landscaped and cared for, prospective residents will be favorably impressed and interested in exploring further. The property can eventually develop the reputation of having a beautiful exterior, thereby attracting more residents. A carefully balanced decision must be made as to the quantity of plantings versus the amount of care and expense that will be required.

The manager is responsible for scheduling not only such routine tasks as watering and mowing, but fertilizing, weeding, mulching, edging, chemical treatments, tree trimming, and other preventive maintenance procedures as well. The use of a calendar, as discussed in chapter 11, can help to prevent oversights. Failure to drain sprinkler lines before the winter freeze, for example, can be an extremely expensive mistake. Placing this function on the maintenance calendar will avoid the problem.

Because of weather conditions, an alternate timetable needs to be built into the lawn care schedule. For example, say that the lawns are scheduled to be mowed on Friday. If it rains on that day, the maintenance staff would have to work overtime on the weekend—not a desirable or viable alternative in most cases. It is better to schedule Wednesday as the regular mowing day. An indoor project, such as cleaning the lobbies, can be scheduled later in the week. If it rains on Wednesday, the indoor project can be done then and the lawnmowing moved to Thursday or Friday.

Lawnmowers will break down if they are not kept clean and well oiled. All moving parts should be inspected before and after each use. Careful attention should be paid to oil levels, lubrication, and belts. There should be a supply of gasoline on the premises (stored in a safe, OSHA-approved container) to avoid unnecessary trips to the gas station during the middle of a job.

Another important landscaping responsibility is disposal of cut grass. The manager must decide whether or not to catch the grass, rake it, or mulch it back into the lawn.

Depending on the climate and the season, any or all of these methods might be used. Some properties use neither catcher nor mulcher, and do not bother to rake the cut grass. This creates an unkempt look that detracts from the appearance of the property. The buildup of dead grass trimmings will eventually harm the lawn.

Edging is the careful trimming of the lawn where it borders plantings, walks, driveways, or buildings, to leave a clean dirt border. Whether to edge or not to edge is determined by whether the owner's objectives are for picture-perfect lawns or a more natural look. An easier solution might be to clear a wide edge of two to three inches along each walk at the beginning of the season, and then using a preparation to sterilize the soil in the groove. This will prevent anything—grass or weeds—from growing in the groove for months at a time, giving the edge of the walks a clean, crisp edge without constant retouching. In applying the sterilization chemical, care must be taken not to spread it beyond the area designated. Grass can be killed and the lawn made unsightly for the entire season.

Sprinkler Care

One of the drudgeries of maintenance work is moving around hundreds of feet of sprinkler hose. Hose is also expensive to maintain. More properties, large and small, are turning to the installation of sprinkler systems of one type or another, capitalizing the expense and reducing labor costs. Sprinkler systems fall into four categories: (1) automatic, where time controls start and stop the system; (2) semi-automatic, where someone must turn the system on, at which time a control box takes over and runs for a specified period of time; (3) manual, where valves in the ground at one or more locations must be turned to start the system; and (4) fully manual, where sprinkler heads must be snapped into outlets across the yard and removed when the watering is complete.

Whichever system is used, the finest quality sprinkler heads should be obtained and installed. Many quality heads can be readily removed, cleaned, replaced, or adjusted by the maintenance staff without special tools. Many others have shut-off valves at strategic locations for repairs. A supply of extra heads and valves is essential.

A grounds map should be drawn, if original plans are unavailable, showing the general run of the system and where each head is located. In the event a leak develops, it will be possible to zero in on the location without a great deal of searching. A map also facilitates periodic inspections of the sprinkler heads.

A self-contained timing system is usually maintenance-free. One problem that does occur is broken cogs on the timer wheel, which can be caused by wear and tear or improper setting by unknowledgeable employees. A lock on the control box and specific printed instructions posted on the wall will help to prevent tampering and unnecessary breakdowns.

The drip system, a new type of sprinkler system for watering shrubs, trees, and plantings, is rapidly gaining attention. Already extensively in use in dry areas in the southwest, this system provides a constant but minimal flow of moisture at specified times. The popularity of this type of system is based in part on its more reasonable costs, its low maintenance needs, and the ease of installation.

Without an automatic system (and sometimes even with one) it is difficult to determine how much water is necessary. America is a country of overwatering and guesswork in lawn care. Here is a simple procedure for determining how much water your system distributes, whether it is automatic or manual:

Place four cans of equal diameter at locations near the sprinkler. Turn on the system for exactly one-half hour. Combine the water caught into one container and measure the depth, dividing by two. This is the number of inches per hour your watering system will distribute. In some cities, the local water department each day publishes the number of inches of water needed the next day.

Streets and Parking Areas

The on-site manager is responsible for controlling, repairing, and cleaning all streets, driveways, and parking areas. In order to maintain the maximum number of parking places, it is necessary to occasionally restripe the spaces. Professional help is often unneeded; a simple paint roller fitted with an appropriate roller cover can recoat the old lines. Through careful planning, some extra spaces can be gained by making some spaces narrower than standard and designating them "small car only" spaces. A graveled area away from the main parking area can be reserved for boats and trucks, freeing regular spaces for in-out traffic.

All pavements require frequent maintenance and attention because of the stress placed on them. Heavy-duty concrete streets are rare in most properties; petroleum-based asphalt is the most common form of paving. Asphalt can break down because of moisture seepage, stress, temperature changes, and lack of preventive maintenance.

Many surface problems begin with alligatoring or small shrinkage cracks. A sealer coat of emulsified asphalt applied regularly can help to prevent cracking which permits moisture to penetrate the surface. If nothing is done to prevent cracking, sooner or later potholes will appear and major repairs will be needed. If a ⅛-inch slurry of asphalt fails to solve the problem, then it may be necessary to fill fine cracks with an overlay coat of asphalt.

When repairing chuckholes or potholes, first identify the source of the problem. Is the drainage slanted toward a particular spot? Is a drain blocked? Is the asphalt in that area improperly installed? The condition causing the problem should be corrected and the damaged asphalt cut out. The hole should be cut with straight sides at least 3 inches wider all around than the broken down area. The hole should be filled in with several layers of new asphalt, each tamped down, and the final layer packed so that a hump is formed about 1½ inches above the finished surface. Vehicle traffic will help to pack this final layer down.

Snow Removal

Snow removal can take up a major portion of the maintenance budget in northern cities, simply because the snow arrives in the fall and ground is not seen until spring. In some cities, such as Denver, snow melts rapidly because of dry air and altitude; in New England, streets just absorb layer after layer of packed snow. The snow removal needs of the property should be ascertained before the onset of winter.

Equipment already within the property should be examined; it may be possible to adapt existing equipment for snow removal. Garden tractors can often be outfitted with a small snowblade for winter use. Heavy-duty maintenance trucks can also be fitted with snowblades. Unless the area to be plowed is quite small, backup arrangements with a contractor should be made in the event of either equipment failure or a massive snowfall. One good rule of thumb used by property managers in midwestern cities with moderate snowfall is that the on-site staff removes snowfall up to 2½ inches, and a contractor removes the snow if more than 2½ inches accumulates.

To prevent accidents, ice should not be allowed to build up on steps and walkways commonly used by residents. Only compounds which will not damage the concrete should be used to melt snow and ice from sidewalks. Pure salt will rapidly disintegrate the concrete's surface; new concrete needs two years to completely cure before it will withstand salt and harsh chemicals. Salt will also kill the dormant grass at the sidewalk edges.

Melting compounds with a mild chemical base are available through suppliers. These compounds can also be mixed with hot sand. Many suppliers maintain accurate snowfall records and can readily estimate the quantity of melting compound you will need for a given area. The compound should be purchased early in the season when prices are best and stored in a cool, dry area. Buckets suitable for moving the compound from location to location should be purchased and stored with the compound, so that all supplies are available when it is time to remove snow.

Sidewalks

In warmer weather, sidewalks need a regular sweeping and an inspection for loose spots. Doorsteps can be made safer by painting the front side of the step a highly visible color. If doormats or runners are used outside, they should be impervious to weather and of a nonskid construction.

An inspection of the grounds often reveals that the residents have created their own new sidewalk, usually a direct path between two areas cutting across a lawn. The grass is worn away and the shortcut looks unsightly. One solution to this problem might be to install fencing or shrubbery at the beginning and ending point of the path, making it less accessible—a costly solution, but effective. Another solution might be to just ignore the problem and continue seeding. A final solution is to accept the will of the people and make a sidewalk of the path they have cut. Flagstone paths are particularly attractive and are less expensive to install than concrete sidewalks.

Trash Removal

Trash removal can be a delight or a burden depending on the system used. Trash may be removed by several means: trash chutes, trash rooms, and dumpsters are commonly used. Each method has its pros and cons; the method chosen should be the most convenient and effective for the property. Nothing deteriorates the curb appeal of your property more than trash scattered around.

Trash chutes can be a potential source of fire, particularly if they are allowed to back up or if greasy items are disposed of through the chute. Doors to each chute should close automatically with a strong spring. If a fire does start, smoke will be hindered in spreading to every floor of the building. The doors should be inspected regularly to insure that they close properly.

Trash rooms within buildings are certainly convenient and effective but present a problem with fire safety and odors. Residents depositing trash in trash rooms should be encouraged to use tie-top plastic bags to help with odor and prevent mess. Shelves may be placed in this room for stacking newspapers and magazines to avoid overloading the containers.

Dumpsters may be placed in convenient locations throughout the property. They need to be screened from sight and yet accessible for the trash removal service's pickup. Again, residents need to be encouraged to use secure bags to avoid loose trash. Dumpsters often become overloaded, particularly when residents are vacating at the end of each month, and trash is simply piled at the base of the container. Dumpsters do need supervision, but with frequent pickups, they can be one of the better solutions to trash removal.

Dumpsters or trash storage areas should be inspected daily for cleanliness. An inspection should immediately follow the pickup by the removal service so that any problems involving the contractor can be noted and reported.

Holiday celebrations generate large amounts of trash, though there may be a missed pickup because of the holiday. Thought should be given in advance to where your residents should place their discarded Christmas trees. Tree removal should be guaranteed with your trash removal service. Residents should then be notified in writing of the correct disposal method.

Individual curbside pickups at each unit can be arranged for large complexes with many separate buildings. The resident keeps the trash inside until pickup day, then places it at the curb. The disadvantage to this system is that the put-out time is often missed and the trash is left all day (or all week) at the curb.

Fencing

Fencing serves a variety of purposes. There are fences for security, for privacy, for cosmetic appearances, or for a combination of all three needs. Maintenance procedures include repainting, repairing, and in the case of shrubbery used for fencing, regular trimming. The key to fence maintenance is frequent inspections.

Fences should be inspected for openings that would breach security, and for structural problems such as loose boards or posts. If there are gates, they should be oiled and adjusted regularly. Combination locks are preferable to keyed locks: keys can be lost, and it is easier to change combinations than it is to rekey.

The fencing itself can be chain link, wood, shrubbery, or fancy brick and block. Because of its high cost, chain-link fencing is usually not as feasible as wood fencing. Unattractive chain-link fencing can be improved by a new coat of paint or by planting vines and training them to grow along the links.

Natural wood, highly attractive and requiring low maintenance, is a good alternative to chain-link fencing.

Shrubbery is also realistic in cost, if the property can afford to wait the four or five years it will take for the shrubbery to grow large enough to provide privacy.

Exterior

Painting

The purpose of exterior painting is twofold: to preserve the structure and to increase the attractiveness of the property. Exterior repainting is a major job and hence is often performed by contract. It is not unusual to spread repainting over three years or more, with one-third of the property being repainted each year. This arrangement allows the expense to be balanced over several years.

Regardless of which service is chosen, in-house or contract, the manager should prepare specifications for the job, including the desired paint quality, type, colors, type of application, and commencement and completion dates. Exactly what is to be painted should also be specified. Perhaps only the walls are to be painted by an outside contractor, with the balconies and trim being done by the in-house staff. If the desired color scheme is an involved one, or you are planning to use bright, modern colors, an expert in color selection should be consulted. Major paint supply companies often provide this decorating service for no extra charge.

It is important to make sure that preparations are made to ensure neatness. Shrubbery and doorways should be draped to avoid paint being spattered on the landscaping. Some kinds of paint will cling to concrete as well as shrubbery, making spills and splashes difficult to remove.

Brick and Stained Wood Walls

The two other types of exteriors—brick and stained wood—also require attention. Brick needs to be inspected for missing mortar, caused by deterioration. If mortar is crumbling or missing, the gap should be scraped and brushed clean. New mortar is then forced into the gap, a process known as *tuck-pointing*.

Stained wood, often of cedar, is popular in many areas of the country. If a good quality stain was applied to start with, restaining may not be necessary for many years. Stained wood walls do, however, need to be inspected for caulking and loose boards. Professional advice should be sought if restaining becomes necessary.

Roof, Gutters, Downspouts

One of the most irritating emergency requests for a resident is a roof leak. Surprisingly enough, few managers emphasize roof areas in their inspection tours, even though regular inspection and troubleshooting can prevent many of these incidents. A roof inspection each spring and fall will take only a short time and can be very rewarding. As already mentioned, it is best to inspect roofs immediately following a rainstorm to check for leaks and drainage.

The areas to be inspected include the roof surface itself, flashings, gutters, downspouts, and fixtures. Many roofing companies will, for a small fee, train an on-site manager to make roof inspections.

If the roof has a flat surface, there should be an even coat of gravel and no puddling an hour after the rain stops. On pitched roofs, the valleys should be smooth and free of debris, the shingles securely fastened. Gutters and downspouts need to be completely clear, with splashblocks placed to carry the rainwater well away from the building. *Flashings* are the metal trim sealed with tar or other sealant which forms a weatherproof joint where the roof meets a different material, such as the side wall, or has a groove. Flashings should rise well above the base of the side wall and be tightly sealed on all sides. A cracked flashing can indicate the beginning of serious problems. Flashings pulled away from the wall can also create leakage. Flashings need to be recoated from time to time to insure watertightness. When in doubt, call in a professional for advice on a suspected problem.

Window Cleaning

The final area of exterior maintenance involves the interior—window cleaning. The owner's objectives as well as the height of the building often govern the attention given to window cleaning. In some properties, window cleaning is left entirely to the residents. In others, professional window cleaners are engaged three times a year for cleaning hard-to-reach exterior windows. In this case, residents should be informed of the scheduled washing well in advance. Residents should be encouraged to clean interior windows and, if accessible, exterior windows. It would be helpful to provide written instructions and to have squeegees and wipers available at the maintenance office for the residents to use.

In some buildings, screens can only be removed from the interior of the unit. In this case, residents can be notified of the cleaning date and asked to remove their own screens:

> Weather permitting, we plan to wash windows on Tuesday, July 14th. If you would like your windows washed on the outside, please remove your screens by 9 A.M. that day. Our "rain date" will be Thursday, July 16th.

A two- or three-person cleaning crew may also be used, with one member of the crew entering the unit and handing the screens down to the ground. Bent or broken screens discovered during window cleaning can be replaced by extra screens held on hand, eliminating the need for a second trip to the unit. The screens may also be cleaned at this time.

At the time the windows are cleaned, a careful inspection should be made for loose, missing, or defective caulking and weatherstripping, so that repairs may all be made at one time.

The solutions used to clean windows can range from old-fashioned ammonia to new liquid cleaners designed to remove window grime and prevent filming or streaking. This is one area of maintenance where new products should be tested for quality, ease of use, and cost. A new product which is a little more expensive may be worth the cost in manpower saved.

Interior Common Areas

The six interior common areas which need attention are lobbies and corridors, walls and ceilings, floors, stairways, and lighting. Most maintenance is directed towards keeping these traffic areas clean.

Lobbies and Corridors

An attractive, well-lighted, clean lobby can add to the marketing effort. If the lobby is unkempt and littered, with stained carpets and dirty tile, the lobby will present a poor image to the public.

The aesthetic appearance of a lobby and its corridors can often be improved with better, more attractive lighting fixtures. Consider replacing standard light bulbs with fluorescent fixtures which screw into the standard light bulb outlet, thereby saving energy. If regular bulbs are used, compare various bulbs for lifetime expectancy before ordering a quantity.

Often overlooked in a building are the lobby doors, and yet poorly adjusted lobby doors can admit intruders or even wandering animals. Lobby doors that close rapidly and completely will not only be secure, but can help keep the lobby warm in the winter and cool in the summer. Many adjustments to the door-closing apparatus are simple and the special tools necessary to make the adjustments reasonably priced.

Walls and Ceilings

Walls and ceilings can be covered with two types of materials—those needing maintenance and those which are virtually maintenance-free. Materials needing frequent maintenance include painted walls or walls covered with wallpaper. Low maintenance surfaces include stone, tile, treated wood, or natural concrete.

Any painted surface will need repainting sooner or later. The frequency of repaintings is governed by (1) the volume of traffic and (2) the color and quality of the paint. The same rules apply to wallpaper. A printed pattern will reduce the visibility of dirt. A high-quality vinyl covering can be cleaned rather than replaced.

Rough-finished ceilings rarely need respraying to maintain an attractive look. If ceiling tiles are used, a supply of replacement tiles should be kept on hand and the brand

name and stock number recorded. If Murphy's Law is in
effect, the manufacturer will discontinue your type of tile
the moment the ceiling leaks. In this case, you may replace
the entire ceiling with a different style and use the old,
leftover tile for repairs in other areas.

Walls and ceilings, no matter how maintenance-free, need
a regular brushing or dusting to remove the webs and
cobwebs that form. Nothing is more distasteful to a
prospective resident than to glance at a corner and see a
spider web forming.

Floors

Caring for floors takes skill and time. Managers are often
unfamiliar with what materials to use on the floors or which
carpet cleaning method to use. Reference books,
professional magazine articles, and mini-seminars run by
floor product companies can help in making the decision.

There are several popular common area floor coverings:
carpeting (commercial grade for durability), vinyl (sheet
goods or tile), and some type of stone or concrete, such as
terrazzo, a mixture of marble and cement. Vinyl tiles may
have a no-wax finish, which means that a shine has been
manufactured into the surface of the tile. The
manufacturer's directions will specify what type of cleaner
should be used—ammonia-based or detergent-based to
prevent damage to the surface. Terazzo surfaces may be
virtually maintenance-free, needing only sweeping, an
occasional damp mopping, and a coat of sealant once a year.

Stairways

Stairways can be gloomy or attractive, depending on their
location. To insure safety, stairways must have good
lighting, secured treads, stable handrails, and clean
surfaces. In a lobby staircase, for example, the treads might
be wrapped with carpet that harmonizes with the lobby
wallpaper. Dust often builds up on the railings and stairway
lighting fixtures. Regular dusting along with a thorough
annual cleaning will help keep stairways attractive.

Lighting

Sooner or later, it comes time to change light bulbs. Difficulties arise when one bulb out of six in a fixture needs changing—and a week later, a second bulb out of the six needs changing, and so forth. Any task of this nature which requires manpower and stepladders should be done on a cost-effective basis: all the bulbs should be changed when the first one goes out. A baby-carrier or similar device can be worn around the maintenance worker's neck. The used bulbs are placed in it as the fresh ones are removed from it, which frees both hands for changing the bulbs. When globes are to be cleaned, start with one clean set, take them up the ladder, replace the dirty ones, and go on to the next, so that only one trip is made to each chandelier.

One effective maintenance man was observed in his building changing sometimes one bulb in a fixture and sometimes all six. The puzzled manager, seeing him take six bulbs up the ladder but occasionally returning with five new ones, inquired how he made his decision. His answer was surprising but logical: when installing six new bulbs, he marked one bulb with the date. If one bulb burned out too soon, he knew that it was just an inferior bulb and that the others had more lifetime left.

If the interior lights are on a timer, the manager needs to be sure they are turning on and off at the most appropriate time. Timers may need to be reset twice in the spring and twice in the fall to accommodate the time change and the lengthening or shortening days. The dates on which the timers are reset should be included in the maintenance calendar. Circuit breaker boxes should be posted with this note:

> If electrical service is interrupted for more than 15 minutes, timers need to be reset.

Unit Interior

Carpeting, Vinyl, Tile

Carpets receive more wear than any other part of the unit interior, yet they receive the least amount of care from the resident. If you manage a building which is largely furnished or which caters to young residents, for instance, you may find that a great number of the residents do not even own a vacuum cleaner. In this situation, it is a smart policy to have several vacuum cleaners available as loaners to sign in and out of the maintenance office as needed. If no provisions are made, some units will not be vacuumed until the current resident vacates many months later. The ground-in dirt will significantly reduce the life of the carpet.

Residents who occupy their apartments year after year are valued, but their long-term occupancy can pose problems when it comes to carpet cleaning. An older couple occupying a unit will generally keep their carpets clean, but a young couple with a child will often put an unusual amount of wear and tear on the carpet. Long-term residents must be encouraged to keep up with vacuuming to help prolong the carpet's life.

A carpet cleaning of the entire property should be scheduled regularly. A scheduled carpet cleaning and a fresh coat of paint may influence residents to take pride in the property and continue their occupancy.

Another consideration is the color of carpeting selected when recarpeting becomes necessary. Neutral beiges are extremely attractive but difficult to maintain. Dark or earthy tones hide stains and dirt well but make rooms look smaller and darker. A variety of carpeting colors will cover a variety of tastes, but all too often the carpeting in a vacant unit will be the wrong color for the prospective residents. In a weak rental market, every technique to turn prospects into residents should be employed, and offering to replace carpeting slightly earlier than is absolutely necessary may attract prospective residents and influence current residents to stay. In a strong rental market, you may not lose prospective residents by less attractive, longer wearing carpeting. If the carpet is still in good shape, dyeing the carpet may be an alternative to replacement.

Vinyl and tile floors have traditionally been used in the kitchen and bath areas for their durability and practicality. Carpeting, sometimes more popular than vinyl or tile, can be extended throughout these two areas, but great care must be taken in the choice of carpeting used. Carpeting in these areas can cause great problems, especially when excess water appears, such as water from backed-up plumbing. When considering floor replacement, balance the cost and manageability of carpet versus tile and decide accordingly.

Carpet installers will often try to convince you to glue carpeting down rather than tack it down. Glued-down carpeting is difficult and expensive to scrape loose and remove, and should be avoided when possible. In bathrooms, carpeting can be secured by using a heavy cement stapler.

Tub and shower enclosures often have ceramic tile walls. Ceramic tile is rich-looking, durable, and easily cleanable. Modular tub/shower/wall units, formed in one piece from fiberglass, are also used, but are not as easily cleanable. Scouring powder used on the wall of these fiberglass units will usually permanently scar the walls.

Appliances

Well-chosen appliances can serve as a marketing tool as well as being a low-maintenance feature. Ranges, refrigerators, dishwashers, and disposals now all have component parts. These can be repaired by an on-site maintenance worker in many cases, eliminating expensive service calls.

Ranges. Ranges manufactured since about 1965 usually come with snap-in elements and burners and interchangeable parts. The common problem of a nonfunctional burner can be handled by snapping out the old element and snapping in the new one. The broiler and baking elements in electric ranges are also easily replaced. Gas ranges are virtually maintenance-free, needing only an occasional replacement of burner rings and pilot light valves.

A supply of elements, racks, broiler pans, and burner guard rings should be stocked in inventory. When a unit is vacated, a new set of burner guard rings can be installed and the ones removed taken to a soaking tub for cleaning before being rotated back into stock. A good oven thermometer and a calibration tool, both inexpensive, are important tools for the maintenance worker. The resident who does a good deal of baking is usually the one who discovers that the stove is out of calibration. Recalibrating the range is a minor adjustment, once the degree of variance has been established with a high-quality thermometer designed for oven testing.

Appliance bulbs for ranges are best changed by the maintenance worker. Too often, an unskilled resident will break off the bulb in the socket while trying to remove it, cutting a hand in the process and necessitating a service call to remove the broken bulb.

Refrigerators. If a resident reports a puddle of water mysteriously appearing in front of the refrigerator from time to time, it merely means that the drain pan has been bumped out of place. Drain pans may also be the cause of the buzzing or vibrating noises residents report. The drain pan can usually be adjusted by removing the front vent grill, reaching underneath until the edge of the pan is grasped, and then wiggling the pan back into position.

Some items to keep in stock for refrigerators would include door bars; a double supply of hinge fasteners, which are easily broken by oversized bottles; plastic flat racks, which crack from overloading; and ice cube trays, which may disappear with the outgoing resident.

Disposals. The most typical disposal problem is blockage caused either by overloading or by a foreign object caught in the disposal. One of the most important instructions given a resident at occupancy is how to free the disposal. Residents should be shown how to remove the guard rings, how to safely unblock and free the blades, and the position of the reset button.

Extra parts to keep in stock for a disposal include guard rings, strainers, and caps. Most modern disposals are sealed units, which means it is easier to replace the entire disposal rather than repair it. For this reason, when disposals start to break down, a supply should be obtained at quantity prices. When ordering new disposals, horsepower and ease of installation are considerations.

Dishwashers. Problems with dishwashers can be serious. A broken dishwasher seal can result in a flood of water on the floor. When the pump motor breaks down, smoke from the oil seal will make it appear that the dishwasher is on fire.

When you receive a panicky call from the resident, you must move quickly to make sure a disaster has not occurred. When the smoke clears, the dishwasher can be pulled and the motor inspected and replaced. Pump motors are an easily replaced unit. When it becomes necessary to replace an entire dishwasher, be sure to salvage the good parts from it to use in repairing other dishwashers. A supply should be kept on hand of the most common parts that break: roller wheels, guides, and spray arms.

Luxury appliances. Luxury items such as microwave ovens and trash compactors have become more popular as amenities in apartments. Care should be taken to retain extra copies of the operating instructions for future residents. Presenting these instructions in a resident kit, rather than leaving them in a drawer or on the counter, can often insure that they will be read and followed. One consideration in adding such luxury appliances to a unit should be the extra cost of repair by an outside serviceman when breakdowns occur.

Plumbing

Simple plumbing repairs can easily be handled in-house. Plumbing parts are one of the biggest stockpiles in inventory because there are such a variety of items that break down. Washers, faucets, sink stoppers and lifts, and aerators are needed for sinks; floats, chains, handles, and lids are needed for toilets—the list goes on. The maintenance department should have a plumber's snake long enough to reach through the plumbing to the end of the building. Use of the snake may be enough to clear a stopped line. An outside plumber can be called if the snake has been pushed to where the building line joins the outside line without clearing the stoppage.

A good basic plumbing repair manual can be the best training guide for both residents and maintenance staff members. Simple guidelines to solve common plumbing problems may be included in the resident handbook.

Extensive damage can often be avoided if every maintenance employee knows exactly where the sewer caps, access points, and traps for each unit are located. Shutoff valves for water should be clearly labeled in utility rooms, so that in an emergency anyone—including a resident—can quickly shut off the water. It is also helpful to know where the main valve shutoff for the property is located and the steps to take in calling the water or fire department in the event that the water must be shut off at the street.

Electrical

Electrical repair techniques need to be studied carefully before any repairs are attempted; a hazardous situation might otherwise result. In most cases, the maintenance staff will only handle the smaller electrical repairs and modifications and leave the major repairs for an electrical contractor. Beware of residents who plan to try making modifications themselves. Special training in replacing breakers, switches, and fixture mountings can be arranged with a local contractor to facilitate making these repairs in-house.

Residents will often have their own chandeliers they wish to exchange for the one already in place in the unit. An effective policy is to make storage of the unused chandelier the resident's responsibility. A charge should be made sufficient to cover installation of the new chandelier and eventual reinstallation of the old chandelier. Quality dimmer switches can be stocked at the maintenance office and added to the unit for a one-time charge including labor; the dimmer then becomes part of the property.

Cleaning

Cleaning units in between occupancies calls for a thorough job to avoid complaints during the walk-through. A checklist should be used to ensure as perfect results as possible (see the sample unit make-ready report in exhibit 12.1). When a unit is turned over to a resident in sparkling condition, the relationship begins on a good note.

The incoming resident must be made aware of the property's cleaning standards. Without being too intrusive, the manager must make sure that those standards are being maintained. The resident who piles papers all over the unit

Exhibit 12.1   Unit Make-Ready Report

Property _____

Unit _____ Type _____

Date Vacated _____ Date To Be Occupied _____

Initial Inspection by _____ Date _____

Checklist Before Move-In	Instructions
☐ Check all plumbing. (Toilets, faucets, all plumbing in unit.) Make sure no leaks.	
☐ Check all appliances. (Run dishwasher once on each cycle, check for proper operation of refrigerator, disposal, and range.)	
☐ Check hardware in unit. (All door knobs, closet hooks, closet rods, door pulls, night locks, door stops, magnetic catches, etc.)	
☐ Check windows and screens. (No breaks in either. All sliding glass windows and screens working correctly.) Clean out tracks on all sliding glass windows and doors. Ensure that all screws are installed where needed.	
☐ Check venetian blinds for proper operation.	
☐ Check all walls for holes, seams, cuts, nail pops.	
☐ Check paint. (All walls, ceilings, woodwork, trim which need to be cleaned or painted. No spots, streaks, or scratches.)	
☐ Check flooring. (All floors cleaned and waxed, parquet block floors or wood strip and asphalt tile included. Carpet vacuumed.)	
☐ Bathroom(s) cleaned. (Tubs, toilets, tile walls, tile floor, vanities, mirrors, medicine cabinets, and sinks clean.)	
☐ All towel bars, toilet paper holders, soap dishes installed and cleaned.	
☐ Check tile in bathroom(s) for cracks or flaws.	

will not be motivated to vacuum thoroughly; the resident who piles dishes to the ceiling will be the first to complain about bugs. The clutter of a unit will often spread onto the balcony or patio. Draperies will be askew and boxes piled around.

Cleaning is often a difficult subject for managers to bring up with residents. No resident likes to hear that his or her unit is not clean enough. If not spelled out in the lease,

Exhibit 12.1 (Continued)

Checklist Before Move-In	Instructions
☐ All baseboard, shelves in closet, electrical outlet plates installed properly.	
☐ All threshholds and metal strips installed where needed.	
☐ Check that all doors close properly, with no rubbing or warping.	
☐ Check that all vents and registers are installed.	
☐ Check heating and air conditioning (when appropriate) to be sure working properly.	
☐ Check that filters are installed in all air handling units or air conditioning units (when appropriate).	
☐ All kitchen cabinets cleaned inside and outside.	
☐ Windows cleaned.	
☐ Check all lighting. (New bulbs in all fixtures, and all fixtures hung and working.)	
☐ Check for chips or cracks in plumbing fixtures and kitchen appliances.	
☐	
☐	
☐	

Final Inspection by _____ Date _____

Approved by _____ Date _____

standards for cleaning and orderliness will be difficult to enforce when a messy, careless resident takes occupancy. Without lease terms to back up the standards, it will be very difficult to evict this type of resident.

Facilities and Amenities

Laundry facilities, swimming pools, clubrooms, playgrounds, and tennis courts can be both a management and maintenance headache, or conversely, one of the smoother-running areas of the property. A prime consideration in maintaining recreational facilities is securing the facilities to prevent misuse and vandalism, which can ultimately turn into large maintenance problems.

Laundry

Laundry rooms need daily inspections and daily cleaning, 365 days a year. Simple operating instructions should be posted. Each washer and dryer should be identified with a large number, so that residents can accurately report problems. A supply of "Out of Order" signs can be hung on a hook on the wall. The resident discovering the problem can use an attached marking pen to date the sign and place it on the out-of-order machine.

A variety of locations for laundry facilities may be considered. There may be an interior location such as a small main floor laundry, a washer/dryer on each floor, central laundry rooms located in separate buildings, and even individuals hookups in each unit. Having washers and dryers scattered over a variety of locations can make maintenance problems difficult. When a single washer is broken, residents must go to a nearby building, increasing the need to have the equipment repaired promptly. A central location can alleviate this problem, but may be difficult to secure.

The hours of laundry facilities should be clearly posted. In central locations, where the noise of the equipment won't disturb residents, late hours might be possible. Inside buildings, where the noise might disturb nearby residents, a 10 P.M. closing time might be necessary. Inside security buildings, where a washer/dryer might be located on each floor, limited hours might not be needed. If there is a reason to shorten hours in any of these locations, a brief explanation should be circulated to all residents.

Laundry equipment is customarily owned by a service company, which takes the responsibility for repairs and maintenance and shares the income with the property. In this arrangement, maintenance personnel should be trained in troubleshooting or minor repairs. Major problems should be left for the company to handle. If a property elects to own its own equipment, complete training in repairs should be arranged for staff members, so that unnecessary delays in securing a repair worker can be avoided.

Swimming Pools

Cleanliness and preventive maintenance are crucial in the care of swimming pools. Constant communication with staff and continual checking will render this area virtually trouble-free. In season, pools need to be cleaned regularly (a daily skimming and vacuuming is suggested). The chemical balance should be checked at least twice daily and adjusted as needed. Many pool maintenance assignments can easily be handled by a minimum-wage, part-time pool manager instead of an expensive maintenance staff member.

Effective rules can help reduce maintenance problems at swimming pools. A policy of no glass containers, no food inside the pool fence, and similar rules can simplify pool maintenance.

Managers should be alert to a variety of free seminars offered each spring by companies supplying pool chemicals. These seminars instruct the maintenance manager or on-site manager in the latest techniques of opening a pool and operating it safely. Pool care is one area of maintenance where changes occur rapidly; suppliers often publish newsletters to keep on-site managers up to date on the latest techniques.

A pool cover should be used during the off season. An unsightly pool can greatly detract from the property's curb appeal.

Clubhouses

Clubhouses tend to be locked up except when a party is arranged, defeating the original purpose for which clubhouses were designed: a gathering place for residents and their guests.

A double-lock system can help to prevent vandalism, a key problem in maintaining clubhouses. The door is outfitted with two locks. All the residents have a key to one lock and the manager the key to the other, making the clubhouse accessible during regular clubhouse hours, but keeping it secure from anyone without a key.

Tennis Courts

Tennis courts require considerably less maintenance than other features on the property. Sweeping tennis courts occasionally, repainting lines and replacing nets when needed, and resurfacing every three to five years will normally be the only services needed.

On the annual calendar, a notation should be made as to when to take down the nets, indicating the season is over. In northern cities, leaving the nets up over the winter will result in new nets being needed frequently. An alternative is to take down all but one net in late fall, leaving it up for mild day use until inclement weather sets in. The process can be reversed in the spring, putting up one net early and adding the others as the weather permits.

Tennis courts should have locked gates to prevent unauthorized persons from using the courts. Security must be provided not only to avoid complaints about outsiders using the courts but to validate insurance coverage. A combination lock can be used; residents then sign for the combination. The combination can be changed frequently and the new combination distributed to those who signed for the old one.

Tennis courts and sprinkler systems do not mix. When the grass near the courts needs to be watered, the courts are rendered useless for several hours. One solution is to surround the courts with a six-foot stretch of asphalt or gravel so that watering is kept away from the courts, leaving them dry and playable all day.

Playgrounds

A playground can be a simple, grassy area with a volleyball net or a large, landscaped area with swingsets and sports equipment. The manufacturer's guidelines need to be carefully followed when installing any playground equipment to ensure its safety for children's use. Chains and other moving parts on swingsets should be checked frequently for wear or damage and repaired or removed immediately when damage is noted. Playground surfaces should be inspected daily for broken glass or sharp objects.

Consideration should be given regarding a playground arrangement that will suit the largest number of children and tend to separate the smaller children from the older. Teenagers might be content with a basketball court area, while preteens might enjoy a shuffleboard court. Smaller children enjoy swings and jungle gyms to climb upon, while very small children need only sandboxes and an area where balls can be rolled. It is not necessary to have extensive playground facilities, but those arranged should be as safe as possible.

Mechanical Equipment

In the category of mechanical equipment are heating, ventilating, and air conditioning (HVAC) systems; water heaters; elevators; pumps; and supporting systems such as alarms, gauges, timers, and thermostats. This equipment can be a bewildering assembly in a basement or modern, individual systems in each unit.

There must be complete operating instructions for every piece of equipment. In the case of older equipment where no factory manuals are available, manuals can be written. A professional maintenance equipment worker, on an hourly fee basis, can come to the mechanical room and examine the systems, reporting on each. From this information a manual can be assembled. The manual should describe the piece of equipment, how it works, and common problems associated with it.

Every piece of equipment, including all gauges, needs to be labeled. There should be an identifying list on the mechanical room wall listing each piece of equipment and its location in the room. The purpose of this identifying system is to make it easy for anyone who enters the mechanical room to identify the operation of the system for inspection. For example, if the boiler is not working, you will not know which of 10 pump-like devices controls the boiler and which controls some other piece of equipment unless each device is labeled.

After everything is organized, another chart should be placed near the entrance to the room identifying where each control valve or shutoff is located and what equipment it controls. One good way to test whether or not the equipment has been properly labeled is to invite the local fire marshall to inspect the mechanical room and assess it from a safety standpoint. In the event of a fire or other disaster, the fire department needs to enter the mechanical room and shut off various systems. Without good identification, this cannot be accomplished.

The mechanical room is not the only location for equipment. While the heating equipment is often located in the mechanical room, the ventilating fans may be located on the outside roof. Main circuitry is often in the mechanical room, but subcontrols may be located on each floor of the building, in addition to circuit-breaker boxes in individual units. All of these locations must also be noted. When a repair is necessary or an emergency occurs, it is critical to be able to shut systems down in an orderly fashion.

Mechanical rooms should be locked to prevent unauthorized persons from entering. These rooms, however, must be easily accessible in the event of an emergency. For security reasons, it is unwise to give a master building key to the fire department. Instead, the fire department should be given a key to the outside doors and the combination to a lockbox outside the mechanical room which will contain all keys the fire department will need in combatting the emergency.

Gauges of mechanical equipment should be inspected daily and any necessary adjustments made. On a weekly, monthly, quarterly, or annual basis, routine servicing of mechanical equipment can be performed. This can be handled in one of two ways:

1. A preventive maintenance contract can be signed with a local service company or vendor. Adjustments, changes, and routine repairs are handled under the contract. Provision is made for a certain number of labor-hours per month for failures.

2. A maintenance employee can be trained to do the servicing or to work with the outside contractor. Simple tasks a maintenance worker might perform would include draining of water from boilers regularly to prevent buildup of deposits or to clean and change filters; more major servicing might

include changing motors or chemicals in a cooling system on a regular basis.

Summary

Maintenance procedures may be divided into six areas: (1) grounds, (2) exterior structure, (3) interior common areas, (4) unit interior, (5) facilities and amenities, and (6) mechanical equipment.

Grounds maintenance covers the following areas:

1. Landscaping.
2. Sprinkler care.
3. Streets and parking areas.
4. Snow removal.
5. Sidewalks.
6. Trash removal.
7. Fencing.

Exterior maintenance includes:

1. Painting.
2. Brick and stained wood walls.
3. Roof, gutters, downspouts.
4. Window cleaning.

Interior common areas which need attention include:

1. Lobbies and corridors.
2. Walls and ceilings.
3. Floors.
4. Stairways.
5. Lighting.

Areas of concern in the unit interiors include:

1. Carpeting, vinyl, tile.
2. Appliances.

3. Plumbing.

4. Electrical.

5. Cleaning.

Maintenance of facilities and amenities includes:

1. Laundry.

2. Swimming pools.

3. Clubhouses.

4. Tennis courts.

5. Playgrounds.

Mechanical equipment includes HVAC systems, water heaters, elevators, pumps, and supporting systems such as alarms, gauges, timers, and thermostats. Every piece of equipment must be labeled and identified. When emergencies occur, it is important that all equipment can be shut down in an orderly fashion.

13

Energy Conservation

Energy conservation is no longer something new or radical. In the world in which we live today, energy conservation is an absolute necessity. Although at the time of this writing the United States faces no serious energy shortage, the cost of gas, oil, coal, and electricity is still extremely high, necessitating conservation. The successful on-site manager will take steps to conserve energy before it becomes crucial.

The study of energy consumption can be complex, but many energy-saving techniques and methods are very simple, require little expense, and add to the value of the building. Energy conservation does not necessarily mean reduced resident comfort; on the contrary, often the opposite is true. Caulking and weatherstripping, for instance, can eliminate unpleasant drafts. Energy conservation will save money for both management and residents: there is really no reason to avoid energy conservation.

To begin conserving energy, an energy audit must be taken of the building to determine what conservation measures can be taken. After the energy audit has been completed, the manager can develop an energy conservation program designed to educate and motivate residents.

Energy Audit

Similar to a management survey in evaluating the operation of a property from a management standpoint, an energy audit pinpoints areas and patterns of waste in the property's usage of energy and makes recommendations on ways to remedy the particular problems. It can delineate between residents' responsibilities and management's responsibilities in saving energy.

Energy conservation is a complex and difficult subject, and professional help is often used in making an energy audit. Your local utility company can provide you with an audit of your electricity and gas usage, along with average figures to compare. Professional engineers can provide a mechanical evaluation of the HVAC system and a structural survey of the building. There are companies which specialize in energy audits, providing a total package for a negotiable fee. The benefit in using any of these services is the on-site training provided for both the manager and the maintenance staff member who accompanies the auditor.

The audit will follow a checklist format, breaking down the items by location or type of use. The audit will look at the following general categories:

HVAC system.

Water heating.

Lighting.

Metering.

Infiltration.

Insulation.

Storm doors and windows.

Roof.

Solar energy (if any).

Landscaping.

Fireplaces.

Appliances.

Common areas.

The condition of each item or area will be listed along with any recommendations for modification. The urgency of each

Exhibit 13.1 Sample from Energy Audit

Item	Condition	Urgency
Water Heaters	Poor. All need flushing.	Very urgent
	Poorly insulated. Wrap with insulation blankets.	When possible
	Draft diverter blocked—creates inefficiency and fire hazard.	Immediately
Estimated savings:	Flushing & cleaning: Insulation blankets: Unblocking: 1–2%	5% 8% Cost: zero

recommendation can be noted—some recommendations will be labeled, "urgent," while others will be labeled, "when possible." A sample item from an energy audit list can be found in exhibit 13.1.

Based upon the energy audit, specifications can be drawn and costs estimated. The entire package is then reviewed by the on-site manager, the maintenance supervisor, and the property manager. A priority list is prepared. This list is compared to the short- and long-range budget and preliminary decisions are reached. Tax benefits may be explored to further justify the merit of a particular modification.

The recommendations for any type of modification will fall into three categories: (1) immediate changes, low- or high-cost; (2) immediate implementation of no-cost methods (usually involving residents); and (3) long-range planned expenditures.

By evaluating the condition of the building, equipment, and fixtures, and analyzing the operational habits of the residents, energy conservation can be approached in a logical fashion, towards the goal of achieving the greatest energy savings.

We will now look individually at each area to be covered in the energy audit.

Utilities

Heating Systems

With a central heating system, energy is often wasted by inefficient equipment, pipes, and ducts, as well as improper preventive maintenance programs. The controls for the heating equipment can often be modified with timers and part replacement to produce a more efficient system, with the cost spread over several budget years.

Energy can be saved by redirecting heat away from certain areas. At one time it was common practice to heat lobbies and hallways. Lines to these areas can be restricted and a cooler temperature maintained.

In individually heated units, where small furnaces or in-wall heaters are used, energy is often wasted through dirty filters or coils. Residents should be shown how to keep filters clean by checking them monthly and replacing dirty filters promptly. (Management should change filters if residents do not follow through.) The following no-cost/low-cost energy saving techniques can be passed along to residents in the resident handbook or in the newsletter:

1. The thermostat must be kept unobstructed and free from dust.

2. Heat registers and cold air returns work best when there is no furniture obstructing them. Radiators should be vacuum-dusted regularly.

3. Drapes should not block registers. By opening the draperies on warm sunny winter days and closing them at dusk, energy can be saved through passive solar heating.

4. Lower the thermostat. In steam and electric heating systems, a constant temperature setting is recommended. For forced air systems, lower the thermostat at night and add a sweater or blanket while sleeping.

5. Close registers or shut off heat in little-used rooms and keep the doors to these rooms closed.

We mentioned passive solar heating. An *active* solar heating system involves collectors, pumps, ducts, storage systems, and sun requirements. A *passive* solar heating system is not a system, but rather the natural and efficient use of sunlight without any equipment. Residents can conserve man-made energy by using the sun's rays at the appropriate times. When remodeling is considered, careful placement of windows can often create natural areas for sunlight.

Cooling Systems

A positive result of the energy shortages of the last decade has been the willingness of the public to reduce their energy consumption during hot weather by setting thermostats higher and using their air conditioners less. Cooling equipment must be checked for its *energy efficiency ratio* (EER). The EER is the ratio of output in Btus per hour to the energy input in watts—the greater the ratio of output to input, the more efficient the unit. This rating is placed on the equipment by the manufacturer.

Individual room units require frequent changes of filters and regular cleaning of the coils if they are to operate at peak efficiency. If the residents are conscientious in changing filters, and if the proper level of freon (coolant) is maintained, residents need only be educated to set their air conditioners at a level that will provide reasonable comfort while conserving energy.

Residents should be made aware of the following:

1. In dry climates, an evaporative cooler works as efficiently as an air conditioner at a much lower cost.

2. During the cooling season, all heat-producing appliances, such as television sets and lamps, should be kept away from thermostats to avoid an artificial call for cooling.

Water Heating

The heating of water can consume as much as 30 percent of the property's total energy costs. A common way to waste energy in heating water is overheating. Settings of 120° F are adequate for most purposes. (Dishwashers without their own heating units do require water heated to 140° F.)

Another common waste of energy comes from lack of proper insulation around older water heaters, lack of proper venting, or improper adjustment of gas flames.

If residents have individual water heaters, they should be encouraged to set the water heater thermostat at a lower setting. Most water heaters can handle household needs at a medium or low setting rather than a high setting. Residents should be encouraged to run the dishwasher and washer only with full loads. When an apartment changes hands, water restrictors can be installed on shower heads and faucets to help conserve heated water.

Lighting

Lighting in hallways can often be reduced without sacrificing safety or security. Using a 100-watt incandescent bulb in an inside hallway would be wasteful if a 40-watt incandescent bulb would provide adequate illumination. There are fluorescent bulbs that are designed for standard sockets; these bulbs use about a fourth of the energy an incandescent bulb uses. All light fixtures should be kept clean to insure maximum efficiency.

Metering

Every on-site manager should be familiar with gas and electric meters. By knowing how to read the meters, the manager can evaluate energy consumption and determine the peak usage hours. Both gas and electric meters are read in the same way.

Most electric meters measure usage in kilowatt hours (kwh). As you face the electric meter you will note four dials. From left to right, these dials represent thousands, hundreds, tens, and ones. The thousands and tens meters run counterclockwise, the hundreds and ones meters run clockwise. The pointer must completely pass a number before it is counted.

Say that you look at the meter and notice that the needle is past the 4 on the ones dial, past the 5 on the tens, past the 6 on the hundreds, and past the 7 on the thousands. The meter reading is 7-6-5-4, or 7,654 kilowatt hours.

Next month, the meter reads past the 4 on the ones dial, past the 7 on the tens, past the 5 on the hundreds, and past

the 8 on the thousands. The reading is 8-5-7-4 or 8,574
kilowatt hours. Subtracting the previous reading (meters do
not reset), you find that in one month's time you have used
920 kilowatt hours. Your utilities company will supply you
with the rate charged per kilowatt hour.

On the gas meter, you will see four similar dials. The gas
meter works in the same way as an electric meter, except
that gas is measured in cubic feet.

There are three basic ways of metering energy in
apartment properties: (1) master metering, (2) individual
metering, and (3) submetering.

In a master metering system, one meter measures energy
consumption for a single building. The meter is owned by
the utilities company; bills are paid by management. A
portion of each resident's monthly rent goes toward this
cost.

In an individual metering system, each apartment unit
has a separate meter. The meters are owned by the utilities
company; residents pay their energy bills directly to the
company.

A submetering or *check metering* system uses both a
master meter and individual meters. The individual meters
are owned and operated by the owner. It is the owner's
responsibility to bill the residents and pay the entire energy
bill to the utilities company.

Residential Utility Billing System

The Residential Utility Billing System (RUBS), a procedure
rather than a metering system, uses established formulas to
pass utility costs on to residents in addition to the rental
rate. Rental rates do not include the cost of utilities; instead,
the master billing is divided equally and passed on to the
residents. These costs, of course, vary from month to month.

To figure a RUBS bill, take the entire utility bill and
subtract a fixed percentage of the total to account for heat
and hot water used in common areas. Take this sum and
divide by the total number of square feet of apartment
space in the property. The individual charge for each unit is
an amount equal to the square footage of that apartment
multiplied by the charge per square foot. Besides dividing

by size, some balancing and adjustments of the calculations may be necessary for certain locations in the building. The assistance of the local utilities company may be sought if an equitable division is difficult to arrange.

Residents may at first object to RUBS, especially if utilities have previously been included in the rent. It should be pointed out that dividing the charge by apartment size is the most fair method outside of individual metering. RUBS will also cut down on frequent rent increases, since utilities costs are not connected with rent. A project at the University of Colorado, sponsored by the Department of Energy, concluded that RUBS heightens resident awareness of energy conservation, and can result in a savings of up to 15 percent in energy use.

Insulation and Infiltration

The purpose of insulation is to prevent infiltration of outside air into the building. Outside air causes the heating or cooling system to work much harder than it needs to. Great savings can be realized through careful insulation of the building.

Much energy is wasted because storm doors and windows are left open when they should be closed, or vice versa. If you notice windows open in the summer with air conditioners going, give your residents a simple reminder.

Weatherstripping and Caulking

Weatherstripping and caulking are forms of insulation used on door frames, window frames, sills, and on any joint where two different materials meet. Once often overlooked, weatherstripping and caulking are now looked upon as a major means of saving energy. It is probable that if one added up all the energy lost in an average apartment building through faulty caulking and weatherstripping, it would compare to the amount lost through a one-foot square hole in an outside wall.

Caulking is usually appropriate where fixed surfaces meet; weatherstripping, where moving surfaces meet, as in a door opening and closing. Often overlooked are infiltration points outside of normal traffic patterns, such as a point where pipes pass through the walls or where the frame meets the foundation. Many electrical outlets leak air; special fireproof foam inserts are available to correct this problem.

Caulking and weatherstripping is relatively inexpensive and is easy to install. The on-site staff can probably do the job with only minimal training. It does take some knowledge to decide which of the various types of weatherstripping (rolled vinyl with metal backing, foam rubber, or thin spring metal) should be used for each situation. However, once the proper choice is made and the material carefully installed, weatherstripping can last for many years.

The on-site manager and/or maintenance worker should inspect caulking and weatherstripping at least annually. The flexible weatherstripping can often become misaligned by excessive slamming of doors; caulking can shrink or crumble over the years. Adjustment or replacement should be made where indicated.

Landscaping

Landscaping is often not thought of as a means of energy conservation, but it can have practical applications. Deciduous trees planted on the south and west sides of your building can provide shade in the summer, reducing the need for fans or air conditioning, and permit sunshine in the winter, to aid in heating the building. A common reservation is the length of time it takes for trees to grow to a beneficial size. As long as landscaping is being done, however, it costs nothing extra to plant the types of trees that will aid in energy conservation and not hinder it.

Fireplaces

Fireplaces are attractive but are energy wasters. All fireplaces need a supply of air when being used. If the fireplace has airtight glass doors and the air is drawn from outside, the fireplace does not draw upon the air inside the apartment. When there are no glass doors, however, then the air inside the apartment—which has already been expensively heated—is drawn into the fireplace and up the chimney. You can prove this to yourself by sitting in front of your fireplace while it is burning and feel the air moving past you into the fireplace.

As the air is drawn into the fireplace, the air pressure is reduced in the apartment. Cold air then infiltrates through cracks and other openings to restore the balance by replacing the air going up the chimney. However, it replaces hot air with cold air. The apartment cools down, the thermostat calls for heat, and energy is wasted in a vicious cycle. The usual result is that a fireplace takes more heat out of the apartment than it puts in, even though it feels warm from the front.

Standard fireplaces were designed to create ambience, not work as a supplemental heat source. During the energy audit, the fireplace should be examined carefully, answering the following questions:

Is there an adequate outside source of air?

Are there glass doors to prevent air from being drawn into the fireplace? Are the doors at least $\frac{3}{16}$-inch thick with strong frames and insulation?

Is the damper closed when the fireplace is not in use, to avoid the natural draft created by the warm air inside the apartment?

Is there a buildup of soot in the chimney, further reducing efficiency?

Fireplaces can be an attractive feature for residents, but an expensive energy-wasting problem for the property.

Common Areas

Since common areas are unsupervised and unoccupied, they are potential sources of energy waste. Waste in these areas is often caused by lack of attention rather than system inefficiencies. Accurate readings on heating, cooling, and lighting need to be taken, a conservative level for each chosen, and adjustments then made.

In the 1960s and 1970s, it was popular to build large apartment properties with expensive clubhouses. Clubhouses stand unused much of the time, yet are kept well heated in the winter and well cooled in the summer.

When parties are held, doors are often left open with heating or cooling equipment running. When the parties are over, no one is delegated to reset the thermostats to a conservative level. Energy is often wasted due to lack of supervision.

Controls can be instituted to prevent energy from being wasted in recreational facilities. Ice machines that run all month but which are used rarely can be shut down. Thermostats can have locking control boxes placed over them, which permit only the staff to change the settings.

Appliances

Use of appliances within the apartment makes up a large percentage of the total energy costs, and is therefore a potential source of waste. Since appliances are the residents' responsibility, the information in this section is largely to be passed on to the residents.

Refrigerators

Refrigerators and freezers are often set much colder than is necessary. 5° F for freezer compartments and 34–37° F for refrigerators will preserve food. The space underneath a refrigerator should be vacuumed at least four times a year and the coils vacuumed annually. If the freezer is not self-defrosting, no more than ¼ inch of frost should be allowed to accumulate. More frost than this greatly reduces the efficiency of the unit. In a frost-free refrigerator, all liquids should be tightly covered, since loosely covered liquids cause a frost-free system to work harder.

There is a smaller chance of spoilage when frozen foods are thawed in the refrigerator compartment, which benefits from the added cold. Opening and closing the refrigerator door as infrequently as possible will aid in maintaining the desired temperature.

Ranges

Foods cook faster when the amount of water used is kept to a minimum. On electric ranges, burners can be turned off a few minutes before cooking is to finish. Enough heat will remain as the burner cools down to finish cooking the food.

Reflector pans under the burners are for just that purpose: to reflect the heat onto the pan bottom, not to catch drips. They should be kept clean for maximum efficiency.

On a gas range, check the color of the flame: a blue flame means the range is operating properly. If the flame is yellow, the burner may be clogged. Clogged burners can be easily cleaned with a pipe cleaner. Aluminum foil should not be used to line an oven. In a gas range, foil can cause a fire; in an electric, it will cut efficiency.

Other baking appliances. Microwave ovens can only save energy when used properly. Using them to defrost food wastes energy, as does using them partially empty. The amount of energy saved depends on how carefully you plan the use of the microwave. Small broiling and baking appliances do often use less energy than a range, but only if the size of the food placed in them and the length of cooking time chosen are appropriate.

Dishwashers

Dishwashers should be run only when there is a full load. Hand-washing dishes and then running them through the cycle to make sure they are clean is a waste of energy. Many dishwashers can be set to let the dishes dry naturally, rather than using the heater element built into the appliance. If you don't need the dishes immediately, let them dry overnight in the dishwasher without heat.

Washers and Dryers

With today's detergents, cold water can often be used for all but extremely soiled loads instead of hot or warm water. In any event, use cold water rinses, fill the washer completely, and don't overwash clothes. The water level can often be set lower for a partial load.

The lint filter in the dryer should be cleaned after each load, to allow proper venting. Fabrics of similar weight will dry more rapidly than a mixed load. The dryer vent (every dryer needs one) should be checked regularly to make sure it is unclogged.

A gas dryer must be vented to the outside for safety. If you need to vent an electric dryer inside, make sure it vents well away from the dryer: the moist air will cause the dryer to work harder and the humidity buildup will eventually clog the vent.

Energy Conservation Program

Once the energy audit of the apartment property is complete and a determination is made as to where energy can be conserved and what modifications are necessary, the manager can turn to designing an energy conservation program for the residents.

Residents must be made aware of the importance of energy conservation—for the good of the property, the country, and the residents' own finances. The first step in making residents aware is to provide them with an example. Don't expect residents to become energy conscious immediately unless the management has taken energy conservation steps within the building and informed the residents of these measures.

Residents often rent apartments rather than buy homes because they want to avoid the responsibilities—such as energy conservation—that ownership involves. Therefore, they may not respond well if they are burdened with extensive checklists, instructions, and procedures on energy conservation. Any suggestions made to residents must be simple and easy to follow. The tips that we have discussed in this chapter can also be made part of the resident handbook.

Many public utility companies will send a representative to a resident's unit shortly after he or she moves in to demonstrate the most efficient ways to use the appliances, equipment, and heating. If this service is available in your area, the name of the representative and where to call for an appointment should be included in the resident handbook and the resident's attention directed to it. A demonstration on energy-saving techniques could also be made by the manager or appropriate staff member at the time of the move-in meeting with the incoming resident.

A logo or slogan created for your energy conservation program can be displayed in the newsletter. A small section can draw attention each month to a particular energy tip. As the residents become accustomed to reading about energy conservation in each newsletter, they should be encouraged to submit their tip of the month for publication in the next newsletter.

If residents prove interested in energy conservation, more elaborate programs may be designed. Residents can be involved in an "energy weekend" where an overall effort is made by the entire property to consume as little energy as possible. A party can be scheduled at the party room so that televisions are not used that evening. The maintenance staff can read the meters on Friday and re-read them on Monday morning; the results compared to the previous weekend can be posted or published. The enthusiasm generated by an "energy weekend" can often continue into the following months.

One property in Colorado ran a contest each month: a goal was set for each size of apartment on electric consumption, and any resident who brought in a billing for that month below the goal amount received a discount on that month's rent. The discount was often only $2, but the incentive worked. The one who brought in the lowest billing for a particular size unit received a $10 discount on the rent.

Rewards of this nature may be illegal in some states. And in any case, recognition should be the primary reward. In the past, it was often thought that energy costs in a property should be carefully concealed from the residents. Now, letting residents share in the knowledge of the increased costs in utility bills can often result in their cooperation—and their enthusiasm, when they realize that they themselves benefit from energy conservation.

For Further Information

The U.S. Department of Energy offers a wealth of information on energy conservation. Their address is: National Energy Information Center, EI20; Energy Information Administration; Forrestal Building, Room 1F048; Washington, DC 20585; 202/252-8800. The Institute of Real Estate Management publishes books on energy conservation, including the following: *No-Cost/Low-Cost Energy Conservation Measures for Multifamily Housing*; *Energy Cost Control Guide for Multifamily Properties*; and *Alternatives to Master Metering in Multifamily Housing*.

IREM also publishes a public service brochure, "30 Ways to Conserve Energy in Apartments, Condominiums, & Other Multi-housing Properties," designed to hand out or mail to residents.

Summary

The first step in developing an energy conservation program for the property is taking an energy audit. This audit studys areas and patterns of waste in the property's consumption of energy and makes recommendations on ways to remedy the particular situation. The following areas are studied in the audit:

HVAC system. Filters for both heating and cooling units should be cleaned regularly. Cooling equipment must be checked for its energy efficiency ratio (EER).

Water heating. The heating of water can consume as much as 30 percent of the property's total energy costs.

Lighting. Lighting in hallways can often be reduced without sacrificing safety or security.

Metering. There are three basic ways of metering energy in apartment properties: (1) master metering, (2) individual metering, and (3) submetering. The Residential Utility Billing System (RUBS) divides up energy costs among residents by the number of square feet in each apartment.

Insulation and infiltration. Weatherstripping and caulking are effective means of preventing infiltration of outside air into the building. Landscaping can also be used as a form of insulation. Fireplaces waste energy unless they have airtight glass doors and an adequate supply of outside air.

Common areas. Since common areas are unsupervised and unoccupied, they are potential sources of energy waste.

Appliances. There are many no-cost steps the resident can take to save energy in the use of refrigerators, ranges and other baking appliances, dishwashers, washer, and dryers.

When the audit is completed, a determination is made as to where energy can be conserved and what modifications are necessary. Residents are brought into the energy conservation effort through education and promotional programs.

Glossary

Abandonment   A relinquishment or surrender of property or rights. Abandonment of leased premises refers to the relinquishing of the premises by the resident without consent of the owner before the lease expires.

Abatement   In real estate, a reduction of rent, interest, or an amount due.

Access   The owner of a leased premises has a "right of access" to the unit in order to show the unit to prospective residents and to make repairs.

Account   A detailed statement of receipts and payments of money or of trade transactions which have taken place between two or more persons.

Accounting   The theory and system of setting up and maintaining the book of a business organization; analyzing the operation of a business from a study of income and expenses.

Accounts payable   Monies due to others for services rendered or goods ordered and received.

Accounts receivable   Monies due for services rendered or goods ordered and delivered.

ACCREDITED RESIDENT MANAGER™ (ARM®)   A designation conferred by the Institute of Real Estate Management to persons who have qualified as resident or on-site managers.

Active solar heating   Solar heating involving machinery and sun requirements. See **Passive solar heating**.

Advance rent   Rent paid in advance. Some states require rents paid more than 31 days in advance to be held in an interest-bearing escrow account.

Advertisement   An individual notice designed to attract public attention.

Advertising   The placing of paid public presentations or announcements about a product, service, or activity, with the objective of persuading the public to buy that good or service or accept a certain point of view or concept.

Aeration   A method for aerating soil, often used in dry or desert areas.

Air space   Space above a property which may be sold or leased. In condominium ownership, the space of air or three-dimensional area located within the walls, floor, and ceiling of a condominium structure to which the condominium owner has title.

Alligatoring   The breaking up of a surface, such as paint or asphalt, into a pattern that resembles the hide of an alligator.

Allowance for vacancies and bad debts   An estimated amount, based on records and statistics, subtracted from the **gross scheduled income** (see) to allow for vacancies and bad debts.

Amenities   Features of a property that render it more useful and/or attractive. Satisfactions of possession and use arising from architectural excellence, scenic beauty, and social environment.

Annual budget   A 12-month estimate of income and expenses for a mature property.

Annual statement   In real estate, a fully detailed and annotated statement of all income and expense items involving cash and covering a 12-consecutive-month period of operation of an individual property. Includes the disposition and application of net funds for the period concerned and accumulated funds from prior periods. Variations in form and content are effected to conform with owner directives.

Apartment   A residential unit found in a variety of properties such as walk-ups, garden-style projects, mid-rises, and condominiums.

Apartment building   A building designed for the separate housing of two or more families and where mutual services are supplied for comfortable and convenient occupancy.

Apportioned rent   System of rent where the number of extra features and amenities determines the rent. Apartment units are graded and a value is assigned.

Appreciation   An increase in the value of property.

Asset management   A sophisticated form of property management under which the managing agent organizes, operates, and assumes the risk of the total real estate business venture and whose concern extends beyond net operating income.

Assignment   The transfer of an interest in a bond, mortgage, lease, or other instrument, by writing.

Balance sheet   Statement of the financial position of a business firm at a particular time, indicating its assets, liabilities, and owner equity.

Bankruptcy   The legal proceeding whereby the affairs of a person or business unable to meet its obligations are turned over to a receiver or trustee in accordance, in the U.S., with the Bankruptcy Act.

Bid   Offer of a price made by a supplier of goods or services.

BMIR   Below-market interest rates, offered by the Department of Housing and Urban Development for mortgage insurance on certain types of housing.

Boldface   A typeface that is bolder than regular typeface, used for emphasis.

Breach of contract   A failure to perform the terms of the contract for which there is no legal excuse.

Brochure   A pamphlet or booklet designed to give, by illustration and narrative, complete information on a specific subject.

Broker   An agent who buys or sells for a principal on a commission without having title to the property.

Brokerage license   License to do business as a broker.

Btu   British thermal unit; a measure of heat.

Budget   An itemized estimate of income and expenses for a given period of time in the future.

Building codes   Ordinances specifying minimum standards of construction of buildings for the protection of public safety and health.

Calibration tool   Tool used in calibrating the temperature of an oven.

Capital   Any form of wealth capable of being used to create more wealth.

Capital asset   An asset needed to create a product or service, normally acquired with the intention of being kept rather than being resold.

Capital cost recovery deduction   Tax deduction allowed for **depreciation** (see).

Capital expenditures   Major one-time costs representing the purchase price of a capital asset.

Capital gain   A profit from the sale of a capital asset.

Capital reserves   Portion of a budget where money is set aside for capital expenditures.

Carport   A roofed, sideless shed for the storage of a motor vehicle.

Cash flow   The amount of cash available after all payments have been made for operating expenses and mortgage principal and interest.

Casualty loss   A deductible loss of property resulting from disaster, accident, or theft.

Caulking   Form of insulation used where fixed surfaces meet.

Certified check   Check that has been presented to the bank on which it is drawn and marked good by the proper officer. Such certification is a warranty that the signature is genuine and that the drawer has funds in the bank to meet it and obligates the bank to pay it on presentation.

CERTIFIED PROPERTY MANAGER® (CPM®)   The professional designation conferred by the Institute of Real Estate Management of the NATIONAL ASSOCIATION OF REALTORS® on individuals who fully comply with the professional standards as specified by the Institute.

Check meter   See **Submeter**.

Civil rights laws   A body of laws which guarantee the rights of all persons, regardless of race, religion, color, sex, or national origin.

Claim   In insurance, an insured's demand for payment as rightfully due.

Classified ad A basic medium for briefly announcing space for rent, which usually appears in a special section of a newspaper.

Closing In salesmanship, persuading the customer to buy the product after the product has been explained and demonstrated; the last step in the sales process.

Coinsurance A form of fire insurance coverage which penalizes the underinsured: If a certain percentage of a property's value is not insured against loss, the property owner shares the risk of loss with the insurance company.

Collections A sum of money collected. In real estate, usually refers to rentals paid or collected.

Commingling of funds The illegal act of a real estate broker or managing agent in mixing the money of other people with his or her own.

Compensation Payment for services received, including salary and benefits.

Completion date In a construction schedule, the date a particular unit is scheduled to be fully completed, inspected and certified, and ready for occupancy; also **delivery date** and **occupancy date**.

Complex A group of buildings that together form a single comprehensive unit.

Compliance In law, fulfilling all the specified requirements of a law.

Concession Things conceded or granted. In real estate, to induce the making of a lease or sale.

Condemnation The taking of private property for public use; also the official act to terminate the use of real property for nonconformance with governmental regulations or because of the existence of hazards to public health and safety.

Condominium The absolute ownership of an apartment or a unit, generally in a multi-unit building, by a legal description of the air space which the unit actually occupies, plus an undivided interest in the ownership of the common elements which are owned jointly with the other condominium unit owners.

Condominium association Private, automatic, usually nonprofit organization responsible for the operation of the condominium community; also **homeowner's association**.

Construction key   Master key used during the construction of a residential building. After the individual unit key has tripped the lock, the construction key can no longer be used.

Constructive eviction   Occurs when an owner creates or allows to exist a condition that makes the leased premises unfit for its intended use or hazardous for occupancy.

Contract   An agreement entered into by two or more legally competent parties by the terms of which one or more of the parties, for a consideration, undertakes to do or refrain from doing some legal act or acts.

Contractor   Company that contracts to perform a service or provide supplies, as in a construction contractor.

Contract rate   In newspaper advertising, reduced rate provided when a contract is signed for a certain number of ads.

Control   System, method, or technique designed to control some aspect of a business.

Cooperative   A corporation that owns real estate, usually a multifamily dwelling, including the building and land on which it is built; individual shareholders do not own their units but own the right to live in them.

Corrective maintenance   Repairs to the property and equipment due to natural wear and tear or faulty **preventive maintenance** (see).

Cosmetic maintenance   Maintenance which does not affect the function of the item but which makes the item more appealing.

Cost-effective   Economical; where the results of an action are worth the money spent.

Council of co-owners   Another name for **condominium association** (see).

Covenant   An agreement written into legal instruments promising performance or nonperformance of certain acts, or stipulating certain uses or nonuses of property.

Credit bureau   A firm specializing in investigating consumers' credit ratings.

Creditor   Person to whom goods or money is owed.

Credit rating   Evaluation of the financial trustworthiness of a company or individual, particularly with regard to meeting obligations.

Credit report   Report, usually made by a credit bureau, on a person's credit rating.

Curable obsolescence   The reversible loss of value caused by deferred maintenance or by the property becoming outmoded.

Curb appeal   The aesthetic appeal of a property as it would affect a prospective resident standing at the curb.

Current rental rate   See **Prevailing rental rate**.

Custom finishing   In construction of new residential property, an option offered to prospective residents allowing them a choice in how the unit is finished.

Damages   Legal compensation for loss or injury.

Death clause   A special clause in a lease which provides for termination of the lease before its expiration date in the event of the death of the resident.

Debt   That which a person is bound to pay or perform for another.

Debt service   Periodic payments made on a loan, with each payment representing an amount for principal plus interest.

Deductible   The amount of loss sustained by the insured before the insurer assumes coverage.

Deduction   Any expense or cost set off against revenue.

Default   The failure to meet an obligation, either of a mortgage or a lease.

Deferred maintenance   Ordinary maintenance of a building that has not been performed, and which may noticeably affect the use, occupancy, welfare, and value of the property.

Delinquency   An overdue debt, as rent not paid when due.

Delivery date   See **Completion date**.

Demand to pay or quit   See **Eviction notice**.

Department of Housing and Urban Development (HUD)   A federal department created in 1968, charged with the supervision of the Federal Housing Authority (FHA) and a number of other government agencies that administer various housing programs.

Deposit   A credit to an individual's or firm's bank account.

Depreciation   Loss of value due to all causes; usually considered to include: (1) physical deterioration (ordinary wear and tear), (2) functional depreciation (see **Obsolescence**), and (3) **economic obsolescence** (see).

Developer   A person or organization that develops real estate on a speculative basis.

Direct banking   Depositing procedure where funds may be mailed to the bank and deposited directly to a particular account.

Direct mail   A form of advertising through letters, cards, or brochures sent by mail to prospective customers which relies heavily on specialized mailing lists.

Disk   In computers, a magnetic storage medium offering random access to information; either a rigid magnetic disk or a flexible ("floppy") disk.

Display advertisement   A large, paid notice designed to attract the public's attention which usually includes a border and artwork or graphics.

Diversification   Expansion of the scope of business activity, usually into related areas of business.

Documentation   Written documentation of an event or act for purposes of supporting a legal claim or action.

Downtime   A period where a residential unit is forced to stand idle.

Double-lock system   Used to restrict access to a common area in a residential property. The door is fitted with two locks; each resident has the key to one lock; the manager has the key to both.

Drip system   Type of sprinkler system used in dry areas, providing a constant but minimal flow of moisture at specified times.

Dumpster   A container for accumulating waste, generally over two cubic yards in size, which must be emptied by hydraulically lifting the container and dumping the contents into a truck.

Economic base   The businesses or industries that provide an area with the basis for its economy.

Economic obsolescence   A loss in value due to factors external to the property.

Economic Recovery Tax Act of 1981 (ERTA)   Federal tax act which made several changes in tax law that attempted to increase productivity and encourage capital investment.

Effective gross income   Final figure in the income portion of a budget; the sum of the **total projected income** (see) and the **miscellaneous income** (see).

Emergency maintenance Maintenance which must be performed in order to rectify a situation where life or property will be endangered if the repairs are not made.

Eminent domain The right of a government body to acquire private property for public use through court action.

Employment agency A firm in the business of finding jobs for persons seeking employment and employees to fill vacant positions.

Empty nester Someone whose children have left home permanently.

Energy audit Careful examination of a property's energy use.

Energy efficiency ratio (EER) A measure of the efficiency of a HVAC device, expressed as the ratio of output in Btus per hour to the energy input in watts.

Equal Employment Opportunity Commission (EEOC) Agency created to oversee and administrate the Equal Opportunity in Employment Act.

Equal Opportunity in Employment Act A section of the Civil Rights Act of 1964 which prohibits all employers with 15 or more employees from discrimination in hiring, firing, or terms of employment on the basis of an individual's race, color, religion, sex, or national origin.

Equal Pay Act 1963 amendment to the Fair Labor Standards Act which guarantees equal pay for equal work regardless of sex.

Equity The interest or value that an owner has in real estate over and above the mortgage against it.

Errors and omissions Type of liability insurance that protects management from business errors.

Escalation clause A provision in a lease that guarantees automatic rent adjustments, usually based on increased operating expenses or a change in some standard index.

Escrow account Bank account used to hold such funds as security deposits separate from the personal funds of the depositor.

Estimate A statement of the cost of services or products to be provided.

Eviction A legal process to eject residents and their possessions from a leased premises.

Eviction notice   A written notice to a resident to pay the rent immediately or leave the leased premises within a specified time; also **demand to pay or quit**.
Expense   Any kind of business cost.
Expense allowance   An allowance to provide for reimbursable expenses.

Fair housing laws   Body of federal law that prohibits discrimination in housing.
Fair Labor Standards Act (FLSA)   Federal law that specifies a minimum hourly wage and policies regarding overtime for nonexecutive employees.
Fair market wage   A fair wage in comparison with wages being offered for the same position in the area.
Federal Housing Administration (FHA)   Federal government agency created in 1934 whose chief function is to insure loans and mortgages issued by private lending institutions for the purchase of single-family dwellings, private residences, rental housing, cooperatives, condominiums, and mobile homes.
Feedback   In communication, signals from the recipient of a message which indicate that he or she has understood the message.
Fidelity bond   A contract under which the insuring company protects an employer against loss of money or other property through the dishonesty of an employee.
Fiduciary   One who has a legal duty toward another because of an established relationship of trust and confidence.
Fill-up budget   Type of budget used in new communities that attempts to account for wide variances in income and expenses; also **rent-up budget**.
Fire door   Door that is made of fire-resistant material in order to prevent fires from spreading through a building.
Fixed fee   A rate or fee which is a fixed sum and not adjustable.
Flashing   Sheets of metal or other material used to weatherproof joints and edges, especially on roofs.
Floor plan   A scale drawing of the layout of rooms, halls, etc., on one floor of a building or in one unit of a building.
Foreclosure   The legal process by which a lender or lienor can enforce payment of a debt or lien by having the court order the sale of the debtor's real estate.

Freon   Trademark name for refrigerants used in air-conditioning systems.

Fringe benefits   Extra compensation to employees such as housing, pension plans, hospitalization and sickness provisions, and vacations.

Functional obsolescence   Defects in a building or structure that detract from its value or marketability.

Garden-style apartments   Two- or three-story walk-up buildings, often with a sunken first floor, usually found in suburban areas; also called **terrace** or **garden apartments**.

Garnishment   A legal proceeding where a portion of a debtor's wages, property, or assets are withheld to satisfy a creditor.

General partner   A co-owner of a partnership who is able to enter into contracts on behalf of the partnership and is fully liable for debts of the partnership; in a **limited partnership** (see), the individual or firm who manages the limited partnership and is its fiduciary.

General partnership   The business activity of two or more persons who agree to pool capital, talents, and other assets according to some agreed-to formula and similarly to divide profits and losses and to commit the partnership to certain obligations.

Grade   To assign a value to a residential unit in comparison with other units in the building.

Grandfather clause   In a new zoning ordinance, an exemption for a previously existing building that is in violation of the new ordinance.

Graphics   Artwork and/or design.

Grievance   A wrong, injury, or injustice that provides cause for complaint.

Gross scheduled income   Total scheduled rental income.

Habitability   Suitable for habitation; in an apartment building, habitability includes adequate protection from the weather, standard utilities, and sanitary conditions.

Heating, ventilation, and air conditioning system (HVAC)   The unit regulating the even distribution of heat and fresh air throughout a building.

High-rise apartment building   A multifamily structure at least 10 stories in height, averaging 25 stories and 300 units, usually located in a major metropolitan area where space is at a premium.

High season   Busiest season of a resort area, when rental rates are highest.

Hold harmless clause   In a lease agreement, an indemnification provision holding the property manager harmless for liability arising from the property's operation.

Homeowner's association   See **Condominium association**.

Income   The returns that come in periodically from all sources.

Income/expense analysis   Analysis of the relationship between gross income and operating expenses.

Income/expense projection   Projection of income and expenses for a future specified period of time.

Independence of clauses   In a lease, a clause stating that if any one clause of the lease is in violation of the law, the clause becomes void but the balance of the lease remains in full force and effect.

Infiltration   The flow of air into a building through cracks around doors, windows, and other openings.

In-house   Within the company.

Institute of Real Estate Management (IREM)   A professional association of men and women, affiliated with the NATIONAL ASSOCIATION OF REALTORS®, who meet professional standards of experience, education, and ethics with the objective of continually improving their respective managerial skills by mutual education and exchange of ideas and experiences.

Insurance   An agreement whereby one party (such as the insurer, carrier, insurance company, etc.) promises to pay a sum of money to another if the latter suffers a particular loss in exchange for a premium paid by the insured.

Insurance portfolio   The various insurance policies held by a property.

Inventory   Materials owned and held by a business firm; a detailed list of such items showing the value of each.

Investment   Purchase of some form of property that will be held for a relatively long period of time, during which the property is expected to increase in value.

Involuntary ownership   Ownership of a property that has been acquired involuntarily, as by inheritance.

Job description   A listing of regular and ongoing tasks to be performed by the person occupying a given position and assignment of parameters of responsibility and authority.

Job specification   A list of the skills, experience, educational background, and working knowledge needed to fill a particular job within an organization.

Jointly and severally   As a group and individually.

Kilowatt hour (kwh)   A unit of electrical power consumption measuring the total energy developed by a power of one kilowatt acting for one hour.

Late fee   Fee charged for late payment of rent.

Late notice   Informal notice that payment of rent is late.

Lawsuit   Legal action between two parties.

Layout   Interior and exterior arrangement of a residential property.

Lease   A contract, written or oral, in which the owner of a property transfers the right to use and occupy that property to another for a specified period of time and in exchange for a specified rental.

Lease conditions   The provisions setting forth the agreed privileges, obligations, and restrictions under which a lease is made; also lease terms.

Lease escalator   See **Escalation clause**.

Leasing   The process of marketing and renting a building's space.

Legal counsel   Legal advice; or an attorney giving such advice and pleading a case in court.

Legal notices   A notice which the law requires to be given for a specific purpose or action.

Lessee   In a lease, the resident.

Lessor   In a lease, the owner.

Liability   In insurance, a legal responsibility for injury or damage.

Lien   The charge against a property making the property security for the payment of a debt.

Lien waiver   An agreement between management, contractor, and subcontractor, that no liens will be placed against the property for failure to meet the contract terms.

Limited partner   A participant in a **limited partnership**.

Limited partnership   A business arrangement with two types of partners: general partners (see), and limited partners, who take no part in the management and assume no liability beyond their investment.

Listing fee   Fee paid to a referral service (see) for listing in their file or database.

Litigation   See **Lawsuit**.

Log   A record of performance.

Logo   A trademark or identifying symbol used for advertising.

Long-range budget   Budget which covers a longer period of time than an annual budget, usually three to five years.

Low-income housing   Government-subsidized housing for persons with low incomes.

Low-rise   An apartment building containing five or fewer stories.

Low season   In a resort area, the months just before and after **high season** (see).

Maintenance   Care and work needed to keep a property in good physical and operating condition and appearance.

Management   The planned process of organizing, controlling, and administering a business enterprise; the persons in the organization who are engaged in management.

Management agreement   A document in which a property owner contracts the management of a property to an individual manager or firm and which details all rights and obligations of both parties.

Management plan   A strategy for a property's physical, fiscal, and operational management that is directed toward achieving the owner's goals.

Market   The interactions between buyers and sellers.

Market analysis   A general study of market conditions that bear upon supply and demand and affect prices for a particular type of property.

Marketing All business activity involved in moving goods and services from producers to consumers.

Market survey The process of gathering information about specific, comparable properties and comparing it to data concerning the subject property in order to weigh its advantages and disadvantages and to establish market rent.

Market value A property's most probable selling or renting price, given the conditions of the market.

Master key A key which opens many or all of a property's locks.

Master meter A single meter, owned and operated by the utility company, which measures the total amount of energy from one source that is required to operate an entire building.

Media Various forms of communication, such as publications and broadcasting, which carry advertising.

Merchandising An aspect of marketing that involves advertising, promoting, and organizing the sale of a particular product or service.

Metered fee Charge for legal services based on the lawyer's time, experience, and expertise.

Mid-rise apartment building A multifamily structure that ranges from six to nine stories and is found in both cities and suburbs.

Minimum wage The lowest hourly wage rate permitted either by state or federal law or a labor contract.

Miscellaneous income Income for sources other than rent, including parking, storage, and late fees.

Model Furnished apartment which serves as a display for prospective residents.

Monthly financial statement Statement which summarizes one month's income and expenses.

Month-to-month tenancy An agreement to rent or lease for consecutive and continuing monthly periods until terminated by proper prior notice by either the owner or the resident. Notice of termination must precede the commencement date of the final month of occupancy. The time period of prior notice is usually established by state law.

Mortgage A written instrument by which property is given as security for the payment of a debt or performance of an obligation.

Mortgage loan insurance A program for insuring mortgages and loans made by private lending institutions for the purchase, construction, rehabilitation, repair, and improvements of single-family and multifamily housing.

Move-in The process of moving a resident into an apartment.

Move-out The process of moving a resident out of an apartment.

Mulching Spreading a protective covering, such as compost, over ground.

Multiperil coverage See **Umbrella policy**.

National Housing Act (1934) The first significant housing legislation; created the **Federal Housing Administration** (see).

Negative cash flow Deficit or loss.

Neighborhood A district or locality often with reference to its character or inhabitants; an area limited in size and used for residential, commercial, or other purposes or a combination of such uses integrated into an accepted pattern.

Neighborhood analysis The study of a neighborhood and comparison of it with the broader economic and geographic area of which it is a part, to determine why individuals and businesses are attracted to it.

Obsolescence A loss in value brought about by a change in design, technology, taste, or demand; an element of depreciation. (See also **Curable obsolescence**, **Economic obsolescence**, and **Functional obsolescence**.)

Occupancy rate The ratio of rented space to the total amount of rentable space.

Occupancy date See **Completion date**.

Occupational Safety and Health Act (OSHA) Law, passed in 1970, that set up an independent U.S. government agency to reduce occupational hazards by requiring employers to comply with certain job safety and health standards.

Off-season Least busy season of a resort area, when rental rates are lowest.

On call   Having an employee available or "on call" outside of normal business hours.

On-site manager   The direct representative of management and ownership on the property site.

Operations manual   A guidebook that contains all necessary information, instructions, policies, procedures, and forms for performing a job.

Operating expenses   The expenditures for salaries, taxes, insurance, utilities, maintenance, and similar items paid in connection with operating a building and which are properly charged against income.

Owner's requirements   Demands made on the budget by the owner's objective for the property.

Partnership   A form of business ownership, in which two or more partners pool finances and administrative skills, agreeing to share both profits and losses.

Passive solar heating   The natural and efficient use of sunlight for heating without any mechanical equipment; see **Active solar heating**.

Payroll   Total amount owed by business to employees for work performed during a given period.

Pegboard   Board perforated with holes for pegs; used in various forms of organizing records and forms.

Pension fund   Fund into which allowance or other regular payment is made by an employer and/or employee to provide means of payments to employee upon retirement.

Performance   Fulfillment of terms of a contract or lease.

Performance review   The periodic and realistic assessment of an employee's progress on the job.

Planned unit development (PUD)   A large-scale group of properties, sometimes with varying uses (e.g., apartment, offices, shops, schools), that is completely planned before groundbreaking and generally built in several phases over a number of years.

Plumber's snake   Tool with a long, flexible rod used to clear pipes.

Possession   Occupancy or control of property; the right to use and enjoy the premises.

Prevailing rental rate   Rental rate which a current resident pays for a unit.

Preventive maintenance   The regular program of inspection and repair needed to extend a building's economic life.

Price fixing   Collusion between a group of owners and managers to set rental rates at an unusually high price.

Probationary status   Step in disciplinary process; status upon which an employee is placed for a specified length of time, during which the employee must rectify the unacceptable behavior or action.

Profit   Any excess of revenues over the costs incurred to obtain those revenues.

Profit sharing   System whereby employees receive a portion of a business's profits.

Projected completion date   Date which the contractor expects to have a unit completed and ready for occupancy; term used in renting up a property when unit is more than 60 days away from completion.

Property analysis   A complete study of a real estate property, including its architectural design and improvements, physical condition, location, services, and resident profile.

Property management   A service profession in which someone other than the owner supervises a property's operation according to the owner's objectives.

Property management fee   The management firm's fee for management of the property.

Property manager   Chief administrator of a particular property or groups of properties; usually a level above that of on-site manager.

Proposed completion date   See **Projected completion date**. Term used when a unit is within 60 days of completion but more than 30 days away.

Prorated   Divided proportionately; as in rent for a period of less than a month.

Prospect   A potential resident.

Public image   Image of a firm created in the public's mind by public relations.

Public relations   The activities, other than advertising, employed by a firm to promote a favorable relationship with the public in order to increase business.

Pump and dump   See **Turnaround investment**.

Punitive damages   In a lawsuit, damages awarded to a

plaintiff over and above what is needed to compensate the loss, for the purpose of consoling the plaintiff or punishing the defendant.

Purchase order (P.O.)   Written authorization to an outside supplier to provide certain goods or services in a given amount, at a given price, and at a certain time and place.

Quiet enjoyment   Resident's right to use and possess the leased premises without interference from the owner or other party.

Quotation   See **Bid**.

Rate holder   Type of **contract rate** (see).

Real estate   The land and any improvements found on it; the term is often applied to nonagricultural property which accommodates individuals, business, and industry.

Real estate investment trust (REIT)   A real estate lending organization set up to sell shares to investors and use the funds to invest in real estate holdings.

Receivership   A special trust set up to hold and administer property under litigation.

Record keeping   The overall process of accurately accounting for income and expenses in order to facilitate budgeting for future operations and preparing regular financial statements for the owner.

Referral fee   Fee paid to a referral service by management or by a prospective resident when a referral results in a signed lease.

Referral service   Organization that specializes in locating apartments for prospective residents or locating residents for vacant apartments.

Regional analysis   Identification of the general economic and demographic conditions and physical aspects of a region and the trends that affect it.

Renewal   Renewing a lease for an additional period upon the expiration of the original term.

Renewal rate   Rental rate a current resident will pay when the lease is renewed.

Renovation   A general term covering the modernization, rehabilitation, or remodeling of existing real estate.

Rent   A fixed, periodic payment made by a tenant to an owner for the exclusive possession and use of leased property.

Rental agent   Staff member responsible for leasing apartments.

Rental grid   Chart used to grade units in an apartment building.

Rental office   Office on the property used for leasing.

Rent control   Government regulation imposed on rents in order to keep rents from rising inordinately.

Rent roll   A balance sheet for the account of each rental area, listing residents' names and their unit numbers, along with all income payable and paid.

Rent schedule   The listing of each unit and its scheduled income.

Rent-up budget   See **Fill-up budget**.

Rent-up period   The time following construction, renovation, or conversion that is required for a rental property to achieve specified occupancy rates and projected income levels.

Resident   Tenant who resides in the leased premises.

Resident handbook   Handbook for resident use containing all resident policies.

Residential utility billing system (RUBS)   Allocation of energy costs to residents using a mathematical formula.

Resident manager   On-site manager who resides on the premises.

Resident profile   A study and listing of the similar and dissimilar characteristics of the present residents of a property.

Retainer   Fee paid to a lawyer in anticipation of services.

Return on investment   Rate of profit earned in relation to investment.

Routine maintenance   Custodial maintenance, basic lawn care, and **service calls** (see).

Scale   Hard calcium deposits which accumulate in vessels in which water is heated.

Scheduled completion date   See **Projected completion date**. Term used when unit is within 30 days of completion.

Seasonal rent   Rent adjusted by season; often used in resort areas. See **High season**, **Low season**, and **Off season**.

Securities and Exchange Commission (SEC)   An independent federal regulatory agency that administers statutes designed to provide the fullest possible disclosure to the investing public.

Security deposit   An established amount of money advanced by a resident and held by an owner or manager for a specific period of time to cover possible damages and ensure the faithful performance of the lease by the resident.

Seizure of assets   Seizure by the court of the property of someone whom judgement has been rendered against.

Service call   Completion of a maintenance task requested by a resident.

Service contract   Contract with a maintenance contractor for certain maintenance tasks.

Service request   A resident's request for maintenance.

Shared insurance   See **Coinsurance**.

Signature block   Section of lease containing statement that all parties have read and understood the lease, with space for signatures.

Slurry   A watery mixture of a substance, such as asphalt, and water that will flow easily.

Small claims court   Special court set up to expedite litigation of small claims on debts.

Software   A computer program.

Sole proprietorship   A form of business organization in which an individual owns and manages the entire enterprise.

Specifications   Written instructions to a contractor or supplier specifying all aspects of the job to be performed or the material to be supplied.

Splashblocks   Concrete blocks placed at the bottom of downspouts which guide water away from the building.

Stabilized budget   See **Long-range budget**.

Stock   See **Inventory**.

Street rate   Rental rate new residents will pay.

Subcontractor   A small, usually specialized contractor who performs part of the contractor's responsibility under contract to the contractor.

Subletting   The leasing of a premises by a resident to a third party for part of the resident's remaining term.

Submeter   An energy-monitoring device used in conjunction with a master meter: A submeter is installed and owned by the property rather than the utility company. The property manager is responsible for operating and maintaining the submeters and for billing residents for the energy they consume.

Subsidized housing   Federal program of housing based on government grants that reduce cost of housing and as a result lower the rent charged to the resident.

Suppliers   Vendors who provide goods and services to the property.

Syndicate   See **Partnership**.

Tax   A governmental levy usually made on a regular basis and based in principle upon the relative value of the object being levied.

Tax shelter   A device whereby a taxpayer may reinvest earnings on capital without paying income tax on them.

Tenant   One who pays rent to occupy or gain possession of real estate.

Tenant organization   Organization of tenants formed to use their collective powers against an owner to achieve certain goals such as improved conditions, expanded facilities, and lower rent.

Termination   Cessation of an employee's employment; firing.

Term   Duration of a resident's lease.

Term rent   Type of rent sometimes collected in resort areas for a specified term—usually the high season—and payable in full in advance.

Terrace apartments   See **Garden-style apartments**.

Theme   Concept for a property or development upon which all marketing efforts will be based.

Tickler file   A record-keeping system that reminds the manager of important dates and duties.

Time clock   Clock used to record arrival and departure of employees.

Title   Evidence of right which a person has to the ownership and possession of property or land.

Total projected income   The figure gained from the subtraction of an **allowance for vacancies and bad debts** (see) from the **gross scheduled income** (see).

Townhouse   A one-, two-, or three-story dwelling sharing common or party walls but with a separate, outside entryway.

Trading   In interviewing, process of gaining information by asking a question in return for each piece of information given.

Traffic   The movement of visitors and prospective residents through a property.

Traffic report   A record summarizing the traffic of a property, including the numbers of visiting prospects and the factors that led them to visit.

Tuck-pointing   Mending of broken, crumbling, or missing mortar between bricks in a wall.

Turnaround investment   Short-term investment in a property; usually includes renovating the property, raising rents, and reselling the property for a profit in a short amount of time.

Turnover   Number of units vacated during a specified period of time, usually expressed as the ratio between the number of new residents to the total number of units in a property.

Umbrella policy   Insurance policy which covers a wide range of liability, also called **multiperil coverage**.

Unemployment compensation   System of insurance whereby those who lose their jobs receive periodic payments from an unemployment compensation fund for a period of time presumably long enough to permit them to find new jobs.

Upcoming inventory   In properties under construction, refers to units nearing completion.

Upward budgeting   Practice of allotting more money in the budget than will probably be needed.

Utility   A public service, such as gas, water, or electricity.

Vacancy rate   The ratio of vacant space to total rentable area.

Wage-hour laws   State and federal statutes that govern the number of hours that may be worked and subsequent compensation.

Walk-up   An apartment building of two or more floors where the only access to the upper floors is by means of stairways.

Water restrictor   Attachment to a shower head that restricts the flow of water.

Weatherstripping   Thin strips of material used as insulation between a door or window and the jamb or sill.

Workers' compensation insurance   An insurance policy that covers payments that may be required by law to be made to an employee who is injured at work, regardless of who is at fault.

Work order   A record of maintenance work, usually stating what was performed, by whom, where, the amount of time required, and materials used.

Writ of execution   A statement issued by a court ordering the enforcement of a judgement.

Zoning   A public regulation determining the character and intensity of land use.

Index

Essential
Property Management Titles
from IREM

Managing the Office Building
Managing the Shopping Center
Marketing and Leasing of Office Space
The Owner's and Manager's Guide
  to Condominium Management
Practical Apartment Management
The Practice of Real Estate Management
  for the Experienced Property Manager
Principles of Real Estate Management
The Successful On-Site Manager
Expense Analysis: Condominiums,
  Cooperatives & P.U.D.'s (annual)
Income/Expense Analysis: Apartments (annual)
Income/Expense Analysis: Office Buildings (annual)